Single with Attitude

**Not Your Typical Take on Health and Happiness,
Love and Money, Marriage and Friendship**

Bella DePaulo, Ph.D.

2009

CONTENTS

Thanks to *Psychology Today* for inviting me to write the "Living Single" blog, and to the Huffington Post for welcoming my writings there as well. Many of these essays first appeared in some form at those two sites. Others originally appeared in publications such as the *Chronicle of Higher Education*, *Forbes*.com, and the *New York Times*.

Most of all, I am grateful to the many readers of my first book, *Singled Out: How Singles Are Stereotyped, Stigmatized, and Ignored, and Still Live Happily Ever After*, for their tremendous outpouring of appreciation that continues to this day, and for all of the enthusiasm from readers of my blogs and other writings on single life. Often, their tips and comments are my greatest source of inspiration.

Bella DePaulo
Summerland, California
August 9, 2009

1.

Living Single: It Is How We Spend the Better Part of Our Adult Lives

Mar 21 2008

Welcome to the Living Single blog! This is my first post, so let me tell you a bit about myself and what you can expect to find in this space.

I'm 54-years old and I've been living single my entire life. So I have quite a lot of experience in the practice of singlehood. Over the past decade or so, I've also become a scholar of the single life.

I started taking mental notes on what it means to be single long before I decided to approach the topic scientifically. Probably my most jarring life transition was going from graduate school, where just about all of my friends were single, to my first job as an Assistant Professor, in 1979, in a psychology department in which just about all of my colleagues were institutionalized (i.e., married) or acting as if they were.

Now, nearly three decades later, fewer single people will find themselves "singled out" in their work or social environments. Each new Census Bureau report points to a growing number of single people in the population. There are now about 92 million Americans, 18 or older, who are divorced, widowed, or have always been single. That's about 42% of the adult population. (Some estimates are even higher. A New York Times story set the blogosphere ablaze with its headline claiming that 51% of women are living without a spouse.)

There are now fewer households consisting of mom, dad, and the kids than of people living solo. And here's my favorite statistic: Americans now spend more years of their adult lives unmarried than married.

What it means to be single has changed dramatically over the decades, especially for women. In 1956, when the age at which Americans first married was as young as it has ever been, and when nearly everyone married at some point in their lives, there was a big bright line separating married life from single life. There were fewer job opportunities for women than there are now, and especially fewer with decent pay. The Food and Drug Administration had not yet approved the pill as a safe form of birth control. Women who had sex or children outside of marriage were stigmatized, and the children of single mothers were not fully protected under the law. In the mid-20th century, the reproductive science that we now take for granted could only be imagined.

Today, many women are no longer tethered to men for economic life support. They can, if they have the resources and the inclination, have sex without having children, and children without having sex. Marriage is not essential to any of it. Increasingly, contemporary singles are no longer waiting to find The One before buying homes, traveling the world, or pursuing their passions.

Our perceptions of people who are single, though, have not kept up with their rapidly changing place in society. Stereotypes persist. As I discovered in my own studies, and while researching my book, Singled Out, there are important ways in which singles are stigmatized and marginalized. For example, in many workplaces, they receive less compensation than their married co-workers for doing the same job. (This is especially true for single men.) Singles also have fewer legal benefits and protections than married people do.

As I was learning about the ways in which singles are targets of stereotyping and discrimination, I was also noticing headlines in the media proclaiming that getting married makes people happier and healthier. I thought there was an obvious story to be told: Getting married makes people happier and healthier in part because it means escaping the stigma of singlehood.

I decided to look closely at the studies behind the headlines, wondering whether there might be some interesting qualifications (for example, does getting married improve the health or happiness of some people more than others?). I was stunned at what I found. When I examined the data reported in the original journal articles, I discovered that the media claims about the benefits of getting married were grossly exaggerated or just plain wrong. (So were the reports of the benefits for children of having two married parents rather than a single parent.)

The first few times, I thought the studies I was finding were the exceptions. I figured that as I kept reading, I would find the research showing that getting married transforms miserable and sickly single people into blissful and healthy married couples. That has not happened. The media stories extolling marriage keep on coming, but it is a rare headline that is an accurate summary of what the relevant study really did show. (See, for example, the stories in the news yesterday about the links between marital status and blood pressure. I'll probably write more about that in a subsequent post.)

Once I realized that I was not the only happy single person, and that getting married does not typically result in remarkable or enduring improvements in happiness or health, I had to rethink what it means to live single in contemporary American society. The new, data-based version of the story that was taking shape in my mind was far more interesting than the one I envisioned from the headlines. In the new version, singles are stereotyped, stigmatized, and ignored, BUT they still live happily ever after! How can that be? What is enriching and fulfilling in the lives of people who are single? What do our negative cultural stereotypes miss about the real lives of single people? Those are some of the key questions I addressed in my book, Singled Out, and they will motivate some of what I write here.

8

A single person's view of the world can raise some interesting challenges to the conventional wisdom. Think back to the early days of the 2008 Presidential campaign, when each side had a long lineup of candidates. On the Republican end were Sam Brownback, Rudy Giuliani, Mike Huckabee, Duncan Hunter, John McCain, Ron Paul, Mitt Romney, Tom Tancredo, Fred Thompson, and Tommy Thompson. The Democratic dance card featured Joe Biden, Hillary Clinton, Chris Dodd, John Edwards, Mike Gravel, Dennis Kucinich, Barack Obama, and Bill Richardson. A quick glance at all the Republicans standing together onstage, compared to the Democrats, suggested a stark difference that became the common knowledge: The Republicans were all white men of a certain age, and the Democrats were diverse.

When I looked at all the candidates on both sides, though, I thought there was an important way in which they were all the same: They were all married.

Does that matter, and if so, how? What, if anything, does it say about 21st century America?

Stay tuned.

Source URL: http://www.psychologytoday.com/node/248

Links:
[1] http://www.census.gov/Press-Release/www/releases/archives/facts_for_features_special_editions/010329.html [2] http://query.nytimes.com/gst/fullpage.html?res=9A01E0D91030F935A25752C0A9619C8B63 [3] http://www.amazon.com/Singled-Out-Singles-Stereotyped-Stigmatized/dp/0312340826/ref=ed_oe_p/002-7432694-6177638?ie=UTF8&qid=1146449667&sr=1-1 [4] http://www.newswise.com/articles/view/538727/?sc=dwhn

---

2.

It's National Singles Week: Here Are 14 Reasons Why We Need It

Sep 21 2008 - 3:02am

Today is the start of National Singles Week, September 21-27 (sometimes called National Unmarried and Single Americans Week), but don't expect to find any greeting cards to celebrate it. That's okay about the cards - I don't care about them. But I do care about increasing awareness of the truth about single life. We need National Singles Week because we need consciousness-raising.

1. We need it because living single is how we spend the better part of our adult lives. Americans now spend more years unmarried than married. But even if we spent only

9

a sliver of our lives single, we should be able to use that sliver to pick any door or puncture any myth.

2. We need it because what it means to live single has changed dramatically over the past half-century, but our perceptions have been left in the dust. Bogus stereotypes rule, and they need to be dethroned.

3. We need it because fairy tales can come true, it can happen to you, if you are a plastic Barbie or Ken doll or you play one on TV. If you are a real person, <u>you are no more likely to live happily ever after if you get married than you were when you were single</u>. We need to know that.

4. We need it because the media has grabbed onto the Marriage Myth Express and taken it for a long and silly ride. I don't just mean the dopey shows like The Bachelor or the Bachelorette. The press does us wrong even in reporting the news. As I've been documenting on <u>this blog</u>, on the <u>Huffington Post</u>, and in <u>Singled Out</u>, media descriptions of the latest scientific studies consistently add a little glitter to the any results that look good for married people, while batting away any promising findings about single people.

5. We need it because our educational institutions - those colleges and universities that should be at the leading edge of scholarship and critical thinking - have been just as smitten by the marital mythology as the rest of society. Those bastions of higher learning are filled with courses, degree programs, textbooks, journals, endowed chairs, research funding and all the other components of the intellectual industry that is the study of marriage. As for the other 42% of the adult population, we're still <u>waiting for the scholarly spotlight</u> to shine as brightly on us.

6. We need it because we are shorted on the 1,136 federal benefits, protections, and privileges that are available only to people who are legally married. We need it because there is <u>housing discrimination</u> and there are <u>tax penalties</u> and <u>pay disparities</u> linked to marital status.

7. We need it not just for the privileges and protections but also for the opportunities to give and to care. Because I am single and don't have any children, no one can take time off under the Family and Medical Leave Act (FMLA) to care for me if I fall ill. That's a missing protection. But I also can't take time off under the same Act to care for a person who is important to me, such as a sibling, a nephew, or a close friend.

8. We need it because there are more than 92 million of us, and even without any of the opportunities offered to married people by policies such as FMLA, we are doing more than our share. In some significant ways, more of the work of <u>holding together our networks, families, and communities</u>, and <u>sustaining intergenerational ties</u>, is done by single people than by married people.

9. We need it because we have <u>untapped political potential</u>. We don't vote as often as married people do. Lately, we've been on the leading edge of national sentiment. We realized that the nation was headed in the wrong direction before other people did. We need to be heard.

10. We need it because if single life were taken more seriously, then the relationship life of all people, single and married and everyone in between or on the side or undecided, would be expanded and enriched. Follow the finger of married people as they point to an important person in their life and you will end up staring at a spouse. Follow the finger of a single person and you may find yourself gazing at a close friend or a sibling or cousin or a mentor or a neighbor. Look more closely at that person and maybe you will newly appreciate the importance of the entire category that person represents. Friends are hardly "just friends."

11. We need it because single people who live solo can show us that living alone is not the same as feeling alone. They remind us of something that is too seldom acknowledged in a society that so celebrates the buzz of social life, something that people of all marital statuses can appreciate - that solitude can be sweet.

12. We need it because the de-stigmatizing of single life does not undermine marriage, it strengthens it. When single people can live their lives with all of the same respect, benefits, protections, and opportunities as people who are married, then those who want to marry are free. They can pursue marriage for the right reasons - not to run away from the stigma of being single, but to embrace the attractions of being married.

13. We need it because, when it comes to kids, love is the answer. Single parents can give quite a lot of that. Add all the other important people in the lives of single parents and their kids, and then you truly have a whole lot of love.

14. We need to value single people because that's what progressive nations do. They look for the people who have been marginalized and diminished, and invite them into the center of society. That way, we can all live happily ever after.

Happy Singles Week.

Source URL: http://www.psychologytoday.com/node/1836

Links:
[1] http://www.sfgate.com/cgi-bin/article.cgi?file=/c/a/2008/09/19/LVAN130G93.DTL
[2] http://www.amazon.com/Singled-Out-Singles-Stereotyped-Stigmatized/dp/0312340826/ref=ed_oe_p/102-4637341-6604139
[3] http://cat.inist.fr/?aModele=afficheN&cpsidt=14763661
[4] http://www.psychologytoday.com/blog/living-single
[5] http://www.huffingtonpost.com/bella-depaulo/
[6] http://chronicle.com/free/v54/i05/05b04401.htm
[7] http://gpi.sagepub.com/cgi/content/abstract/10/4/457
[8] http://www.amazon.com/Beyond-Straight-Gay-Marriage-Families/dp/product-description/0807044326
[9] http://caliber.ucpress.net/doi/abs/10.1525/ctx.2006.5.4.toc
[10] http://www3.interscience.wiley.com/journal/119393014/abstract
[11] http://www.huffingtonpost.com/bella-depaulo/anyone-want-a-few-million_b_100062.html
[12] http://www.sfgate.com/cgi-bin/article.cgi?file=/chronicle/archive/2007/01/14/INGJINGKTE1.DTL

[13] http://www.psychologytoday.com/blog/living-single/200808/the-american-psyche-tipping-toward-solitude
[14] http://www.springerlink.com/content/q525812276602356/

3.

Marital Mentalities: The Changes are Historic, and We're Living Them

Jul 12 2009

I think this is a moment in social history that scholars and critics will be analyzing long into the future. There's a lot of matrimania going on - the over-the-top hyping of weddings and marriage. But as I argued in Singled Out, I suspect that's not a sign of how secure we are about the place of marriage in our lives, but how insecure.

There are at least two ongoing rhetorical maelstroms. The first, and more narrow one, is over marriage itself. On one side is the "everyone into the marital pool" movement; lined up against it are the lifeguards cautioning, "not so fast."

The second has yet to make quite as much noise as the first, but it is more profound. It asks why marriage is so central to our conversations, our politics, our scholarship, and our culture wars, at a time when it is so inessential to our lives. This perspective takes a step back - no, many steps back to get a good long view - and looks at the entirety of our lives, as we live them today, and what makes them meaningful.

The first societal face-off was lucidly illustrated by two high-profile magazine articles on marriage published in the last few weeks. The "get in the pool, NOW, and stay there!" side was Caitlin Flanagan's cover story for *Time* magazine, titled "Why Marriage Matters." The skeptical lifeguard was played by Sandra Tsing Loh in the *Atlantic*, who said of marriage, "Let's Call the Whole Thing Off."

I've written about both articles previously (*Time*, here, and the *Atlantic*, here – also reprinted in this section of this *Single with Attitude* collection), so I won't recap the themes in this post, but instead underscore some starkly divergent takes on the same data.

First, consider how the two characterize the place of marriage in contemporary American society.

From *Time*'s "everyone into the marital pool":

> "Getting married for life, having children and raising them with your partner - this is still the way most Americans are conducting adult life."

From the pages of the *Atlantic*:

> "we both divorce and marry at some of the highest rates anywhere on the globe."

Loh's claim about America's extraordinarily high rates of marriage and divorce is from Andrew Cherlin's new book, The Marriage-Go-Round. I have no idea how Flanagan comes up with the notion that "most" Americans - that would be more than 50% -- get married for life, have children, and raise them with their partner. First, somewhere between 43 and 46% of all marriages end in divorce. Second, some 10% (probably more) of Americans will live single all their lives. Third, as of 2004, more than 19% of women between the ages of 40 and 44 had never had any children (Census Bureau). Flanagan's numbers just don't compute. Yet neither she nor any of the editors at *Time* seemed to notice. They are clinging to that white picket fence for dear life. Accuracy be damned.

Here's one more example, showing two different portrayals of the implications of single-parenting.

From *Time*'s "marriage matters" story:

> "on every significant outcome related to short-term well-being and long-term success, children from intact, two-parent families outperform those from single-parent households...in all cases, the kids living with both parents drastically outperform the others."

Now here's the *Atlantic* on the same theme:

> "while having two biological parents at home is, the statistics tell us, best for children, a single-parent household is almost as good. The harm comes, Cherlin argues, from parents continually coupling with new partners, so that the children are forced to bond, or compete for attention, with ever new actors."

If there is just one study showing one way in which kids from single-parent homes outperform kids from two-parent homes, or even perform just a bit different rather than drastically so, then Flanagan's reckless statement simply cannot be true. In previous posts (here and here) and in Singled Out, I've rounded up a list of such studies.

Flanagan's argument that marriage matters, that it makes a "drastic" difference, is the traditional perspective. It is the reigning American worldview. That's the story that made the cover of *Time*, a magazine with a circulation in the millions. Loh's account, less compliant with our mythologies but also more consistent with the facts, was in the back of a magazine with far fewer readers (but more intellectual cache).

In the days surrounding the publication of the "marriage matters" story, Richard Stengel, *Time*'s managing editor, made the rounds of the television shows, proudly touting Flanagan's work and repeating her misleading claims. He seems, in other ways, to be a smart and interesting person. These marriage wars, though, take their toll on all sorts of people who should know better.

Here's just one more example of the marital mythology making people lose their good sense. It's from the halls of academe. Recently, I've been rereading studies of marital status and depression for an academic paper I'm writing. To see whether people who get married become less depressed, ideally you'd want to follow the same people over time as they get married or stay single and see what difference that makes to their mental health. There actually are several such longitudinal studies. One 7-year study compared the depression scores of people who got married during the study to those who stayed single. But the authors did not compare the singles to all of the people who got married. Instead, they excluded anyone who got married but then got separated or divorced "because they clearly are not deriving any benefits from marriage." So in a study designed to see whether getting married was beneficial to mental health, the authors excluded anyone who got married and then split, because obviously they weren't getting any benefits from marriage. And they say so, apparently with no shame.

You can't make this stuff up.

(Still, even with that blatantly unfair advantage accorded to the married group, only the men, and not the women, showed any decrease in depression after they married. I'll tell you where to find that study - the *Journal of Marriage and the Family*, 1996; the quote is on p. 899. Unfortunately, though, it is not the only example of that methodological sleight-of-hand.)

Maybe, just maybe, the new and more accurate perspective is beginning to strike people as the more intriguing one. I don't have any good evidence for that, just one promising anecdote. The magazine The Week chooses one story per week to excerpt, from all of the possible magazine and newspaper long-form essays that appeared during that time. This week, they chose Loh's unconventional piece, not Flanagan's tired old tale.

Source URL: http://www.psychologytoday.com/node/30805

Links:
[1] http://www.amazon.com/Singled-Out-Singles-Stereotyped-Stigmatized/dp/0312340826/ref=ed_oe_p/102-4637341-6604139 [2] http://www.time.com/time/nation/article/0,8599,1908243,00.html [3] http://www.theatlantic.com/doc/200907/divorce [4] http://www.psychologytoday.com/blog/living-single/200907/time-s-misleading-cover-story-marriage [5] http://www.psychologytoday.com/blog/living-single/200906/avoid-marriage-advises-atlantic-writer [6] http://www.randomhouse.com/catalog/display.pperl/9780307266897.html [7] http://www.psychologytoday.com/blog/living-single/200804/it-takes-single-person-create-village [8] http://www.theweek.com/home

4.

Marital Mentality #2: The More Profound Historic Change

Jul 15 2009

Previously, I started to describe the historic changes that are occurring around the way we think about marriage and single life. The first set of transformative changes, discussed in my last post, focus on marriage itself. How important is it to your life experiences whether you ever marry and if so, whether your marriage ends? How important is it to children's fate whether they are raised in a 1-parent or a 2-parent home (or some other type)? What's striking about these questions is that they are being raised at all. Once upon a time, there was little or no debate over these issues. Now, the consensus that has been so unquestioned for so long is beginning to dissolve. That's historic.

The cultural confrontations over same-sex marriage are part of this first set of historic changes. Proponents ask why they have to be with an other-sex partner in order to have access to all of the benefits, protections, and respect that comes with legal marriage. Opponents balk at the threat to what they regard as the very definition of marriage.

All of that is small stuff compared to the second change, a true paradigm shift. Finally, what may be a critical mass of thinkers and critics, with and without formal credentials, has suggested a complete de-centering from marriage and coupling. Their question is, why should you have to be any kind of a couple to have access to basic rights, protections, dignity, and respect?

The old paradigm puts marriage at the center of our society and our individual lives. The law still treats it as the gateway to privilege, and citizens - and not just the most traditional ones - treat it like an elite social club that accords status. The United States is the odd-nation-out in this regard. As Nancy Polikoff noted in her important book:

> "No other Western country, including those that allow same-sex couples to marry, creates the rigid dividing line between the law for the married and the law for the unmarried that exists in the United States (p. 2)."

Polikoff is among those leading the revolution in our thinking. Rather than focusing on marriage and who should get let into the club, she suggests, we should "start by identifying what all families need and then seek just laws and policies to meet those needs (p. 7)." (Personally, I'd substitute "individuals" for "families," but we both favor a broad vision over a narrow one.)

It is especially important to see the big picture now that Americans are spending more years of their adult lives unmarried than married. The relevant questions in contemporary American society are not, are you married and to whom, but:

• Who are the important people in your life?
• What are the defining passions and pursuits of your life?
• What makes your life meaningful and worthwhile?
• What particular combination of solitude and sociability is most conducive to your best work and your most significant contributions to society?

It is not just in our laws and policies, but in our everyday interactions with friends, family, neighbors, co-workers, and people in the street, that these kinds of considerations should be paramount. The presumption that marriage matters most would then fall away - but it would not disappear as an individual option. People who want to follow the traditional path would still be able do so.

The new mentality asks why a pair of siblings who have lived with one another for decades, and whose lives are interdependent in every way that a married couple's is (except for the sex), should not be accorded the same benefits and protections as a conjugal couple. It asks why we measure relationships only in pairs and why we look only at complete interdependencies. Why not recognize that we all have concentric circles of people who make up our personal communities, and that different people can be important to us in different ways? When assessing a trend such as the growing number of people living solo, why not resist the temptation to assume that we are suffering from an epidemic of loneliness and instead ask another set of questions first: Is this how you prefer to live? Do you find your solo living isolating and depressing or refreshing and conducive to your very best creative work? Is your time alone complemented by time with others?

If we can de-center from marriage, and value more of the important people, relationships, preferences and passions in our lives, then future demographic shifts - which we really can't predict - will be far less consequential. Even if our society as a whole took an unpredicted turn back to the 1950s model of marriage happening early, for almost everyone, and often for life, nothing would be lost. Both the married and the single would remain equal under the law. Maybe our new enlightened habits of the mind would have become so entrenched that singles could live stigma-free even if they were to become a small minority once again.

Source URL: http://www.psychologytoday.com/node/30931

Links:
[1] http://www.psychologytoday.com/blog/living-single/200907/marital-mentalities-the-changes-are-historic-and-we-re-living-them[2] http://www.psychologytoday.com/blog/living-single/200904/marriage-wars-the-real-fight-is-over-moral-superiority[3] http://www.amazon.com/Beyond-Straight-Gay-Marriage-Families/dp/0807044326[4] http://www.amazon.com/Singled-Out-Singles-Stereotyped-Stigmatized/dp/0312340826/ref=ed_oe_p/102-4637341-6604139[5] http://www.psychologytoday.com/blog/living-single/200903/what-matters-is-whether-you-matter-others[6] http://www.psychologytoday.com/blog/living-single/200808/the-american-

psyche-tipping-toward-solitude[7] http://www.psychologytoday.com/blog/living-single/200811/the-fragile-spouse-and-the-resilient-single-person[8] http://www.psychologytoday.com/blog/living-single/200805/bigger-broader-meanings-love-and-romance

---

5.

"Avoid Marriage," Advises *Atlantic* Writer

Jun 26 2009

The *Atlantic* magazine has peddled its share of misguided matrimania and scolding of singles - both mothers and others - but not this month. Just look at this tease for a story by Sandra Tsing Loh: "The author is ending her marriage. Isn't it time you did the same?"

Skipping straight to the conclusion, here is Loh's final piece of advice:

> "avoid marriage - or you too may suffer the emotional pain, the humiliation, and the logistical difficulty, not to mention the expense, of breaking up a long-term union at midlife for something so demonstrably fleeting as love."

Let us all pause for a moment of silence, the better to hear the sounds of the tectonic plates of contemporary American culture shifting beneath our feet.

True, the tease may have been a bit tongue-in-cheek, and Loh may at times be having a wisp of fun with her readers, but there is a serious message in the pages of this essay, and it is not the party line. Loh is floating the idea that maybe we should all just get over our love affair with marriage.

Loh embraces the traditionalists' view that divorce hurts, then turns it upside down. The moral of the story, she suggests, is not the old, boring, bedraggled one: Get married and stay that way - no divorcing! Instead, she says, just skip the marriage.

So what do the data say? Is she right that people who stay single are better off than those who marry and then divorce? That's a point I addressed in a previous *Psychology Today* post, "Is it better to have loved and lost than never to have loved at all?" and of course in Singled Out.

I don't equate being married with being loved; my view of love is far broader and less hackneyed. So the question I actually do address is this: Who is happier, physically healthier, psychologically stronger, less lonely, more likely to live longer, and more engaged with neighbors, friends, and family - people who got married and then got unmarried, or people who stayed single? The answer, in just about every study I've ever reviewed, is people who have stayed single. Those who have studied individual lives over time (examples are here and here) have often found that crossing the threshold from singlehood into marriage is of little lasting consequence for health or well-being; it is the transition out of marriage that can be problematic, at least at first.

I'm not saying, though, that you should not get married if that's what you want to do. You may have your reasons. Those reasons, though, should not include the misperception that if only you marry, you will live happily ever after.

Unless you've managed to tune out the cultural altercations over marriage, you know the objection that will be raised next: But what about the children? Impressively, Loh resists the conventional wisdom even on that score, noting that "a single-parent household is almost as good" as having two biological parents. (And because she got so much right, I'll ignore the snippet of singlism in her article that made me cringe.)

The data on single-parent households are on Loh's side. As I've noted here and in Singled Out, there are even ways in which children from single-parent households do better than children of married parents. I'm not arguing that you should create a single-parent household for the good of your children, but let's also not pretend that the children of single parents are doomed.

It is possible, you know, to value two-parent families without denigrating other family forms. It is even possible to acknowledge the potential positive power of the experience of growing up in a single-parent home, without denying the good that can come with having two (or even more) adults at home. And maybe, at last, there is some cultural space for such claims.

Consider, for instance, what Melissa Harris-Lacewell (whom you may have seen on the Rachel Maddow Show) has said about Barack Obama in her thoughtful essay in the Nation:

"Had his father been present he might have had less adolescent angst, but then again that angst was part of what sent him into a world of books from which he emerged a formidable intellectual. Part of Barack Obama's greatness is his fatherlessness."

Her conclusion: "We can assert the value of fathers and still create government and community structures that more fully support families of all kinds."

My conclusion? Hurry up, please. It's time.

Source URL: http://www.psychologytoday.com/node/30333

Links:
[1] http://www.theatlantic.com/doc/200803/single-marry [2]
http://www.huffingtonpost.com/bella-depaulo/marry-him-atlantic-ma_b_87045.html
[3] http://www.theatlantic.com/politics/family/danquayl.htm [4]
http://www.sandratsingloh.com/ [5] http://www.theatlantic.com/doc/200907/divorce
[6] http://www.psychologytoday.com/blog/living-single/200808/is-it-better-have-loved-and-lost-never-have-loved-all [7] http://www.amazon.com/Singled-Out-Singles-Stereotyped-

Stigmatized/dp/0312340826/ref=ed_oe_p/102-4637341-6604139 [8]
http://www.psychologytoday.com/blog/living-single/200805/bigger-broader-meanings-love-and-romance [9] http://www3.interscience.wiley.com/journal/118000098/abstract [10]
http://www.ncbi.nlm.nih.gov/pubmed/15179909 [11]
http://blogs.psychologytoday.com/blog/living-single/200804/it-takes-single-person-create-village 12] http://www.msnbc.msn.com/id/26315908/ 13]
http://www.thenation.com/blogs/notion/444069/obama_and_the_black_daddy_dilemma

6.

TIME's Misleading Cover Story on Marriage

Jul 4 2009

There's a lot not to like in the cover story for Time written by the smugly-married Caitlin Flanagan. There is, for example, the predictable singlism (Mark Sanford's soulmate is not just a single woman but an "emotionally needy single woman," because really, what other kind could there be), the obliviousness to any moral compass other than Flanagan's own (if parents are unmarried, it is because they "simply can't be bothered to marry each other"), and more. For this post, though, I will focus on the statement that is, by scientific standards, the most egregious and indefensible:

"On every single significant outcome related to short-tem well-being and long-term success, children from intact, two-parent families outperform those from single-parent households...if you can measure it, a sociologist has; and *in all cases, the kids living with both parents drastically outperform* the others." (emphasis mine)

Actually, they don't.

I will draw from the most impressive studies I can find (typically, those based on large, nationally representative samples) to show that:

• Sometimes children from single-parent homes do just as well, or even better, than children from two-parent families.

• Sometimes they do worse, but not "drastically" so, as Flanagan misleadingly suggests.

• When children living with one divorced parent do worse than those from two-parent homes, sometimes they were already having problems long before their parents divorced.

• Factors such as the quality of a parent's relationship with the child and the stability in a child's life can be more powerful than the number of parents in the household.

• The simple-minded "just get (re)married" advice can be misguided.

I. Here are a few examples, from large nationally representative samples, in which children from 2-parent households hardly differed at all from the others.

• In a large, nationally representative sample of two-parent biological households, adoptive households, stepmother, stepfather, and single (divorced) mother households, there were *no significant differences* across the different households in the children's **grades**, or in the **children's relationships with their siblings or their friends**. What mattered to the children was whether the parents were constantly arguing with them or with each other. The authors concluded: "Our findings suggest that adoption, divorce, and remarriage are not necessarily associated with the host of adjustment problems that have at times been reported in the clinical literature...It is not enough to know that an individual lives within a particular family structure without also knowing what takes place in that structure."

• What about sex? Are adolescents who are not being raised in two-parent households having **earlier and more wanton sex**? An answer comes from a national sample of more than 12,000 adolescents between the ages of 11 and 18. Four different family types were compared to intact 2-parent families: single-parent families, stepfamilies, cohabiting families, and lesbian families. The authors looked at the age at which the adolescents first had sex, and for the sexually active ones, their number of partners. They did this separately for the boys and the girls. That means there were 16 opportunities for the authors to find evidence for Flanagan's claim that kids living with both parents are drastically better off (4 types of comparison families X 2 measures of sexual behavior, X 2 kinds of kids, boys and girls). There were no significant differences at all for the boys. It just didn't matter what kind of household they were living in. For the girls, they had sex earlier if they were from single-parent households, but they had fewer sexual partners if they were from cohabiting families. For the other 6 comparisons involving girls, household type made no difference. So what did matter? In the authors' words: "the familial context - primarily familial involvement as measured by the mother-child relationship and familial culture as measured by maternal attitudes regarding adolescent sexual activity - is a more relevant factor."

• For other examples and further discussion, see Chapter 9 of <u>Singled Out</u>.

II. Here's an example from a large nationally representative sample in which children from two-parent families did better, but hardly "drastically" so.

A national substance abuse survey, based on 22,000 adolescents, found more substance abuse among the children of single mothers than among the children of two biological parents. But the difference was small: 5.7% of the children of single mothers had substance abuse problems, compared to 4.5% for the children of two biological parents. That also means that more than 94% of the children from single-parent homes did NOT have problems with drugs or alcohol. What's more, two was not a magical number of parents - on the average, the kids did better living with a single mom than they did with a dad who was married to a stepmother. The best living arrangement of all (with regard to substance abuse) included three adults - typically, mom, dad, and a grandparent.

III. **Around the world: Here are examples in which children from single-parent households did the same or BETTER.**

Hey Caitlin, can you see Austria from your house?

If the effects of growing up in a single-parent household were as sweepingly, spectacularly, and uniformly damning as Flanagan claims they are, then we should find that the children of single parents are doomed around the world.

They're not.

Consider, for example, a study of the math and science achievement of grade-schoolers in 11 industrialized countries. How equal was the performance of children from single-parent vs. two-parent households? The U.S. and New Zealand were dead last in equality - their children of single-parent families did worse than the children of two-parent families. In Austria and Iceland, there is no achievement gap at all. (In Australia, Canada, England, Ireland, the Netherlands, Norway, and Scotland, the gap is smaller than it is in the US and NZ.) Why the differences? Here's what the authors suggest:

"The United States and New Zealand lag behind other industrialized countries in providing financial assistance, in the form of universal child benefits, tax benefits, and maternity leave to poor and single-parent households. The same can be said about the quality and the generosity of parental leave packages (p. 695)."

Now let's look at children's reading skills in five Asian countries and compare them to the U.S. In Japan, there's a difference favoring the children of married parents, but it is smaller than in the US. In Hong Kong and Korea, there is no difference. In Thailand and Indonesia, the children of single parents are *better* readers than the children in two-parent intact families. If this seems like a puzzling possibility, maybe that's because Americans are so focused on marriage and nuclear families that we miss all of the other important people in our lives and the lives of our children. Extended family is more valued in some Asian countries than it is here; social, emotional, and economic resources are more readily shared. If a dad isn't around to pitch in, maybe an aunt or an uncle or a grandparent or a whole network of relatives is.

III. **What was going on BEFORE the parents split? What if they had stayed together?**

In many studies of the implications of divorce for children, researchers assess how the kids are doing at just one point in time - after the divorce has taken place. But maybe that's like skipping to the last page of a novel, and missing out on all that happened to bring the kids to the place they're at.

Flanagan seems to take Jon and Kate Gosselin a bit too seriously. To her, Jon left Kate because he "had gotten bored with being bossed around by Kate" and had a fling. Other unnamed parents, she tells us, "drift in and out of their children's lives." Maybe there are some actual humans who are that casual about divorce, but I think that for most real people, divorce - including the period leading up to it - involves intense emotional turmoil. The question then becomes: What is happening in the lives of children when they are still living in "intact" married-parent homes in which the two parents are, perhaps, arguing relentlessly?

In studies of some of the difficulties that Flanagan so recklessly pins on single parenting, such as substance abuse and behavioral problems, evidence of those difficulties can be traced back as far as 12 years BEFORE the parents divorced. (References are in Singled Out.) The timeline is not: parents split, kids freak out. Rather, the kids are already troubled well in advance of the divorce, while they are living in the supposedly ideal household run by two married parents.

Another relevant study was based on a nationally representative sample of more than 10,000 high school students followed over time. The author compared the students whose parents spit up over the course of the study to those whose parents stayed together. He found that the students whose parents would eventually split were already doing less well on math and reading and had more behavioral problems even while their parents were still together. Their family environments were different - they saw their parents as getting along less well with them (the adolescents) and with each other. Their parents were also less involved in their educations (such as by discussing school-related issues with them).

The "just get married" advice of marriage-promotion programs (and of those who would simplify or caricature the issues) rests on a teetering assumption - that if those parents who fight constantly or endure each other in icy silence would just stay together, then their kids (who are already having problems) would be just fine.

I do not want in any way to minimize the emotional pain and other difficulties that can face children in any type of household, including single-parent homes. But it is also wrong to blatantly misrepresent and exaggerate those problems.

One Last Reason to Stop the Stigmatizing

The utter inaccuracy of the claim that kids living with both parents "drastically outperform" children of single parents "in all cases" is more than enough reason to make that sort of irresponsible stigmatizing stop. Here's another. Single parenting can't all be pinned on wandering, lying, hypocritical South Carolina governors who spend Fathers Day with a South American mistress instead of their kids. Death happens. Ongoing wars mean that scores of children who go to sleep at night with two parents wake up in the morning with just one. Medical calamities outside of war zones create instant one-parent families, too.

If readers were to take Caitlin Flanagan's proclamations at face value, then they may be tempted to conclude that if death or anything else turns their two-parent household into a one-parent home, then they should hurry and marry again. Perhaps

Flanagan should have said a word about the conclusion of the book she mentions. In The Marriage-Go-Round, Andrew Cherlin ends with this piece of advice - "Slow down":

> "Americans' pattern of going quickly from partner to partner is problematic for children...we should focus not only on Americans' tendency to end relationships too quickly - the most common critique - but also on their tendency to start relationships too quickly (p. 194)."

The message, in a way, is a familiar one: Stability is good for kids. The difference between Flanagan's argument and Cherlin's or mine, though, is that Flanagan seems to locate stability only within two-parent households. Sure, it can be there, but if that's the only place you see it, then you are standing out in the rainstorm of conventional wisdom and need to invest in an intellectual umbrella.

After reading stacks of research papers in the professional journals (and not just going by the claims of people such as Judith Wallerstein or members of the Heritage Foundation), I came to this conclusion in Singled Out:

> "Single parents can provide stability, too. When they settle in with their kids, maintain a good connection with them, and do not jump from one marriage to another, they are probably going to have children who are as healthy and secure as anyone else's (p. 182)."

REFERENCES

Davis, E. C., & Friel, L. V. (2001). Adolescent sexuality: Disentangling the effects of family structure and family context. Journal of Marriage and Family, 63, 669-681.

Hoffman, J. P., & Johnson, R. A. (1998). A national portrait of family structure and adolescent drug use. Journal of Marriage and the Family, 60, 633-645.

Lansford, J. E., Ceballo, R., Abbey, A., & Stewart, A. J. (2001). Does family structure matter? A comparison of adoptive, two-parent biological, single-mother, stepfather, and stepmother households. Journal of Marriage and Family, 63, 840-851.

Park, H. (2007). Single parenthood and children's reading performance in Asia. Journal of Marriage and Family, 69, 863-877.

Pong, S.-L., Dronkers, J., & Hampden-Thompson, G. (2003). Family policies and children's school achievement in single- versus two-parent families. Journal of Marriage and Family, 65, 681-699.

Sun, Y. (2001). Family environment and adolescents' well-being before and after parents' marital disruption: A longitudinal analysis. Journal of Marriage and Family, 63, 697-713.

Source URL: http://www.psychologytoday.com/node/30559

Links:
[1] http://www.time.com/time/nation/article/0,8599,1908243,00.html [2]
http://www.unmarried.org/ [3] http://www.amazon.com/Singled-Out-Singles-Stereotyped-Stigmatized/dp/0312340826/ref=ed_oe_p/102-4637341-6604139 [4]
http://www.randomhouse.com/catalog/display.pperl/9780307266897.html

7.

Marriage Wars: The Real Fight is Over Moral Superiority

Apr 12 2009

Have you seen the "Gathering Storm" ad? It is the latest from the anti-gay marriage machine. Set against a grey, lightening-pocked, ominous background, it begins with the words: "There's a storm gathering. The clouds are dark and the winds are strong and I am afraid." It continues with one person after another (actors, all) declaring that same-sex marriage advocates are a threat. "Those advocates want to change the way I live," says one.

The ad touched off a televised maelstrom, with pairs of pundits yelling at and over each other with arguments that go round and round and never seem to come to any sensible resolution. The key question that befuddles gays who want to marry, and straights who have no problem with that, is this: How can one person's marriage threaten another person's? How is that even possible or plausible?

As Mike Barnicle asked when he was guest hosting Hardball, "I still don't get it. How, you know, if the couple upstairs, Ray and Tommy - what do they have to do with my life downstairs?"

The predictable arguments are trotted out: God doesn't want it. Marriage is for procreation. It is the foundation of civilization. By now, all of these are high hanging curve balls for the batters on the other team who have been swinging away at these pitches for so long. (See, for example, this parody of the "Gathering Storm" ad, and this blog.)

Even if granted, though, none of the anti arguments answer that puzzling question - what does one person's marriage have to do with another person's? Just how, exactly, are gay marriage advocates going to "change the way [opponents] live?"

They aren't. But they are a threat nonetheless. If advocates were to succeed in achieving complete cultural and legal acceptance - maybe even celebration - of same-sex marriage, something truly significant would be lost by the other side. It is not something that those opponents can see or feel or hold in their hands, but they cling to it nonetheless. It is their view of the world.

Both sides have a worldview and wish fervently for theirs to prevail. Among some of those who oppose same-sex marriage, marriage really does have a sacred place. In their minds, it truly is the bedrock of civilization (anthropologists be damned!). Getting married is, to them personally, a transformative experience. It doesn't just make them more mature or more adult or just different from those who are not married - it makes them better.

That, I think, is the real reason why some (though not all) of the opponents of same-sex marriage are so vehement. It is why they feel so threatened. To open the door of marriage to gays is to let them in on the one resource that opponents are most reluctant to share (especially with gays) - their own sense of moral superiority.

The dark and scary motif of the gathering-storm ad aptly expresses a genuine sense of foreboding. Even though the arguments in the ad may be bogus, the fear is real.

If it really is a sense of moral superiority that is at stake, then it is also easy to understand the passion on the side of the advocates of gay marriage. The GLBT community has been so vilified for so long. They've been scorned as moral misfits. Now imagine if the mantle of marriage - the official, legal, federal, no-holds-barred kind - could confer instant respectability. No, not just respectability - superiority. MORAL superiority. Who wouldn't be tempted to reach for that diamond ring?

The marriage wars are not only about the moral high ground. I think there are sincerely-held motives on both sides that are worthy of respect. On the side of the opponents, they often are <u>religious</u> ones. On the side of the advocates, there is the wish to lean against that long arc, and <u>bend it toward justice</u>.

There are weighty practical matters as well, such as the 1,138 federal rights and protections afforded only to heterosexual married couples. The LGBT community is currently protesting their unequal opportunities in their very own <u>tea party</u>. The press release notes, for instance, that "LGBT individuals are blocked access to their partner's social security benefits, often making retirement financially difficult, if not impossible." The <u>Family and Medical Leave Act</u> (FMLA) is another example. Official marriage would mean that LGBT people could take time off under that policy to care for their partners.

I'd never stand in the way of non-discrimination, so same-sex marriage has my vote. Still, I don't like this route to fairness. Any attempt to achieve social justice simply by expanding membership in the Married Couples Club is always going to come up short. As a single person, I don't have access to anyone's social security benefits, and I can't leave my own for anyone else - they just go back into the system. Were I to fall ill, no one can take leave under FMLA to care for me, nor can I tap its protections in order to care for a peer who is especially important in my life. Where's the justice in that?

Fortunately, there is growing momentum for more inclusive approaches that do not make the marital door the sole point of access for caring, sharing, and fairness. The "<u>Beyond Sane-Sex Marriage</u>" project, Canada's "<u>Beyond Conjugality</u>" project, and

Nancy Polikoff's Beyond (Straight and Gay) Marriage book are just a few of those efforts. Now there's a storm I'd like to gather in my arms and run with!

I started writing this post because Jen, a Living Single reader, asked whether I thought that people on both sides of the same-sex marriage debate were making arguments that are matrimaniacal. Were they, she wondered, viewing marriage as an all-purpose magical solution to everyone's problems? And, she asked, isn't all this incessant promotion of marriage, in a way, a devaluing of marriage?

I like Jen's questions. So much so, that I concluded the first chapter of Singled Out by raising just those sorts of issues:

> This is not a book about the "plight" of singles as victims, but about their resilience. Obviously, I'm going to moan about the many ways that singles are viewed and treated unfairly. I've already started. But I will not end with the predictable "woe is us." Instead, I will express pride at how well so many singles do despite all the singlism and the matrimania. Singles, by definition, do not have that one special Sex and Everything Else Partner who is supposed to fill up all of their empty spaces with happiness, maturity, and meaning. Yet, as we will see, the singles who actually are miserable and immature and who believe their lives have no meaning are the exceptions. How can this be? And if married people so obviously have so much going for them, why do they need swarms of scientists, pundits, politicians, experts, authors, reporters, and entertainers making their case for them? (from p. 27 of Singled Out)

Source URL: http://www.psychologytoday.com/node/4272

Links:
[1] http://www.youtube.com/watch?v=Wp76ly2_NoI[2] http://www.msnbc.msn.com/id/30135702/[3] http://www.youtube.com/watch?v=7YGe8DwBs-s&feature=related[4] http://andrewsullivan.theatlantic.com/the_daily_dish/2009/04/vermont-and-rods-giant-sigh.html[5] http://blow.blogs.nytimes.com/2009/04/11/vermont-victory-revisited/[6] http://www.democraticunderground.com/discuss/duboard.php?az=view_all&address=132x5 382479[7] http://www.huffingtonpost.com/2009/04/10/lgtb-tea-party-planned_n_185780.html[8] http://www.dol.gov/esa/whd/fmla/[9] http://www.beyondmarriage.org/[10] http://www.samesexmarriage.ca/legal/law_commission.htm[11] http://www.amazon.com/Beyond-Straight-Gay-Marriage-Families/dp/0807044326[12] http://www.amazon.com/Singled-Out-Singles-Stereotyped-Stigmatized/dp/0312340826/ref=ed_oe_p/102-4637341-6604139[13]

8.

Newsweek **Is Still Wrong**

June 11, 2006

Newsweek, it turns out, was just kidding about the terrorists. Twenty years ago, the magazine infamously quipped that 40-year-old women who had not yet married were "more likely to be killed by a terrorist" than to ever get married. The news was considered traumatic. In 1986, a therapist told *Newsweek* that "everybody was talking about it and everybody was hysterical."

Now *Newsweek* has recanted. The chances of marrying after 40 are actually much higher than the initially reported 2.6%.

Newsweek wants to know why they were so wrong. I have a different question: Why did it matter? Even if the original statistics had been true, why should that have been a cause for trauma or hysteria? At my age (52), the chances that I will ever be a butcher, a baker, or a candlestick maker are surely less than 2.6%, but that awareness does not send me scurrying fretfully into the offices of a therapist. The myth about low marital odds can have the power to incite panic only if it is co-dependent on a second myth that is even more pernicious -- that life as a single person is shameful and sad.

It isn't. But *Newsweek* has yet to get that part of the story straight. In its pictures and in its prose, *Newsweek* is still peddling the myth of the poor single women, who -- even if they thought they were happy -- really did not know what true happiness was.

The morality tale of the virtuous married people and the clueless singles is unfurled through the words of a handful of women who had been interviewed as singletons for the 1986 story, and then again in 2006.

Take, for example, the story of Penny Sohn:

<u>Then</u>, in 1986, she was totally "focused on her career" as a director of the NJ Department of Higher Education. Friends used to comment on her glamorous life.

<u>Now</u>, in 2006, she is married with children. According to *Newsweek*, Penny now "realizes that family, not work, is what constitutes a person's real legacy." Adds Penny, "Now I really do know what I was missing."

Or consider Laurie Anderson:

<u>Then</u>, in 1986, she said: "I have a meaningful life with meaningful relationships."

<u>Now</u> she's married and she's "ecstatic" -- in fact, she wishes she'd married earlier.

Sally Jackson's life lessons are also celebrated.

Then, 20 years ago, she was described as the "President of a successful public-relations firm," and enjoying her "charming 18th-century cottage overlooking Ipswich Bay."

Now *Newsweek* quotes her as saying that "it is much more fun" to be married. In fact, the caption next to the picture of Sally and her husband says "pure bliss."

So, in twenty years, *Newsweek* has gone from terrorist sensationalism to marriage triumphalism.

The myth of marital superiority will not be lost on those who merely flip through the pages of the magazine, looking at the pictures. Five big pictures, sometimes sprawled across two pages, show women who have married. Their husbands are right there with them, as are their children, if they have any, and even a pet. There are also smaller pictures of the women and their husbands on their wedding day.

The last two pictures are of women who stayed single. They are squeezed onto one page. The bigger picture goes to the glum-faced Nancy Rigg. In a quote next to her picture, she says that even if she lives to be 100, she will still be open to the possibility of marrying. Of all people in all the pictures -- 18 of them, if you include husbands and kids -- the ever-single Nancy Riggs is the only one who is not smiling or kissing.

The other single woman posed a real problem for *Newsweek*. The magazine could not get Lillian Brown to bemoan her single status, nor to pine for a partner, either then or now. Instead, she talked about how happy she was with her friends, her child, her grandchild, and her life. Plus, when they took her picture, she had the audacity to smile! What was *Newsweek* to do?

They showed her! They literally stuck her in the basement corner. Her picture is in the very bottom of the last page of the story, right next to the binding. The important people in her life are not included. Lillian, *Newsweek* is telling us, is single: by definition, she is alone.

If scientific studies really did show that marriage transforms people from miserable singletons into blissfully happy couples, then *Newsweek* would have every right to rub it in. But they don't. On average, people who marry and stay married show a small blip in happiness around the time of the wedding, but then they go back to being about as happy as they were when they were single. As for the people who marry and then divorce, they are already becoming a little less happy as the wedding day approaches, a trend that typically does not reverse until about a year before the divorce becomes final.

In touting its marriage triumphalism, *Newsweek* was missing out on the better part of our adult lives. The magazine is right in claiming that most people (probably about 90%) eventually do get married. But that statistic hides a more significant one: Americans now spend more years of their adult lives single than married. People who do marry often don't get around to it for a good long while, and then, many do not stay married for long. After divorce or widowhood, remarriage (especially for women) is hardly inevitable.

Newsweek spells out its moral for us: "The real story of this anniversary is the unexpected happily-ever-afters." *Newsweek* was referring to the women who were single two decades ago, and now are married. I think they've still missed the real story: Often, the women who are living happily ever after are -- and always have been -- single.

Source URL: http://www.huffingtonpost.com/bella-depaulo/newsweek-is-still-wrong_b_22765.html

9.

"Marry Him!": Atlantic Magazine Back-of-the-Book Backlash Porn

February 17, 2008

Lori Gottlieb, writing in the Atlantic magazine, has one word for single women of any age: Settle!

Settle, she exhorts us, even for the guy who smells bad or who gives you "a cold shiver down your spine at the thought of embracing" him. Settle for the man who has "a long history of major depression," is enthralled by terrorists, and is obnoxious to the wait staff. Settle for the guy so boring that you "preferred reading during dinner to sitting through another tedious conversation." Settle for "a widower who has three nightmarish kids and is still grieving for his dead wife."

HER OWN LITTLE WORLD

I'm a social scientist, and in the next section I'll show that Gottlieb is peddling myths about singlehood and marriage that do not pass scientific muster. I don't expect Gottlieb to be open to data, though. She's already gathered all of the evidence she believes she needs, from every 30-year old single woman that she knows. No matter how successful these women are, Gottlieb proclaims, they are all panicked about their unmarried state.

Now look at the line that comes next - the one that the Atlantic has turned into a printed shout-out:

"If you're a single 30-year old and you say you're not panicked about your marriage prospects, then you're in denial or you're lying."

29

Try telling a person who would say a thing like this that you feel differently. Gottlieb is creating her own reality.

She is also the mom telling all her kiddie readers that they must do as she says "because I said so!!!"

SCIENCE - THAT PESKY PROTESTER

Gottlieb buys into just about all of the myths about singles that I debunk in my book, Singled Out. She believes, for example, that singles are interested in just one thing - getting married. She warns that even if they have great jobs, their jobs won't love them back. She thinks that if single women wait too long, the available men will all be "damaged goods." Most of all, she seems to believe that single people are miserable and lonely, and that the cure for what ails them is to get married.

Science demurs. A study in which thousands of people have been followed for 18 years (and counting) shows that people who get married enjoy, at best, a brief and tiny bubble of happiness around the time of the wedding (a honeymoon effect); then they go back to being as happy or as unhappy as they were when they were single. Moreover, only those who marry and stay married experience the early blip in happiness; those who marry and then divorce are already becoming less happy, not more so, as the day of the wedding draws near. (See Chapter 2 of Singled Out.)

The words "lonely" or "alone" occur a dozen times in "Marry Him." Gottlieb seems to be channeling Bridget Jones's fear of ending up "dying alone and found three weeks later half-eaten by an Alsatian," only without the humor.

I've studied the scientific research on loneliness in later life (Chapter 11 of Singled Out). It shows that no group is LESS likely to be lonely in their senior years than women who have always been single.

Gottlieb also believes that mothers who settle, regret that they did, and then divorce, will still be better off financially than if they had never married. The science does not support that, either.

I will give Gottlieb this, though: Scientific findings are about averages. There are always exceptions. Perhaps if Gottlieb marries the rude, terrorist-enthralled depressive, she will indeed be happier than she is now. And maybe she will be wealthier, too, even if she eventually divorces him.

That's more than Gottlieb will grant me, or any other single woman. Recall her insistence that any report of single life that differs from her own is disingenuous.

Oh, and by the way, she's wrong, too, about the history of love and marriage. It is not true that the dream of women "from time immemorial was to fall in love, get married, and live happily ever after."

WHAT DOES LORI GOTTLIEB WANT?

After trudging through all of Gottlieb's admonishments to single women to settle even if it "involves selling your very soul," I was surprised to learn what she was fantasizing about finding upon entering the gates of marriage. For one thing, it wasn't sex.

Here are her "role models" for marriage: "the television characters Will and Grace, who, though Will was gay and his relationship with Grace was platonic, were one of the most romantic couples I can think of. What I long for in a marriage is that sense of having a partner in crime. Someone who knows your day-to-day trivia...So what if Will and Grace weren't having sex with each other?"

Gottlieb opened her piece by recalling a time when she and her son were picnicking with a close friend and her daughter. The two adults - single mothers both, whose children arrived by way of sperm donors rather than storks - looked longingly at other mothers who were there not just with their children but also with their husbands.

Here's how she explained the longing: "The couples my friend and I saw at the park that summer were enviable not because they seemed so in love [but] because the husbands played with the kids for 20 minutes so their wives could eat lunch."

THE TRAGEDY OF GOTTLIEB'S HUSBAND-FIXATION

I have to admit that there was one paragraph in Gottlieb's essay that I loved. It was a description of a typical single woman in her 30s:

"She has friends who have known her since childhood, friends who will know her more intimately and understand her more viscerally than any man she meets in midlife. Her tastes and sense of self are more solidly formed."

Tellingly, Gottlieb did not intend this description as a compliment. Instead, she was explaining why 30-something single women are so dense when it comes to realizing that they should settle.

I think it explains something very different. It is a great big hint as to why women who have always been single are so unlikely to be lonely in later life - they have close friendships that have outlasted many marriages.

Gottlieb's husband-fixation is tragic not just because she is trying to foist it on all other single women, but because it leaves her oblivious to, and unappreciative of, some of the most important relationships in life.

Wouldn't the person she calls a close friend, a fellow single mom who had her child in the same way that Gottlieb did, be willing to play with the kids for 20 minutes so Gottlieb could eat lunch? And considering the significant experiences that the two women shared, weren't they, in a way, partners who knew one another's day-to-day trivia?

In 2000, a pair of scholars reviewed 286 studies to find out what predicts feelings of well-being in later life. One answer? Spending time with friends. (See p. 205 of Singled Out.)

ATLANTIC MAGAZINE: THE GO-TO PLACE FOR BACK-OF-THE-BOOK BACKLASH PORN

I think what Lori Gottlieb is writing is *Atlantic* magazine back-of-the-book backlash porn. It is nakedly and proudly regressive - taunting and in-your-face. Egged on, perhaps, by all the sound and fury set off years ago by Barbara Dafoe Whitehead's piece, "Dan Quayle Was Right," the *Atlantic* now offers us the likes of Caitlin Flanagan and Lori Gottlieb.

It's a shtick. Consider Gottlieb's style as she scolds fully-grown single women:

"take a good look in the mirror and try to convince yourself that you're not worried, because you'll see how silly your face looks when you're being disingenuous."

Now compare it to this, from Caitlin Flanagan:

"If you want to make an upper-middle-class woman squeal in indignation, tell her she can't have something."

They're interchangeable.

UTTERLY CONVENTIONAL

I suspect that Flanagan, Gottlieb, and their ilk fashion themselves as shockingly unconventional. Look at me, they seem to be saying: I'm smart, I'm educated, and I alone am daring enough to say what those deluded feminists will not - that a woman's place is in the arms of her husband. Even if he stinks - literally.

In fact, though, their positions are profoundly conventional. Women have long been told, even by other educated women, and even now, that they belong with a man. The more progress women make, the more insistent the message becomes.

It takes an utterly unoriginal voice to pose the question, "Is it better to be alone or to settle?" and think that the universe of options has thereby been delineated. It is also kind of dopey to think that women who are single are alone.

MY ADVICE TO LORI GOTTLIEB AND THE *ATLANTIC* MAGAZINE

I have some advice of my own for the *Atlantic*. In the famous words of Jon Stewart, as he stuck a fork in CNN's *Crossfire* and declared it done:

"Stop, stop, stop, stop hurting America."

10.

Living Single Longer: It's a Global Phenomenon

Nov 1 2008

One of my favorite statistics about single life in the United States is that Americans now spend more years of their adult life unmarried than married. Recently, I've been trying to learn more about single life in other nations. I have yet to find any tallies of the number of years spent unmarried vs. married in various countries. However, one demographic trend seems indisputable: The number of years that people spend living single is growing, and the phenomenon has gone global.

It is not just people who stay single who are giving the globe a new look. Even people who eventually do marry are contributing to the worldwide trend of living single for more years of their adult lives. They don't marry as young as they used to, so more and more years of early adulthood are spent single. They are also more likely to divorce than they were in the past.

Stephanie Coontz, who wrote the book on the history of marriage, succinctly summarizes where we now stand: "Everywhere marriage is becoming more optional and more fragile." We are, she proclaims, "in the middle of a world-historic transformation of marriage and family life."

Not-So-Youthful Brides and Grooms

Around the world, the median age at which people first marry - if they marry - is increasing. In the United States, that age is nearly 26 for women (compared to a low of 20 in 1956) and 27.5 for men (compared to 22.5 in 1956). That means that by age 27.5, half of American men have never been married.

Compared to men in all other countries, that puts them near the middle. In United Nations data from 192 countries, the age of first marriage for men, worldwide (as of the 1990s), was 27.2. When only the countries classified as "developed" are considered, then American men look like youthful grooms. Across all developed nations, the age at first marriage for men is nearly 29. (For women, it is 26.1.)

Here are some examples of developed nations in which the age at which people first marry (if they marry at all) has increased by more than 4 years from the 1970s to the 1990s:

Australia Belgium Canada Denmark France Finland Hungary Iceland
Ireland Italy Netherlands Norway Sweden Switzerland United Kingdom
United States

Even in countries the U.N. classifies as "developing" (rather than developed), many
have reported increases of at least 3 years, from the 1970s to the 1990s, in the age at
which people first marry. Here are some of them:

Algeria Bahamas Guyana Kuwait Malaysia Martinique Morocco Qatar
Sudan Tunisia Virgin Islands

Divorce: It Is Becoming Increasingly Ordinary

Also contributing to the time that people spend living single around the globe is the
increase in the rate of divorce. In three-quarters of all of the countries - both
developed and developing - in the U.N. report, the rate of divorce increased from the
1970s to the 1990s.

Single for Life?

Most people marry sooner or later. Many are serial marriers, trying it over and over
again. The more difficult question is whether more people are staying single for life.
We won't know how many people in the current generation will be lifelong
singletons until they have lived their whole lives. We can, though, look at people
who have already reached a particular age - say, 50 - and see how many of them
have always been single.

In the United States (as of 2007), 12.3% of women in their 40s had always been
single. In Australia (according to their 2006 Census report) the numbers are even
higher, at 13.5%.

An article on "The demography of the Arab world and the Middle East," based on
1998 data, reports lower rates of lifelong singlehood overall, but considerable
variation.

Under 2% of women in their 40s have always been single in:
1.0, Oman
1.3, Yemen
1.6, Iran
1.9, Egypt

More than 5% of women in their 40s have always been single in:
5.1, Morocco
6.0, Kuwait
6.4, Israel
8.2, Palestine

A New Attitude

The singlism in the U.S. that I've described is hardly unique to America. That's not surprising. What has been heartening, though, are some of the creative ways that singles here and in other countries are taking on singlism. I've read, for example, that in Japan there is a derogatory term for 30-something singles that translates to something like "losers" or "loser dogs." In the same spirit as gays and lesbians who co-opted the term "queer," Japanese author Junko Sakai wrote a book titled The Howl of the Loser Dogs, about happy, independent singles; with true poetic justice, it became a best-seller.

Even when the number of singles in a society is relatively small, enlightened attitudes can take hold. An example was described in a previous post in which I interviewed Kay Trimberger about single women in India; they write unapologetically about single life and march in the streets to advocate for reforms. [That's the next article in this *Single with Attitude* collection.]

It Is a World-Historic Time to be Single, and We're Living It

Despite the demographic transformations that have swept the world, some things will never change. People will always love other people - sometimes platonically, sometimes romantically. They will always love and nurture the next generation. What will change - what is changing - are the many ways that people reach out to other people and care for children.

I'll give historian Stephanie Coontz the last word: "We can never reinstate marriage as the primary source of commitment and caregiving in the modern world."

Source URL: http://www.psychologytoday.com/node/2226

Links:
[1] http://www.amazon.com/Singled-Out-Singles-Stereotyped-Stigmatized/dp/0312340826/ref=ed_oe_p/102-4637341-6604139[2] http://www.amazon.com/Marriage-History-How-Love-Conquered/dp/014303667X/ref=sr_1_1?ie=UTF8&s=books&qid=1225591690&sr=1-1[3] http://www3.interscience.wiley.com/journal/118756837/abstract?CRETRY=1&SRETRY=0
[4] http://unstats.un.org/unsd/demographic/products/dyb/dyb2006.htm[5] http://www.popline.org/docs/1767/308523.html[6] http://www.city-journal.org/html/17_4_new_girl_order.html[7] http://www.cbsnews.com/stories/2004/11/22/world/main657109.shtml[8] http://www.psychologytoday.com/blog/living-single/200810/single-women-in-india-a-conversation-with-kay-trimberger[9] http://www.psychologytoday.com/blog/living-single

11.

Single Women in India

Oct 15 2008

A Conversation with Kay Trimberger

When I give talks about singles or readings from <u>Singled Out</u>, one of my favorite parts is the question and answer session at the end. I love hearing about other people's experiences, and discovering what they are wondering about. For most of the questions that come up, I have some sort of answer to offer. However, there is one big exception. Lots of people want to know how the experience of living single is different in other countries. I know way too little about that.

It is my great fortune to have a friend and colleague who has spent some time in India and has studied the experiences of single women there. E. Kay Trimberger, author of the insightful book, <u>The New Single Woman</u>, kindly accepted my invitation to share some of what she has learned with *Psychology Today* readers. (By the way, Kay's work has resonated in other countries. Already, there are Taiwanese and Polish editions of her book.)

Bella: Hi, Kay. Thanks for participating. Why don't you start by telling us how you got interested in studying single women in India?

Kay: I had the opportunity to go to a Women's Studies Conference in New Delhi in January 2008. In preparation, I looked up the English language books and articles on single women in India. I was surprised on how much had been written, both in terms of scholarly research and popular novels and essays. For example, I found a 2006 book, <u>Chasing the Good Life: On Being Single</u> - a book where some of India's best known male and female writers, journalists and artists, contribute essays on their mainly positive experiences as singles. The book was widely reviewed affirmatively. I can think of nothing comparable in the U.S. I also read the 2007 Indian "chic lit" novel, <u>Almost Single</u>, which is more skeptical about romantic love and more positive about remaining single than counterparts in the U.S. (Those interested in the scholarly research on single women in India can find it listed in the bibliography on the <u>Singles Studies</u> website.)

Bella: Here in the U.S., people who are single are a growing portion of the adult population, closing in on half of all Americans who are 18 or older. How do the numbers compare in India?

Kay: The number of mature, single women is much smaller in India. Between the ages of 25-59, 89.5% of Indian women are married, as compared with 65% of American women in the same age group. As for the unmarried women in that age range, the "never married" account for 2.5% in India versus 16% in the U.S., while the percentage of divorced women in that population is 17% in the U.S. as opposed to a mere 1% in India The percentage of Indian widows is 7%, higher than the 2% U.S. rate. (Numbers are from the 2000 U.S. Census and the 2001 Indian Census.)

Bella: I would guess that if you are single, living in a country where lots of other people are single, too, can only help. By that way of thinking, it could be particularly difficult to be single in India. Is that what you found?

Kay: Single women in India face more overt discrimination, but culturally they are more accepted. Let me explain. Single people - men as well as women - face discrimination in rental housing, and single women in India are seen as objects of sexual prey, especially vulnerable to sexual exploitation and violence. [Bella's aside: There is also housing discrimination against singles in the U.S.] The first Indian self help book for single women, Single in the City (2000) by Sunny Singh, gives much more attention to issues of safety than such books in the U.S. But psychologically it is easier to be single in India, because of cultural factors.

First, Hindi has no word comparable to the English spinster, with its negative, asexual connotations. Moreover, Hindu culture has a positive image of celibacy. Madhu Kishwar, a writer and activist on women's issues, says: "We are still heavily steeped in the old Indian tradition which holds that voluntary sexual abstinence bestows extraordinary power on human beings." Voluntary is rarely used with spinster in our culture, and certainly respect and extraordinary power are never part of the image.

Second, the arranged marriage system in India serves to liberate unmarried women from the self esteem trap. The author Sunny Singh, in a private communication, recently remarked: "A never-married woman in India is never assumed to be unattractive because arranging the marriage is generally a family enterprise. So people assume that there wasn't enough dowry, not the right match, irresponsible parents (my favorite), a wrong astrological chart and so forth." Perhaps this is one reason that polls show that most Indians, even the educated, urban elite, still favor arranged marriage, although perhaps in modified form with some personal choice involved.

The third difference that stands out is the cultural imperative in the U.S. that being coupled is essential to human happiness. Marriage in India is more highly valued, but its purpose is family ties, not coupled happiness. Compatibility between spouses is not linked to finding a soul mate, but is seen as the result of patient work, along with family support. As a result, single women in India are not pitied because they are not coupled.

To illustrate the implications, let me quote from a one of India's feminist intellectuals, Urvashi Butalia, a publisher who founded the feminist press Kali for Women. She says, "Oddly enough, the first time I really became conscious of my singleness was in, of all places, England. . . . [I found myself] in a culture that so privileges relationships, especially heterosexual one, that if you are not in one (and even if you have been in one that may have broken up you are expected to jump into another almost immediately), there has to be something wrong with you. So I was always the odd one out, the one without the man, the one to be felt sorry for. And it always bewildered me, because I did not feel sorry for myself, so why did they? It wasn't a nice feeling."

Bella: Wow, that's really interesting. So if people in India do not think that coupling is the royal road to happiness, then what do they think is the route to happiness? Or is happiness just not that important a goal for them?

Kay: Traditionally, individual happiness was less important in India, but westernization is leading to more emphasis on personal fulfillment. Western individualism in our own country, however, is culturally in conflict with the idea of the couple as the primary source of contentment. I see western influence in India strengthening the positive image of single women and men, enabling more people to reject marriage all together, rather than adopting a Western ideal of the couple as soul mates.

Bella: I've heard that there is a strong women's movement in India. Do feminists in India address issues important to single women?

Kay: Yes they do, much more so than U.S. feminists. The Indian women's movement, like that in the U.S., dates to the 19th century, and also had a strong second wave in the late 1960s and 1970s. As in the U.S., the Indian women's movement today consists of many different organizations focusing on distinct feminist issues. But in India, a few women's organizations create a nationwide constituency.

The All India Democratic Women's Association (AIDWA) - founded in 1981 from the women's divisions of two of India's communist parties - today is the largest independent women's organization in India, with 9 million members and 600 paid organizers. Moreover one of their current seven top goals is single women. AIDWA's new Commission on Single Women gives most emphasis to the continuing discrimination against widows, but it includes a section on "single, deserted and divorced women," articulating similarities among all single women, cutting across class and caste distinctions.

Even more impressive to me was the actual mobilization of single women. A current example: In late March and early April 2008 in the north India state of Himachal Pradesh, another woman's organization, ENSS (explicitly an association of single women whose aim is to secure their rights to live with dignity and justice), held a march of 5000 single women demanding a number of specific reforms, including free healthcare, land for poor single women, and pensions for older single women. Nor is this organizing around single women only of recent origin. I have found examples going back to the late 1980s and early 1990s.

No woman's organization in the U.S. - not NOW, The Feminist Majority, nor any more specialized woman's group - has ever articulated a program to organize single women. The difference stems, I believe, from the cultural differences I outlined above.

Bella: From your research on singles in India and the U.S., can you suggest any more general understandings of single life in different countries? So, for example, what kinds of factors are likely to make it easier or harder to live single in particular nations?

Kay: My research leads me to give more emphasis to cultural differences between countries. Those countries with a culture hostile to single women need to make a greater academic and popular effort to expose and change their cultural bias. Just the opposite happened in the second wave of the U.S. women's movement. Betty Friedan and Gloria Steinem -- the two best-known American feminists -- both distanced themselves from spinsters without providing an alternative model for life as a mature, single woman. Before we get to the point in the U.S. where single women and men hold demonstrations protesting how, for example, the social security system discriminates against them, we will need a cultural transformation.

The word spinster is rarely used today, but the negative stereotypes of single life over age forty - especially for women - are still strong. We must bombard the cultural wall separating couples and singles with evidence that the good life includes singleness and single living, usually with many close ties to family and friends, along with strong community participation. Some of us have begun this cultural work, but we need much more participation.

Bella: Thanks so much, Kay. I remember when I first heard from you after you returned from India, and I've been intrigued by your findings ever since. To readers: You can find links to more of Kay Trimberger's writings on her website.

Source URL: http://www.psychologytoday.com/node/2076

Links:
[1] http://www.amazon.com/Singled-Out-Singles-Stereotyped-Stigmatized/dp/0312340826/ref=ed_oe_p/102-4637341-6604139[2]
http://www.amazon.com/New-Single-Woman-Kay-Trimberger/dp/0807065234/ref=pd_bxgy_b_img_b[3]
http://www.bookfinder4u.com/IsbnSearch.aspx?isbn=0670999024&mode=direct[4]
http://www.amazon.com/Almost-Single-Advaita-Kala/dp/0553386107/ref=pd_bbs_sr_1?ie=UTF8&s=books&qid=1224046726&sr=1-1[5]
http://issc.berkeley.edu/singlesstudies/[6]
http://gpi.sagepub.com/cgi/content/abstract/10/4/457[7]
http://www.bookfinder4u.com/IsbnSearch.aspx?isbn=9780141000244&mode=direct[8]
http://nceuis.nic.in/madhu_kishwar.htm[9] http://www.sunnysingh.net/[10]
http://www.arenaonline.org/fellows/archives/000027.html[11]
http://www.indiatogether.org/women/resources/DL.htm[12] http://sutra.org.in/enss.htm[13]
http://www.now.org/[14] http://feminist.org/[15]
http://www.greatwomen.org/women.php?action=viewone&id=62[16]
http://www.feminist.com/gloriasteinem/[17] http://www.KayTrimberger.com[18]

12.

Singlism: Should We Just Shrug It Off?

Dec 13 2008

Thanks to Governor Ed Rendell's proclamation that single woman Janet Napolitano will be "perfect" for the job of Secretary of Homeland Security because she has "no life," and Gail Collins's glorious send-up of the matter in her op-ed in the New York Times, singlism is having its day. This matter of stereotyping and stigmatizing people who are single has now been addressed in the Wall Street Journal, on CNN's American Morning, on the ABC news website, and on the Ron Reagan Show on Air America, to name just a few national venues. It also made the cover of The Week magazine, and it is all over the blogs. (A few examples are here and here and here.)

I love all this attention that singlism is garnering, and not because the commentary has been uniformly approving or affirming. It hasn't.

Consider, for example, the 205 comments that were posted in response to Gail Collins' column before the comments option was closed. Many were positive, and I was heartened by them. The readers thanked Collins for her insight and her wit, and recounted their own experiences of singlism in the workplace and beyond.

I was most intrigued, though, by the nasty stuff. One said that if the choice for the position of Homeland Security chief was between someone "with a spouse and kids" and another "with no responsibilities other than filling the cat's food bowl at night," then he would "pick the loner every time." (Singlism, anyone?)

More than a few commenters chastised Collins for writing about the topic at all. They said it was "much ado about nothing," it was "silly" and "ridiculous," and that she should have instead discussed "an issue, ANY issue, that actually matters."

Several said that we single people are just crying victim, that we are hypersensitive and resentful, and that we should just "let it go." One person even made the clever (if obnoxious) suggestion that anyone who thought Rendell's "no life" comment was offensive should "get a life."

What made all these dismissive and derogatory comments especially interesting to me was that I've heard similar versions from fellow scholars. In an academic publication, they have suggested that singles are not really perceived negatively, that any stereotyping or discrimination they experience is small potatoes and is doled out only very selectively (for instance, to people who remain single after the age when most others are married). Some have advised me and my colleagues to put aside the study of singlism and focus on something else.

I thought long and hard about how such otherwise intelligent people could be so apparently resistant to the idea that singlism really does exist and that it matters.

Even more importantly, I thought about how I could make my case more persuasively.

I went through all the predictable options. I pointed to data documenting the practice of singlism, and showing that even young singles are perceived negatively, relative to young people who are coupled. I repeated an important qualification that I had already articulated - that in the degree of viciousness and violence it can engender, singlism is not akin to some of the other isms such as racism and heterosexism. I tried making my case with logic, asking how extreme or hurtful an unfair behavior would have to be before it would be considered appropriate to try to address it. And: who should decide this?

Then I came up with this thought experiment. If you think that singlism really is "much ado about nothing," that we singles are just being hypersensitive and should "let it go," then it should also be perfectly fine to turn the tables. I liked this approach so much that I made it the opening page of my book, Singled Out. Here it is:

EXCERPT FROM PAGE 1 OF SINGLED OUT: *How Singles are Stereotyped, Stigmatized, and Ignored, and Still Live Happily Ever After*:

I think married people should be treated fairly. They should not be stereotyped, stigmatized, discriminated against, or ignored. They deserve every bit as much respect as single people do.

I can imagine a world in which married people were not treated appropriately, and if that world ever materialized, I would protest. Here are a few examples of what I would find offensive:

• When you tell people you are married, they tilt their heads and say things like "aaaawww" or "don't worry honey, your turn to divorce will come."

• When you browse the bookstores, you see shelves bursting with titles such as If I'm So Wonderful, Why Am I Still Married and How to Ditch Your Husband After Age 35 Using What I Learned at Harvard Business School.

• Every time you get married, you feel obligated to give expensive presents to single people.

• When you travel with your spouse, you each have to pay more than when you travel alone.

• At work, the single people just assume that you can cover the holidays and all of the other inconvenient assignments; they figure that as a married person, you don't have anything better to do.

• Single employees can add another adult to their health care plan; you can't.

41

• When your single co-workers die, they can leave their Social Security benefits to the person who is most important to them; you are not allowed to leave yours to anyone - they just go back into the system.

• Candidates for public office boast about how much they value single people. Some even propose spending more than a billion dollars in federal funding to convince people to stay single, or to get divorced if they already made the mistake of marrying.

• Moreover, no one thinks there is anything wrong with any of this.

Married people do not have any of these experiences, of course, but single people do. People who do not have a serious coupled relationship (my definition - for now - of single people) are stereotyped, discriminated against, and treated dismissively. This stigmatizing of people who are single - whether divorced, widowed, or ever-single -- is the 21st century problem that has no name. I'll call it singlism.

END OF EXCERPT

If these kinds of things really did happen to married people, how long do you think it would take before we would all start hearing about the unfairness of it all? Like I said, I wouldn't want that. I want fairness for all, and I'm searching for ways to make my case.

Source URL: http://www.psychologytoday.com/node/2655

Links:
[1] http://www.psychologytoday.com/blog/living-single/200812/ed-rendell-says-janet-napolitano-has-no-life-because-she-is-single[2] http://www.nytimes.com/2008/12/04/opinion/04collins.html?_r=1[3] http://blogs.wsj.com/juggle/2008/12/05/janet-napolitano-and-the-persistence-of-singlism/[4] http://transcripts.cnn.com/TRANSCRIPTS/0812/05/ltm.03.html[5] http://abcnews.go.com/Politics/President44/story?id=6394768&page=1[6] http://airamerica.com/ronreagan[7] http://www.theweek.com/article/index/91552/3/Singlism_Do_only_married_people_have_li ves[8] http://femlegaltheory.blogspot.com/2008/12/is-this-comment-gendered.html[9] http://blogs.parentcenter.babycenter.com/parenting-blogs/2008/12/10/singlism-is-it-fair-for-people-without-kids-to-be-expected-to-put-in-longer-hours/[10] http://nocheapshots.blogspot.com/2008/12/singlism.html[11] http://community.nytimes.com/article/comments/2008/12/04/opinion/04collins.html?s=2&pg =9[12] http://www.informaworld.com/smpp/content~content=a785830591~db=all~order=page[13] http://www.amazon.com/Singled-Out-Singles-Stereotyped-Stigmatized/dp/0312340826/ref=ed_oe_p/102-4637341-6604139[14] http://www.belladepaulo.com

---

13.

Singlism and Matrimania in Everyday Life

Apr 29 2008

One of the most tenacious myths about single people is that they are miserable and lonely, and suffer from ill-health and low self-esteem because, after all, they "don't have anyone." All that is pure nonsense - that's why I get to call these notions myths rather than realities.

In many ways, though, it is understandable that people THINK singles are miserable. Singlism (the stereotyping and stigmatizing of people who are single) and matrimania (the over-the-top hyping of marriage and coupling) are the wallpaper of contemporary American life.

SNIPPETS OF SINGLISM

Here are 6 sample snippets of everyday singlism and matrimania:

1. On April 23, the day after the Pennsylvania primary, Jack Cafferty of CNN posed this question: "Why can't Barack Obama close the deal?" Of the hundreds of responses that viewers sent in, only 5 were read on the air. This, from Steve in Atlanta, was one of them: "Jack, Obama can't close the deal because all of the older women are voting for the Clintons. Every family has a crazy aunt. I just found out that mine thinks Hillary is the best candidate. These women should stay out of politics and go play with their 11 cats."

2. A few months ago, *Time* magazine published a special issue on the science of romance. In an article called "Marry Me," *Time* claimed that getting married makes you healthier. (In Singled Out, I debunked that claim, and showed why some of the very studies cited by *Time* really do not support that conclusion.) To explain this (false) statement, *Time* said, "Marriage means no more drinking at singles' bars until closing, no more eating uncooked ramen noodles out of the bag and calling it a meal."

3. During the Pope's recent visit to the U.S., CNN commentators did the play-by-play of the Bushes meeting the pontiff at the airport. One of them noted, "I know that the Pope was very interested in meeting the president's family, especially Jenna, since she's going to be married soon." Wolf Blitzer then speculated that the Pope must be planning a blessing for the occasion. The reporter replied, "Well, I understand that the gift that he's going to give is going to be designed for Jenna."

Personally, I don't know why anyone should be more interested in meeting someone about to be married than someone who is single and not planning to become unsingle anytime soon. But the POPE? Isn't HE single? Here, I want to give a shout-out to the wonderful title of a book written by Karen Salmansohn, another *Psychology Today* blogger: Even God is Single (so stop giving me a hard time).

4. During the *Hardball* College Tour, Chris Matthews asked Barack Obama how he manages to stay away from smoking. The Democratic Presidential candidate replied, "I think that it is important to just keep in mind, I have a nine-year-old daughter and a six-year-old daughter. And <u>I want to give them away at their weddings</u>."

5. A few weeks later, on the day after one of the Democratic Presidential debates, Chris Matthews offered this guess about what the debate watchers were thinking as the evening progressed: "They stopped listening a half-hour in, and they noticed how pretty she is - Michelle - and they said, '<u>I like the fact he's [Obama] got this pretty wife</u>. He's happily married. I like that.'"

6. I have in front of me a March 2008 magazine that includes a <u>story on wedding planning</u>. It is a straightforward how-to guide, with tips such as "Get organized," "Enlist help," and "Enjoy the day." What magazine was this in? *GradPSYCH*, a professional magazine for graduate students published by the American Psychological Association. I swear I am not making this up.

SO WHAT?

For those of you already set to pounce, let me concede your point: This is all small stuff.

1. Jack Cafferty reads lots of outrageous responses.

2. Most grown-ups know better than to believe everything they read in *Time*.

3. Maybe Jenna's single sister was thrilled to be exempt from the Pope-a-thon.

4. Perhaps Barack Obama did not mean to imply that he would be disappointed if his daughters stayed single.

5. Chris Matthews makes so many insensitive remarks that Media Matters keeps tabs on them.

6. Who cares if a professional magazine prints a story on wedding planning.

There are instances of singlism that are more serious than the ones I've described here. (I reviewed some of them in Chapter 12 of <u>Singled Out</u>.) Still, in its level of intensity, vitriol, and destructiveness, the discrimination faced by people who are single is not on a par with that faced by the targets of, say, racism or heterosexism.

Unlike the better-known isms, however, singlism is often <u>practiced without apology or even awareness</u>. Also, although singlism is not likely to be as scathing as racism, the steady drip, drip, drip of it could drive single people over the edge - if they were not so amazingly resilient.

Links:
[1] http://caffertyfile.blogs.cnn.com/2008/04/23/why-cant-barack-obama-close-the-deal/#more-331[2] http://www.amazon.com/Singled-Out-Singles-Stereotyped-Stigmatized/dp/0312340826/ref=ed_oe_p/102-4637341-6604139[3] http://www.time.com/time/magazine/article/0,9171,1704686,00.html[4] http://transcripts.cnn.com/TRANSCRIPTS/0804/15/sitroom.01.html[5] http://www.amazon.com/Even-Single-Stop-Giving-Hard/dp/076112134X/ref=pd_bbs_sr_1?ie=UTF8&s=books&qid=1209462257&sr=1-1[6] http://www.hiphopdx.com/index/news/id.6680/title.obama-discusses-smoking-gay-marriage-college-loans[7] http://72.14.253.104/search?q=cache:I8p_3hK4UV4J:mediamatters.org/items/200801170001 "chris matthews" jenna married&hl=en&ct=clnk&cd=2&gl=us&client=firefox-a[8] http://gradpsych.apags.org/2008/03/weddings.html[9] http://www.blackwell-synergy.com/doi/abs/10.1111/j.1467-8721.2006.00446.x?journalCode=cdir

14.

A Wife Is Not a "Scoot Out of Jail Free" Card

February 23, 2007

As the jury ponders Scooter Libby's fate, I'm still obsessing about Ted Wells's closing. I find it only mildly interesting that the high-powered defense attorney ended not with a bang but with a whimper, and not even a metaphorical one. I'm only a tad more intrigued by the attorney's creepy cry for help that immediately preceded his parting sob. Said Wells of his client: "He's been under my protection for the last month. I give him to you. Give him back to me."

No, what bothered me is the statement that came just before that one. It was Ted Wells's final argument:

"This is a man with a wife and two children; he is a good person."

If it is not instantly obvious what is wrong with that argument, imagine that Wells had instead said this of Scooter Libby, for all the world to hear about:

"This man is white; he is a good person."

It would never happen. A greatly respected American attorney would not rest on the defense that white people are good people, and by implication, better than people who are not white. Neither Ted Wells, nor anyone else of his ilk, would try shamelessly to suggest that perjury is less offensive when committed by a white person, and should therefore be forgiven.

But to say to a jury - my client is married, he has kids, he is a good person - that, apparently, is no problem.

45

I disagree. I think it is an example of a problem I call singlism - the stereotyping, stigmatizing, and discrimination that is directed at people who are single. At a time of heightened sensitivity to all sorts of isms, singlism has slipped under the cultural radar.

What was Wells thinking? Maybe he was implying that a married father has people who depend on him, whereas single people do not. But the law does not dispense "scoot out of jail free" cards to defendants simply because they are married or have children. And perhaps Libby should have thought about his wife and kids before he pursued his life of crime. (Okay, allegedly.)

There is one more problem with the argument that married people have others who depend on them whereas single people do not - it is wrong. Two national studies have shown that adults who have always been single are more likely to support, advise, contact, and visit their parents and siblings than are people who are currently married or were previously married. Singles are also more likely to help, encourage, and spend time with their neighbors and friends.

In researching my book, Singled Out: How Singles Are Stereotyped, Stigmatized, and Ignored, and Still Live Happily Ever After, I found that the practice of singlism is rampant. Acts of singlism are committed by the right and the left, and singlistic sentiments appear in low-brow and high-brow publications.

When singlism is perpetrated, unchallenged, in the courtroom, one possible outcome is lesser justice for single than for married people. When it is practiced in the political arena, the risk is lost elections.

The left has the most to gain by speaking the language and promoting the policies that include single as well as married people. Single people tilt strongly progressive when they vote, but they show up at the polls less often than married people. Their numbers are growing, and have been for decades. In fact, there are now fewer households consisting of mom, dad, and the kids than of single people living alone. (And most single people don't live alone.) Yet Democrats have been slow to appeal to the very people who are most likely to share their values.

A recent example is Senator Chuck Schumer's new book, Positively American. The subtitle is "Winning Back the Middle-Class Majority One Family at a Time." At the center of Schumer's story is the fictional family comprised of the married Joe and Eileen and their three kids.

I think Senator Schumer is right to care about traditional families. But in showcasing that demographic and, by implication, marginalizing the others, I think he is treading a path to the past. No matter how laudable Schumer's policy recommendations may be, his message about the fictional Joe may strike single people as a lot like Ted Wells's description of the real Scooter:

"This is a man with a wife and children; he is a good person."

15.

"So Why Have You Never Been Married?": A Case Study in Accidental Singlism

Jul 3 2008

"So Why Have You Never Been Married?" That's the title of a book sent to me by its author, Carl Weisman.

Questions like that push my perversity button, and I can't help generating Q & A sequences. For example:

Clueless Question: "So why have you never been married?"
My Perverse Answer: So why have you never been an accountant?

Clueless Question: "Why aren't you married?"
My Perverse Answer: Why aren't you a Christmas tree?

Clueless Question: "When are you going to get married?"
My Perverse Answer: When did you last have sex?

Clueless Question: "Will you ever marry?"
My Perverse Answer: Maybe if I get hit on the head with a rock and turn into a different person.

Seriously, though, I was delighted to get Weisman's book, not because I'd ever stand behind it, but because it is so (inadvertently) telling about what it is like to be single in contemporary American society. Weisman's interest is in single men, but what I find so intriguing and disappointing about his book is relevant to single women, too.

I ended a previous post with the question, "Why is there such a disconnect between the negative perceptions of single men and the actual life experiences of those men?" Readers contributed some thoughtful answers to the comments section. Weisman's book provides another set of responses. The author did not mean to address that question, but wow, did he ever leave some delicious clues to those who are not content to take what they read at face value!

First, I'll give you some background about the book. Then I'll provide some examples that I found particularly intriguing and ask whether you can see the accidental singlism in them. Then, after each one, I'll tell you what I think about it.

47

About the Book

Carl Weisman, the author, is 48, heterosexual, and has always been single. He wanted to know how other men similar to himself - over 40 and (in his words) "never married" - would answer the question, "So why have you never been married?"

He collected responses to an online survey from 1,533 men. Then he interviewed 33 of them by phone, for at least a half-hour.

Upfront, Weisman tells his readers what he thinks: Marriage isn't for everyone. "I just wish," he adds, "that was the prevailing sentiment in our culture today, rather than what it is: that there is something wrong with you if you are not married or have never been married."

If that is truly his wish, I think he undermines it at just about every turn of the page. He's practicing singlism, albeit unintentionally. Here are eleven examples.

Accidental Singlism - the Examples

EXAMPLE #1. The title of the book is "So Why Have You Never Been Married?"

The author said he wanted to answer two questions for himself:
1. So why have I never been married? and
2. What's wrong with me?

Question #1: What (if anything) is wrong with the title of the book, and the author's two goals in writing the book?

(Think about your own answer, then read on.)

One possible answer (mine) to #1: The singlism in the author's second question is obvious, and even he recognizes the "built-in negative bias" that he has created. But I object to the "why" question as well. As I said to Weisman when he first offered to send me his book, I don't think any single people should have to answer the question of why they are not married.

The "why aren't you married" question teeters on the assumption that if you are past a certain age and still single, you have some explaining to do. I don't buy it. To me, the question is akin to the infamous "when did you stop beating your wife" in its presumption of wrongdoing.

EXAMPLE #2. The author said he wanted to make sure he "investigated every possible factor that may have had an influence on the men to get them to avoid or postpone marriage."

Question #2: What (if anything) is wrong with the author's framing of this goal?

One possible answer (mine) to #2: I'll make my answer personal. I'm not "avoiding" marriage, I'm living my single life - fully and joyfully.

EXAMPLE #3. Here is a list of topics covered in the author's online survey:
• Demographic information (age, race, education, salary, do you own or rent)
• Information about family and friends (e.g., are your siblings, parents, friends married? divorced? Do you have kids?)
• Information about past relationships (e.g., how many sexual partners, cohabiting partners, serious love relationships?)
• Information about current situation (e.g., are you currently in a love relationship? Are you afraid of marriage? Why have you never married?)
• Outlook for the future (e.g., will you be married some day? Do you have any regrets about not being married?)

Question #3: What (if anything) is missing from this list of topics? What else would you want to know if you were interested in all of the important factors in a single person's life? (For now, just consider the overall categories. Later, I'll get to the question of what is missing within the categories.)

One possible answer (mine) to #3: Even if I answered every question that the author posed, he would have no idea why I love my single life. He asks nothing about my work, nothing about my passions, nothing about what I appreciate about the texture of my everyday life. There is no place to tell him that I enjoy socializing and I also cherish my solitude, and as a single person with a place of my own, I can have both.

EXAMPLE #4. Weisman's online questions about my siblings include only the following: How many do I have? Are they younger or older than me? Have they been married? Have they been divorced?

What (if anything) is wrong with that?

One possible answer (mine): I'll start with an anecdote. Coincidentally, while I was studying the items in Weisman's online survey, I got a call from my "baby brother." (That's my term of endearment for him; actually, he's in his mid-40s.) I adore him. Just about every time I finish a conversation with him, I'm in a better mood than I was before.

But Weisman's questions in his online survey do not offer me an opportunity to mention any of that. If Weisman had interviewed me by phone, I think he would have asked me something like the following: How does it make me feel that my younger brother is married and I am not?

Here's my answer (and I think it is safe to say that it is not the one Weisman is expecting): It makes me smile. My brother likes being married; I like being single. We're both happy.

EXAMPLE #5. Weisman's online survey includes one question about my physical living situation: Do I own or rent?

49

What (if anything) is wrong with that?

One possible answer (mine): It is true - I rent. I wish I owned the place where I live. I did own a home when I lived in Virginia, but I can't afford one out here in California.

Now here's what I don't get to include in my response to the online survey: The place I rent is a beach house with a spectacular view of the Pacific Ocean. I've lived here for eight years and I never habituate to it. Every day when I wake up, I look out the window and I am in awe of my great good fortune.

EXAMPLE #6. One of the men interviewed for the book was Martin, a 54-year old who, for the past 10 years, has been caring for elderly relatives. The author tells us that the care-giving experience has made Martin realize that he is a selfish person.

What (if anything) is wrong with that?

One possible answer (mine): Martin has spent a decade of his life caring for elderly relatives. He wishes he did not have the obligation to provide this care, and that's why he sees himself as selfish. But he IS providing the care. That is not the least bit selfish. And, because he is doing this care work, others (perhaps married siblings or other relatives) are not. I wonder if they see themselves as selfish?

EXAMPLE #7. Here's how the author described one of the men he interviewed: "Ryan is a forty-two-year-old sculptor from Wisconsin who wanted to be an artist from a young age, which distracted him from forming any real long-term relationships."

What (if anything) is wrong with that?

One possible answer (mine): If Ryan has wanted to be a sculptor since he was very young, then maybe art, to him, is not a distraction - it is a passion.

EXAMPLE #8. Donald told the author that if he were to marry, he would miss the ballgames, the golf, and all the other experiences he shares with his friends. The author muses (to his readers, not to Donald): "Even if [marriage] is about giving things up and sacrificing, surely we get things in return." For example, Weisman says, we get companionship.

What (if anything) is wrong with that?

One possible answer (mine): Donald already has companionship. He values his friends and the time he spends with them. The author seems to imply that the only companionship that really counts is kind that comes packaged with a romantic partner.

EXAMPLE #9. Sandy told the author that he is in a relationship with a woman who is emotionally and physically abusive. She is getting no professional help. Sandy thinks that maybe she is getting better.

Here's what the author says to his readers: "Sometimes it's one thing, one character flaw, that keeps the ball from crossing the goal line. It's that way for Sandy and his girlfriend. He wants her to win and he is rooting for her, so there is hope they could succeed."

What (if anything) is wrong with that?

One possible answer (mine): Apparently the author is rooting for this couple, too. But should he be rooting for them to marry, or for them to not even consider marriage until the woman gets professional help? Is this an example in which the mythical tug of marriage is so compelling that (to some people) even abuse should not stand in its way?

EXAMPLE #10. The author acknowledges that some men have no desire to ever marry. He's sure there are women like that, too. His conclusion: "these two groups should do their best to find each other."

What (if anything) is wrong with that?

One possible answer (mine): Okay, author, let me spell it out. I'm single. I want to be single. You acknowledge that. You also recognize that there are men who want to be single. Yet your conclusion is that you hope we find each other?

EXAMPLE #11. The author notes that before he even started this project, he was confident about one of the things he would find - that the fear of divorce would be one of the reasons why 40+ year-old men had never married. After interviewing 33 of the men, he concluded that he was right all along. Some, for example, had parents who divorced; others had parents who should have divorced.

What (if anything) is wrong with that?

One possible answer (mine): The author articulated an utterly conventional point of view: the assumption that "broken homes" (as the author calls them) produce adult children who stay single for life. He doesn't tally the numbers (even within his own unrepresentative sample) or cite scientific research. He just found some men whose stories seem consistent with the conventional wisdom, and that was good enough.

I don't know of any relevant studies, either. But I wonder what the author would make of my story. My parents were married for 42 years, until the day my father died.

That's just an example, not a piece of evidence. But here's my point: Why is lifelong singlehood seen only as something bad, that needs to be explained by damaging or distressing experiences? Why not at least entertain entirely different possibilities?

51

Maybe, for instance, some parents are secure enough to live the life that works for them, without assuming that the same life would work best for each of their children. Maybe what parents can give to their children, that is more valuable than just about anything else, is faith in themselves and the confidence to live an authentic life and not just an expected one.

Well, I have pages of additional examples, but you've probably already read more than enough. I'm not saying I'm right about these men. Weisman interviewed them; I did not. But by asking the men one question after another such as
• What is your biggest fear about being married?
• What is your nightmare scenario?
• Do you think you have a commitment problem?
the author made it quite clear what he believed. He also aptly represented the prevailing societal view of single life: Wanting to be single is not a plausible option.

If there were men in the author's study who feel as joyful and unconflicted about being single as I do, I think they may have had a hard time making their true feelings known.

Until authors, reporters, parents, friends, and everyone else can accept "I'm single and I like it that way" as an answer, there will continue to be a disconnect between perceptions of people who are single and their actual life experiences.

Source URL: http://www.psychologytoday.com/node/1221

Links:
[1] http://www.amazon.com/Why-Have-Never-Been-Married/dp/0882823264/ref=sr_1_2?ie=UTF8&s=books&qid=1215080054&sr=1-2[2] http://www.psychologytoday.com/blog/living-single/200806/but-what-about-single-men[3] http://www.amazon.com/Singled-Out-Singles-Stereotyped-Stigmatized/dp/0312340826/ref=ed_oe_p

16.

Veterans Day: The Fairest of Them All?

November 11, 2007

On most days of the year, some members of the service seem to be chosen as media favorites; they garner more attention, gratitude, and concern than others. Watch the clips of warriors returning home and notice how often they are rushing into the outstretched arms of a spouse.

Listen to the coverage and take notes. I started doing this a few years ago. One of my first entries was from a Nightline broadcast from December of 2004 about seriously wounded soldiers. Nightline noted that these soldiers "may not be able to do any of the things they did before. And that means the lives of their spouses are changed forever too."

There is a risk to selective coverage: It makes the service members who are not married - about half of them - seem invisible or insignificant. Where are the pictures of the friends, siblings, parents, and neighbors anxiously waiting to embrace them? Where is the empathy for the people caring for the wounded warriors who are single?

On the webpage "Reconnect America - Give Back to Those Who Give It All," visitors are asked to show their support for the members of the Armed Forces by donating to seven nonprofit organizations. Four of them describe their mission as helping the spouses or families of service members. Those people deserve support. But so do the important people in the lives of the soldiers who are not married.

When I interviewed service members for my book, Singled Out, some claimed that even the perks that were not targeted specifically to married soldiers, such as free phone calls, were sometimes doled out preferentially to them. I don't know if those perceptions were accurate. Some of the preferential treatment of married soldiers, though, is on the books.

Take pay, for example. Married soldiers have been paid more than single soldiers of the same rank as far back as World War I. By 2006, the disparity had grown to a 25% advantage for the married service members. (I describe other categories of differential treatment in Singled Out.)

I don't think single soldiers should get special treatment. They should get the same treatment. When an IED is about to explode, it does not stop to check the marital status of the person in the way, then go off with a whimper instead of a bang if the soldier is single.

Today, however, I have no complaints. When it comes to acknowledging the contributions of all service members, Veterans Day strikes me as one of the fairest days of all. On that one day of the year, only two questions seem relevant: Did you serve? And, did you serve honorably? If the answer to both is yes, that's all that matters.

That's why Veterans Day has a special place in my heart.

Source URL: http://www.huffingtonpost.com/bella-depaulo/veterans-day-the-fairest-_b_72074.html

17.

Is It Bad to Notice Discrimination?

May 24 2008

It still amazes me that at a time of such exquisite sensitivity to all sorts of isms (such as racism, sexism, ageism, and heterosexism), singlism is so often practiced without apology or even awareness. But if singlism is unrecognized, and - as I have acknowledged - it is not as vicious as some of the other isms, why not let it stay unrecognized? What's the point of increasing people's awareness of still another form of stereotyping and discrimination?

FIRST, HOW (IF AT ALL) DO YOU THINK IT WOULD MATTER IF STEREOTYPES OF SINGLES AND DISCRIMINATION AGAINST SINGLES WENT UNRECOGNIZED?

Let's generate some possibilities for what it might mean if the stigma of singlehood were to go unnoticed. Then in the next section, I'll tell you about some of the relevant research.

I think that if stereotypes of singles were to go unchallenged, then single people (and everyone else) would believe that singles are miserable, lonely, and self-centered. They might further assume that if only single people would marry, they would be transformed into blissfully happy and altruistic beings. They might also presume that people who stay single "too long" need to answer for their "condition," explaining what it is about them that keeps them from marrying. This is the deficit or tragic-flaw perspective on singlehood - which, by the way, does not pass scientific muster (as I explained in Chapter 2 of <u>Singled Out</u>).

Another component of the stigma of being single is interpersonal exclusion. Sometimes people who have gotten married ditch their single friends not because the single friends have done anything wrong, or because they like their single friends any less, but simply because they have joined the Married Couples Club. Although there are many enlightened exceptions, couples often socialize primarily with other couples. If singles were more aware of the pervasiveness of this custom of exclusion, maybe they would stop searching for their personal tragic flaws to explain their own experiences of rejection.

Occasionally, single people claim that they have never experienced singlism. In some instances, the wording of their claims undermines their points. In a discussion of how solo diners are treated in restaurants, for instance, one single woman said that she is never seated near the swinging kitchen doors because whenever a hostess leads her in that direction, she objects and insists on being seated elsewhere.

More importantly, all singles experience singlism, because it is <u>institutionalized in our laws and public policies</u>. Think through the many arguments you have heard in favor of same-sex marriage. Often, they sound something like this: Gay men and lesbians should be able to marry because then they, too, could have access to the important benefits and protections available only to married people. There are more than 1,000 such privileges, including access to health insurance through a partner's employer-provided policy; estate tax protections; and medical decision-making rights. But even if same-sex marriage were legal everywhere, discrimination against people who are single - gay or straight - would still remain. If colleagues can put their spouse on their health-care plan at a reduced rate, but I can't put my sister or my best friend on my plan (and no such person can put me on their plan), then I am getting less compensation for the same work.

The view I am describing here is this: An awareness of the stereotypes, prejudices, and instances of discrimination that really do exist is mostly a good thing. As Jenny Crocker and Brenda Major suggested (in a paper that is now considered a modern classic), stigmatized people's self-esteem can be protected if they realize that sometimes, when things go wrong, the reason is not their own incompetence or unattractiveness. Instead, the blame should be pinned on other people's biases.

It is not just academics who believe in the possibilities of stigma-awareness. To many activists, consciousness-raising is one of the first steps toward powerful social movements and meaningful social change.

Still, there are other important points of view. For example, how can it not hurt to realize that you are devalued simply because you are single?

With regard to the more recognized isms, such as sexism and racism, there is an abundance of relevant research. We now know, for example, that whether it pains you to perceive discrimination depends on whether you are a member of a stigmatized group and you identify with that group. It also depends on your worldview. If you believe in a meritocracy, whereby people are rewarded because they deserve to be, then that first personal experience of undeniable discrimination can send a shudder down your spine and a jolt to your belief system.

When it comes to singlism, however, the research has only just begun. We cannot assume that the psychological dynamics will be the same for singlism as for other isms, because it differs in its contours and its intensity, and because awareness of it is so new.

IS IT BAD TO NOTICE DISCRIMINATION: WHAT DOES THE RESEARCH SHOW?

Recently, Monica Pignotti has been developing a scale to measure the negative stereotyping of people who are single. She has found, in correlational research, that singles who believe the negative stereotypes have lower self-esteem.

But as Wendy Morris has shown in her dissertation research, many single people do not even realize that there is a stigma to being single. What happens if you hasten the dawn of their awareness?

Wendy thought it would depend on what singles could do with their newfound knowledge that stereotyping and discrimination against singles really does exist. If, just after becoming sensitized to the stereotypes, singles also learned that the stereotypes were inaccurate, then maybe awareness would be a good thing. Or, if singles could look back on a time when they were treated negatively and realize that singlism may have been the reason, then that sort of "rearview revision" might also be helpful.

Across three studies, Wendy found no evidence that awareness of singlism was harmful to self-esteem. She found some indications that it could be good for single people's self-esteem and for their mood. Women were especially likely to benefit from becoming newly sensitized to singlism.

Readers of <u>Singled Out</u> and of this blog already know that in my opinion, when it comes to what singles face in contemporary American society, singlism is just the half of it. The other half is matrimania - the over-the-top hyping of marriage and coupling and all the accompanying myths. So here's another question: Does it matter if singles believe the myths about the magical transformations awaiting them if only they marry?

As always, there is not much relevant research, but what is available is tantalizing. Laurie Rudman and Jessica Heppen used an <u>implicit association test</u> to see <u>what the word boyfriend seemed to mean</u> to different women. Some women made quick mental leaps from "boyfriend" to words or phrases such as "hero" and "Prince Charming." Perhaps they thought of boyfriends as Knights in Shining Armor, who rescue poor bedraggled maidens and transform them into ravishing and everlastingly happy princesses. For other women, phrases such as "Average Joe" were more readily linked to the "boyfriend" idea.

If you are thinking that the fantasy life of the Prince Charming women sounds much more lively than that of the Average Joe women, consider this: The authors found that the women who were quickest to associate boyfriends with rescue heroes "showed less interest in high-status occupations, the economic rewards that accompany them, and the educational commitment they require." Who needs a fabulous job or a great education when you can just step into the glass slipper and live happily ever after?

Many of you already know how most research papers end - with the caution that more research is needed. Same here. Still, from what we've learned so far, I'd say that increasing sensitivity to singlism may well be good for your mental health. This is especially so if you learn not just that singles are stereotyped, but that the stereotype-peddlers are on the wrong side of the scientific fence. As your singlism-awareness develops, you may be less inclined to blame yourself when that blame is not deserved. With a mind unmuddled by matrimania, perhaps you will be more likely to pursue your educational degrees and your professional dreams. Those achievements can never be taken away from you, even if you do decide, at some point, that you want to be married.

A WHOLE OTHER QUESTION: WHAT IF YOU NOTICE SINGLISM AND COMPLAIN ABOUT IT?

Obviously, I think it is mostly good for your own peace of mind to be aware of the psychological dynamics set off by singlism. But once you get outside of your own head and into the world, a whole other set of issues awaits you. What if you don't just notice singlism, but also call it to the attention of others? Unfortunately, that terrain is more treacherous. Whistle-blowers are often treated very badly, even when their claims are meticulously documented.

Source URL: http://www.psychologytoday.com/node/794

Links:
[1] http://www.amazon.com/Singled-Out-Singles-Stereotyped-Stigmatized/dp/0312340826/ref=ed_oe_p/102-4637341-6604139[2] http://psycnet.apa.org/index.cfm?fa=main.doiLanding&uid=1990-04498-001[3] http://www.understandingprejudice.org/readroom/[4] http://cat.inist.fr/?aModele=afficheN&cpsidt=1883274[5] http://psycnet.apa.org/index.cfm?fa=search.displayRecord&uid=2007-07951-008[6] http://psp.sagepub.com/cgi/content/abstract/31/12/1730[7] http://psychjourney_blogs.typepad.com/monica_pignotti_/[8] http://www.mcdaniel.edu/4258.htm[9] https://implicit.harvard.edu/implicit/demo/[10] http://psp.sagepub.com/cgi/content/abstract/29/11/1357[11] http://www.psychologytoday.com/blog/living-single

18.

What We Can Learn from Boneheaded Bigotry about Single People

Jan 2 2009

There is an aspect of singlism (the stereotyping, stigmatizing, and discrimination against people who are single) that continues to amaze me - it is often practiced without apology or even awareness. Those who engage in singlism can be clueless about their bigotry.

Example #1. Dumb Statement from "Smart Marriages"

One example comes the group, Smart Marriages. The goal of the group, according to their website, is to make marriage education widely available. In a recent e-mail, the listserv moderator included a group member's recommendation of the movie "Marley and Me." Now I haven't seen the movie or read the book, so my post is not about that. What is important is what was said about the movie.

The person recommending the movie began by explaining why she thought that the couple who owned Marley (the dog) had such a great marriage. Then she describes the contrast between the husband and his friend who is single, and expresses her approval that the movie never portrays the husband as wanting to be single and carefree like his friend. Here's the money quote:

"The contrast doesn't come across as judgmental. It just makes it seem like the friend doesn't have roots and that his life has a lot of emptiness while John has his family and a life with meaning."

Think about this for a moment while you shake your head in dismay. Here is someone describing a single person's life as rootless and empty, and the married person's as full of family and meaning, AND at the same time claiming that there's nothing judgmental here!

I wondered if other Smart Marriage members would have any response. Sure enough, in the next e-mail, another member complimented the first on her astute assessment. The movie, she added, is "a really good lesson on tolerance and empathy."

I'm not just complaining or making my own value judgments, though I am doing both. (I value people who do not practice singlism over people who do, and I vow to continue complaining about the latter.) I think we can learn a thing or two from the practice of bigotry toward singles.

First, this is an example of how singlism gets perpetrated. Dismissive statements about single people are e-mailed to probably thousands of people, and go unchallenged.

Second, notice the implicit strategy for promoting marriage. If you don't get married and join the ranks of people with meaningful lives, "Smart Marriages" seems to be saying, you will live out your single life rootless and empty. The group is not content to promote marriage; it wants to threaten, scare, and humiliate you out of your single life. Somehow I doubt that's an effective route to a smart and strong marriage.

The example is not an exception for the Smart Marriage group. In fact, they offer their visitors a page of quotes about marriage, including this one from Franz Kafka:

"It seems so dreadful to stay a bachelor, to become an old man struggling to keep one's dignity while begging for an invitation whenever one wants to spend an evening in company, to lie ill gazing for weeks into an empty room from the corner where one's bed is..." [and so on for several more miserable and insulting lines].

Example #2. Heard on C-SPAN: Singles Are Like Obese People - They Lack Discipline

At a panel hosted by the <u>American Enterprise Institute</u>, and later broadcast on C-SPAN, James Q. Wilson of Pepperdine University introduced Linda Waite as:

"co-author, with Maggie Gallagher, of a remarkable book about the benefits, in terms of health, well-being, longevity, etc., of marriage. So compelling is the book that you wonder why any man and woman of the appropriate age doesn't get married immediately. Well, that's akin to explaining obesity. Everyone knows that remaining slender is in your long-term interest but then someone puts fudge in front of you or chocolate cake and you can't resist the immediate temptation."

This is a twofer. In one brief introduction, Wilson flaunts his ignorance and bigotry both toward obese people and single people. I'll leave it to my <u>fellow PT bloggers</u> who are more knowledgeable about such matters to debunk the claim that obese people got that way by their utter lack of willpower in the face of fudge and cake.

As for the singlism, well, which is it? Is single life empty (as the Smart Marriage people would have us believe) or is it filled with tempting and delicious delicacies? Are we single people hanging onto our single states because we don't have the willpower to set aside those brownies and eat our peas? (And is James Q. Wilson really trying to persuade us of the appeal of getting married by comparing it to eating peas?)

The two examples, taken side-by-side, show how the practitioners of singlism get singles coming and going. First, claim that the lives of single people are rootless, meaningless, and empty. If that doesn't stick, then try this: Okay single people, so you think your lives are full? Well, they are full of frivolity, like eating nothing but dessert.

There are lots of these "heads I win, tails you lose" takes on single life. (I've described some of them in <u>Singled Out</u>.) For example, if you are a young single man, you need to "settle down." If you are an older single man with a home, a good job, and people you care about, well, then, you are "set in your ways." If you are a single woman, then maybe you are a slut. That doesn't fit? Poor thing - you don't get any.

The lesson is this: **Live your single life fully, in the ways that seem most meaningful to you. Don't try to construct your life so as to dodge the slings of singlism - there's always another arrow of bigotry where the first one came from.**

Once, when I was describing these gotcha dilemmas to the host of a radio show, she said the dynamic was familiar to her as a married woman who had decided, along with her husband, that she did not want kids. Sometimes she is told that she's just selfish - she's like a kid who just wants to have fun and does not want to accept the responsibilities of parenting. Other times she's told that she is missing out on all the fun and joy of having children. Either way, her decision is derided and dismissed.

One last and very important note. That supposedly "remarkable" book showing that getting married brings health, well-being, and a longer life? I've read it very closely, even going back to the original sources to check out the claims. Don't buy it (the book or the conclusions). As I explain in Chapter 2 of Singled Out, most of the claims made by Waite and Gallagher about the transformative power of marriage are misrepresented, grossly exaggerated, or just plain wrong.

Source URL: http://www.psychologytoday.com/node/2842

Links:
[1] http://www.smartmarriages.com/index.html[2] http://www.smartmarriages.com/marriage.quotes.html[3] http://74.125.45.132/search?q=cache:jv8Dxf8wW88J:www.aei.org/events/filter.all,eventID.1 691/transcript.asp "linda waite" may 2008 c-span&hl=en&ct=clnk&cd=2&gl=us&client=firefox-a [4] http://www.psychologytoday.com/topics/diet[5] http://www.amazon.com/Singled-Out-Singles-Stereotyped-Stigmatized/dp/0312340826/ref=ed_oe_p/102-4637341-6604139

19.

Those Pitied, Mocked, Envied Years Between the Late Teens and Late Twenties: What Are They Really About?

Dec 7 2008

A Conversation with Jeffrey Jensen Arnett

This is the "Living Single" blog, but what it means to live single can be very different depending on the phase of life you are in. Today, I've invited an expert on "emerging adulthood" to tell us what life is really like for people in the ages between the late teens and late 20s. I think that's a very interesting group because it is one that does get a lot of media attention, but not always in an accurate way.

Jeffrey Jensen Arnett is one of the leading scholars of this group. He wrote the book, Emerging Adulthood: The Winding Road from the Late Teens through the Twenties, and I invited him to answer some questions. I'm delighted that he agreed.

Bella: Once upon a time, it was easy to say when adulthood began - it was when you got married. One of the findings from your work that I have found most intriguing is that young people today do not use marriage as the criterion for deciding when they have, in fact, become adults. What are the criteria they use now?

Jeff: Today the criteria are more individualistic and gradual, specifically these 3: accepting responsibility for yourself, making independent decisions, and becoming financially independent. I've been amazed by how the same 3 criteria have come out on top in over a dozen studies by me and others, in every American social class and ethnic group, and in countries all over the world. And it's not just emerging adults who place these 3 criteria on top, it's also adolescents and young and middle adults. Where the heck did marriage go, and finishing your education, and turning 18 or 21? My interpretation is that these old-fashioned criteria are all social criteria that can be measured and judged by others. I think in today's individualistic world, emerging adults like to make their own judgments about whether they have reached adulthood-or not.

Bella: In the first chapter of your book, <u>Emerging Adulthood</u>, you caution that emerging adulthood is NOT the same as late adolescence, young adulthood, transition to adulthood, or youth. Can you explain what emerging adulthood really is?

Jeff: I don't think it's just "late adolescence," because they are not going through puberty, they're not in high school, and most don't live in their parents' household. I don't think "young adulthood" fits because they haven't entered the roles that we associate with adulthood, such as stable work and (for many but not all) marriage and parenthood, and most are not financially independent. I don't think "the transition to adulthood" works because it lasts so long. Ten years seems a bit long for a "transition" to adulthood. And "youth" is the worst of all, because it has been applied to people from age 6 to 40, so it doesn't have a clear meaning. This is really a new life stage, so it needs a new name. Never in human history have we had such a long gap between the time people reach the end of puberty and the time they feel fully adult and have taken on the full range of adult responsibilities. I've found "emerging adulthood" resonates well with many of the people who are in this age period now. It describes their sense of being on the way to adulthood but not there yet.

So what is "emerging adulthood"? It's a period of making your way gradually toward constructing an adult life, in love and work. In my book I describe emerging adulthood has having 5 features that make it distinct: it's the age of identity explorations, the age of instability, the self-focused age, the age of feeling in-between, and the age of possibilities. These features don't necessarily start or end in emerging adulthood, but I think that's when they're most prominent.

Bella: This is a blog about singles, so I'm interested in how you see singles in relation to emerging adulthood. On the one hand, you say marriage is not an important criterion for adulthood, but on the other, you use marriage as one of the "adult roles" that mark the end of emerging adulthood and the beginning of young adulthood.

Jeff: I think young people today reach adulthood according to the 3 subjective, individualistic criteria I described above, then they may or may not marry and become parents. Most people-about 75% of Americans-marry and become parents by age 30, but I think the subjective criteria are more important for marking the end of emerging adulthood and the beginning of young adulthood. As you've described so well, there are still lots of prejudices against singles, especially after age 30, this sniggering sense that they never really grow up, but I don't think that's true.

Bella: One of my missions in researching and <u>writing about singles</u> is to separate the stereotypes and myths from the truths. One relatively new claim is that people today experience a "quarterlife crisis." Can you explain what is meant by that term and where you think it falls on the myth vs. truth dimension?

Jeff: I think you've done great work combating the stereotypes about singles, in "<u>Singled Out</u>" and in your blog. I've tried to do the same for emerging adults. It's amazing to me how many unflattering myths there are about them-they're lazy, they're selfish, they're miserable, they're depraved. I've found them to be quite wonderful in my interviews, by and large. I love their energy and their optimism. They are far less sexist, racist, and homophobic than their parents or grandparents were; national surveys show this. They also do far more volunteer work, in organizations like the Peace Corps and Teach for America. And they are more aware of the suffering of people in the rest of the world than young people ever were before, and more determined to do something about it. So, I think we should be celebrating them instead of tearing them down.

I do think there is something to the "quarterlife crisis" claim, although it has been exaggerated. Few of them are quivering masses of anxieties, but most of them experience stress in emerging adulthood, because they are dealing with the identity issues of who they are and what kind of adult life they want to make for themselves, and because most have no money. But their sense of stress coexists with their high hopes. They struggle in emerging adulthood, most of them, but nearly all of them believe life is going to smile on them eventually. That's why I call it "the age of possibilities." I find it touching to hear them talk about their high hopes, because I know that life's smiles are granted a lot more sparingly than they realize.

Bella: Jeff, the first time I knew I just had to get your insights represented in this blog was when I saw a <u>review of a new book</u> called *Guyland: The Perilous World Where Boys Become Men*. I have to confess that before I read even a word of the review or the book, I had a bad feeling about it. That was because of a giant picture that was printed along with the review. It showed a gathering of shapely, attractive, bikini-clad young women, holding drinks and frolicking in a pool with their male counterparts, one of whom was pumping a fist. Talk about stereotypes! Plus, to make it even worse, the caption said that this "never-ending party" was, for some, the "new normal for guys." Now I know better than to believe everything I read, so this could have been a matter of a reporter getting it wrong. Since you've read the book, and your academic expertise on these matters is probably unparalleled, why don't you tell us what you think of it.

Jeff: I read the book, and it was disappointing. Yet another slander against emerging adults, still more negative stereotyping. Sure, there are guys who get drunk a lot, act like jerks toward women, and have a shallow view of life. But the author's mistake is to imply that all young guys today are like this, and that they're worse than ever. Neither of these claims is true. What's really striking is how much less sexist, racist, and homophobic young guys are now than in the past. Most want an equal partner in a romantic and sexual relationship, not just someone who will serve them. Most have friends who are of different ethnic groups, and most have gay or lesbian friends and don't make a big deal out of it. What's more, rates of every type of "guy problem" have declined sharply in the past 30 years among emerging adults-including alcohol use, crime, and unprotected sex. So the assertion that the typical young guy today is a drunken porno-mad potential rapist is nonsense. It's untrue and unfair.

Bella: During the same week that review of Guyland appeared, there was a story about single men in the *New York Times*. The take on single men in this article could not have been more different. The *Times* was writing about the growing trend of single men raising children, and the great devotion to fatherhood so many of them show. One of the men in the story was an attorney who had a crib set up in his office. The reporter pointed out that many of these single men are similar to the single women who have jobs that pay well and allow them to support themselves and some children, too. Did you think the article was accurate? If this is a real trend and not just hype, do you see any significance in it?

Jeff: I didn't see the article, but it sounds exaggerated in the other direction. I doubt if there are many attorneys with cribs in their offices. Single men are still a very small proportion of single parents, only about 10%. Parenting is one area that is still really unequal between the genders. Even when there are two partners and both work full-time, women still end up doing most of the child care and household work. But I'm hopeful that will change when the emerging adults of today enter parenthood. Young men say they want to be involved fathers, and I think they mean it.

Bella: What have you learned about the importance of people's friends in emerging adulthood? Do you have any sense of how the role of friends is different today than it was for 20-somethings in the past? For example, are attitudes such as political preferences less likely to be passed on from generation to generation, and more likely to be influenced by friends, than they were before?

Jeff: This a fascinating area, something I want to research more. There's not much research on it yet. My sense is that because more people now stay single for longer, friends are more important than ever during emerging adulthood. However, a lot depends on whether they have a current romantic partner. When they're not involved with anyone, they look to their friends for companionship and support, but when they're in love, the love partner comes first.

With regard to political preferences, it was certainly striking how Obama's election was driven so much by emerging adults. Not only did they vote for Obama by the largest margin of any age group, tens of thousands of them worked for him all over the country. Emerging adults have the freedom to get up and go in a way that people can't once they have a stable job and family responsibilities, so they were able to go to Ohio, Virginia, Florida, wherever they were needed. Obama is an inspiring figure, but I'm sure the camaraderie of working with other emerging adults and making friends was also part of the draw for those who worked for him. I'm sure those who were inspired by him early on influenced their friends, who also became inspired to work for him.

Bella: I know that you've studied how people's relationships with their parents change during emerging adulthood. Do any of those relationships become true friendships during that time? Should they?

Jeff: I've been struck by how highly emerging adults think of their parents and how well they get along with them. Of course, it's easier to get along with someone once you don't live with them, and emerging adults who move out get along better with their parents than those who stay home. But it's more than that. Emerging adults really come to respect and value their parents as friends. I can't tell you how many emerging adults have told me that they regret treating their parents badly as adolescents, and that now they see their parents as persons in a way they didn't before. I think it's a great thing for both sides. Emerging adults benefit from having a parent who acts as a supportive and nurturing friend, and of course the change is gratifying to parents, to be loved and respected more. Emerging adulthood is the big payoff of parenting, after all the years of stress and sacrifice.

Many thanks, Jeff. It was great of you to share your important work with us.

Source URL: http://www.psychologytoday.com/node/2593

Links:
[1] http://www.jeffreyarnett.com/[2] http://www.amazon.com/Emerging-Adulthood-Winding-through-Twenties/dp/0195309375/ref=sr_1_1?ie=UTF8&s=books&qid=1227670471&sr=1-1[3] http://www.amazon.com/Singled-Out-Singles-Stereotyped-Stigmatized/dp/0312340826/ref=ed_oe_p/102-4637341-6604139[4] http://www.newsweek.com/id/156372[5] http://www.psychologytoday.com/blog/about-fathers/200811/michael-kimmels-sketchy-tour-guyland[6] http://www.nytimes.com/2008/09/07/fashion/07single.html?ref=fashion

20.

Living Single: Are the Early Adult Years the Hardest? Part I

Feb 1 2009

As much as I love living single - and I do - I also recognize that not everyone is as smitten by the single state as I am. Sometimes other singles tell me so in their comments to this blog or in their e-mails to me. Fellow *Psychology Today* bloggers have had their say, too. Jenna Baddeley, for instance, has written about her single friends who are not in a romantic relationship and who wonder, "What's wrong with me?"

As long as there is <u>singlism</u> (stereotyping and stigmatizing of singles), there will be challenges to living single, and some - such as getting excluded from social events simply because you are not part of a couple - can be truly painful. I'll talk more about that in a later post. Today, though, I want to start a discussion of the question: What does age have to do with it?

Often (though not always), the singles who wish they were coupled, and wonder what is holding them back, are in their early adult years - 20s, maybe early 30s. Sometimes I discern an underlying fear that things are only going to get worse for them if they stay single as the years go by.

That belief is not unusual. Wendy Morris and I, in a <u>series of experiments</u>, have documented a widely shared presumption that single people, relative to married ones, become more dissatisfied with their lives as they grow older. Any loneliness or discontent experienced in their twenties, they assume, only intensifies with age.

My guess is that just the opposite is true. I think that as people move into their late 30s, 40s, and beyond, they become more sure of themselves, and less susceptible to being influenced or hurt by other people's opinions about how they should lead their lives. Also, they have often created full and satisfying lives by then - pursuing their passions, making their house into a home, finding rewarding work or fulfilling after-work interests, making a contribution to society, and developing and maintaining a network of friends and family.

In fact, compared to people who marry and then practice intensive coupling (looking to their spouse to be their everything, and moving everyone and everything else to the back burner), <u>single people may end up less vulnerable than married people</u>. They are not placing all of their life's eggs into the marital basket.

The type of study that would be needed to test my ideas has never been done. It would follow people throughout the course of their adult years, and ask many questions all along the way - questions, for example, about their life experiences, life satisfaction, feelings of autonomy and personal growth, about the difference they have made, and about the important people in their lives.

Short of that, what I have collected in support of my hunches are snippets of research from here and there. Here are a few examples.

• A study of well-being at midlife revealed some challenges to living single (such as lower household income) but also some signs of strength and resilience - for instance, women who were separated, divorced, or had always been single were <u>more open to new experience</u> than were married women.

• A <u>MacArthur Foundation</u> study of social well being in midlife also showed that singles had some difficulties (for example, they were less likely than married people to say that they had much in common with the people in their neighborhood) but also some points of pride - for example, they were more likely than married people to feel that they have <u>something valuable to contribute to society</u>. (See the chapter by Keyes and Shapiro.)

• A comparison of midlife adults who had always been single to similar younger adults found that the midlife single women reported <u>fewer negative feelings</u> (such as sadness, anxiety, worthlessness, or restlessness) than the younger single women. (See the chapter by Marks, Bumpass, & Jun. Note, though, that the midlife and younger singles were different people; the ideal study would track the same people as they made their way through all of the decades of their adult life.)

• Some studies of later life have shown that women who have always been single have extraordinarily low levels of loneliness (reviewed in Chapter 11 of <u>Singled Out</u>).

These empirical snippets have left me unsatisfied, so I was delighted to have the chance to discuss these ideas with psychotherapist <u>Wendy Wasson</u>. The next post in this series will begin my Q and A with her.

Source URL: <u>http://www.psychologytoday.com/node/3223</u>

Links:
[1] <u>http://www.psychologytoday.com/blog/embracing-the-dark-side/200812/singlehood-a-normative-discontent</u>[2] <u>http://www.amazon.com/Singled-Out-Singles-Stereotyped-Stigmatized/dp/0312340826/ref=ed_oe_p/102-4637341-6604139</u>[3] <u>http://www3.interscience.wiley.com/journal/118584107/abstract?CRETRY=1&SRETRY=0</u>[4] <u>http://www.psychologytoday.com/blog/living-single/200811/the-fragile-spouse-and-the-resilient-single-person</u>[5] http://library.pop.upenn.edu/athcgi/athweb.pl?a=f&ci=DL&pg=20&st=std&in=19&fr=1&lr=25&li=31100820&nh=25&kw=MARKS, NADINE F.&k1=MARKS, NADINE F.&k2=&k3=&o1=1&o2=1&l1=3&l2=1&l3=1&loc=&fmt=&vrss=&vrps=&jw=1&tx=000014964 [6] <u>http://www.macfound.org/site/c.lkLXJ8MQKrH/b.3599935/k.66CA/MacArthur_Foundation_Home.htm</u>[7] <u>http://www.amazon.com/How-Healthy-Are-Well-Being-Foundation/dp/0226074773/ref=sr_1_1?ie=UTF8&s=books&qid=1233524708&sr=1-1</u>[8] <u>http://www.mysinglespace.org/aboutus.html</u>[9] <u>http://www.mysinglespace.org/</u>

21.

Are the Early Years of Single Life the Hardest? Part II: Approaching Age 30

Feb 12 2009

A conversation with Wendy Wasson

In the <u>first post</u> in this series, I described the widespread belief that living single only gets harder as you proceed through midlife and then through later life. I also said that my guess, in most cases, is that just the opposite is true. I think that single people are likely to find their lives full of more joy and less angst as they proceed through their adult years. I found a few snippets of research that supported that possibility. Still, I admitted that the most convincing study of this question has yet to be done.

Within just the first few hours of when that entry was posted, hundreds of people had already clicked on to view the post. So I think there is a lot of interest in the topic. That's one of the reasons I am so pleased to discuss this topic with Wendy Wasson.

Wendy is a psychotherapist who, in her practice, has worked with many single women of different ages. She is also one of the creators of the website MySingleSpace, and for nearly a decade had conducted SingleSpace workshops. She has a Ph.D. in Clinical Psychology from Northwestern University, where she was previously on the faculty of the Feinberg School of Medicine. She is also associated with the Cathedral Counseling Center in Chicago.

Wendy Wasson's clinical perspective adds a complementary point of view to the research approach I described in the first post in this series. I thought this Q & A would be one post, but Wendy had so much of value to offer that I'm going to present our conversation in three posts, Parts II, III, and IV of this series. In this initial part of our conversation, Wendy will tell us about her experiences working with single women who are approaching their 30th birthday.

[One more aside before we begin: I know many "Living Single" readers would like to hear more about single men. Previously, I've shared my own frustration with the lesser attention accorded to single men. I promise to return to the topic in the future.]

Bella: Before we talk about single women in their late 20s, let me get your overall take on the question that motivated this series of posts: Is it your experience, in working with singles, that the early adult years of single life are the hardest for them?

Wendy: So many choices and decisions face young women as they explore life on their own, take on adult responsibilities, and develop the initial structures of their adult life. What is my career? How do I want my relationships to look? What are the "things I want to do before I settle down"? What really matters to me?

And there is a lot of change...new jobs, new apartments; new boyfriends...and then dealing with shifting friendships, as peers begin to choose different paths. All of these possibilities for growth and development can also raise concerns. Am I making the right decisions? Will I be able to handle these things on my own? What will I do without my best friend?

Bella: Let's talk about those younger single women, say around 25 to 30 years old. What are the main worries or concerns that they bring to you in your practice?

Wendy: As they approach their 30th birthday, many women (particularly those for whom marriage and children are an important part of their hoped-for future) are attuned to whether they are "on or off time" in relation to their biological clock, their own timetable of when certain events should be happening in their lives, and their social clock- that is, how they are progressing in relation to their peers. They watch friends partnering and are often attending the numerous parties that celebrate marriage (engagement parties, showers, weddings). Many women that I have worked with begin to wonder: "When is my turn?" "Why is it so easy for others?" "Am I doing something wrong?" For these women, there can be a sense of failure and discouragement, resulting in pessimism and/or urgency in finding or holding onto a partner.

It can also be lonely. It can feel isolating to be surrounded by friends who are discussing details of their weddings, or are sharing with excitement having found the perfect guy. Susan, single and 29, described this feeling as "Everyone is opening presents, and you are the only one who Santa Claus forgot." Another woman described attending a wedding and sitting at a table of mostly couples, feeling like she was disrupting the seating plan. These women are not "complainers"...they are describing the very real sense of feeling like the "odd woman out."

Even those women who are enjoying their single lives have moments of worry and doubt. Are they missing something, and if they do want to consider marriage and children, will it be too late when they are ready? (After all, family and friends and Aunt Jennie keep implying such urgency when they ask, "Have you met anyone yet?") Some women feel that no one believes them if they say they enjoy being single. "You're just being defensive!" It is difficult to feel supported and affirmed in being a single woman at 30.

Another challenge that single women at this age face is managing the changing landscape of friendships. As friends chose different paths and interests (e.g. some moving, disappearing when they date, marry, or have children), the single woman has to grieve these losses and recreate new friendship networks and community. Dealing with loss and recreation can sometimes feel exhausting, tiring, and lonely, even though the resilience and self confidence that ultimately comes from learning to manage these experiences is one of the powerful gifts of being single.

Finally, one of the aspects of being young is that we have less "real experience" to draw on, so we tend to fantasize about the future and are prone to believe that stereotypes and assumptions are true. Many young adult women who feel lonely blame it on being single, imagining with horror what it would be like to be 50 and single. It doesn't matter that there is a growing body of research (thank you Bella for conducting and reviewing such research studies) that indicates that Always-Single women show surprisingly low levels of loneliness (perhaps because they have learned to be confident, take responsibility for their lives, and create strong friendships.)

Bella: So as a therapist, what is your goal in dealing with singles in this age group?

Wendy: Part of the work of therapy is providing perspective, and helping the younger single woman appreciate the many possibilities in being single - one of which is to have the space to reflect and deepen one's self awareness.

It also can be relieving for women to actually voice their fears about being single, and to acknowledge the reality of stereotypes they confront every day. They realize that neither are they alone in their feelings, nor deficient because they are single. This groundwork of accepting and understanding some of the realities of being single (and not the myths) makes it possible to explore what being single (and married, having children) really means to THEM, and how to better understand their own needs and motivations.

For example, some young women discover (with surprise) that they really want permission to enjoy the space of being single. Jenny struggled with having a "nice marriage-material' boyfriend whom she liked, and her parents and friends adored. However, she became depressed and insecure, because she felt she should love him and should marry him, even though she was constantly annoyed with him. Jenny needed to understand that remaining single was a viable and important option. But she feared she would disappoint her parents, worried she might be wrong in her judgments, and would never meet anyone as good as Brian in the future. Jennie felt considerable relief when she could let go of her fears, listen to her instincts, and enjoy being single. In the space of being single, she was able to hear what really made HER happy and gain confidence in developing her life in consonance with who she is and where she was in her life..

Other young women become confused and discouraged in their wish to find a boyfriend. Either they don't meet available partners, or end up in relationships that don't work. Sometimes they find relief in getting off the "gerbil wheel" of compulsive dating and activity, to see what is really going on for them. They may discover conflicting desires: "I want to meet someone, but I totally act aloof and avoid situations where I might be rejected." or "I worry that I become so focused on a relationship, that I lose Me," "or "If I'm really honest with myself, I see that as the oldest sibling with a depressed mom, I ended up taking care of everyone else while growing up; now I really relish being able to construct my life around what I need. And that's not being selfish!!"

The point of these deeper explorations is to allow the young woman to become more self aware, so that she has freedom to make choices that fit her. Single doesn't become a refuge, nor does it become a place she has to flee from. Being single becomes a legitimate and powerful place to live, love, and build a life.

Source URL: http://www.psychologytoday.com/node/3384

Links:
[1] http://www.psychologytoday.com/blog/living-single/200902/living-single-are-the-early-adult-years-the-hardest-part-i[2] http://www.wendywassonphd.com/[3] http://www.mysinglespace.org/[4] http://www.northwestern.edu/[5] http://www.medschool.northwestern.edu/[6] http://www.psychologytoday.com/blog/living-single/200806/but-what-about-single-men[7] http://www.springerlink.com/content/n34087714p406323/[8] http://www.psychologytoday.com/blog/living-single/200902/step-away-spouse-another-take-the-value-friends[9] http://www.amazon.com/Singled-Out-Singles-Stereotyped-

22.

Are the Early Years of Single Life the Hardest? Part III: Fears and Misperceptions

Feb 13 2009

Our Conversation with Wendy Wasson Continues

This is Part III of a four-part series on how the experience of living single changes over the course of the adult years. In Part I, I introduced the series. Part II was the beginning of my conversation with therapist Wendy Wasson; we focused on singles approaching the age of 30. In this Part, we discuss the fears and misperceptions facing singles in early adulthood.

Bella: One thing that really bothers me is the conflation of being single with being alone. Sometimes single people are assumed, by definition, to be alone. It is not just in everyday informal conversation that you hear insinuations like this; it is in the media and even in some scientific writings. Is this something that comes up in the clinical setting?

Wendy: Absolutely. In fact this is one of the most important assumptions and fears that is associated with singleness that oppresses both single AND married people. This assumption leads single people to compulsively date (to avoid being alone), and on the other hand, encourages partnered or married people to cling to relationships that are clearly not working.

If you feel secure, you can enjoy being alone, and solitude is a state that people seek to deepen their connection with nature, the spiritual, and their own being. The "being alone" that people dread is that state of being out of connection with others: not belonging, not being understood, feeling invisible, like you don't matter. It's the sense of isolation, being on the outside looking in, feeling left behind. Although being lonely is associated with "single," it actually is not the province of being single. (See Bella's review of research in Part I and in Singled Out).

As a therapist you want to help the client distinguish that single does not, in and of itself, mean you are destined to be lonely. Instead, you want to distinguish what is contributing to the feeling of loneliness. For example, Susan felt lonely when one friend after another fell off the face of the earth when they got a boyfriend, married, and started having babies. Jane felt lonely after she had broken up with her boyfriend of two years. Jessica felt a deep sense of isolation when her friends and family didn't really understand her experience, and she didn't want to burden them with her worries. Erica felt considerable shame about being single when she went home at Thanksgiving and was surrounded by her younger cousins who were engaged or married; she withdrew from others as she felt they were judging her - and she felt very alone.

As a therapist you want to move beyond the explanation (e.g., I'm lonely because I am single) and find out what the experience really means. Why is the young woman feeling lonely? Is she grieving losses? Is she having difficulty sharing her feelings and being authentic with others? Is she convinced that finding a "soulmate" will solve her problems, and doesn't attend to building friendships and going after experiences she wants? Is she feeling shame? Are experiences from childhood coloring her current interpretations of what is happening? Once you establish what is really happening, you can then begin to productively address the problems.

When we feel secure in ourselves and have the confidence that we can build and maintain the emotional connections that are necessary for a fulfilled life, we can manage the expectable periods of aloneness that are part of life, and even relish aloneness and solitude. Many single women talk with pleasure about having peace and quiet, and the ability to read a book all Saturday afternoon

Being single is also seen as an explanation for being depressed. People will sometimes feel that they are depressed because they are single - the fantasy being, "if I had THE relationship I needed, I would feel happy, whole, and complete." Similar to the process of understanding loneliness, it is important to discover the real reasons a person is depressed. Depression is not an inevitable byproduct of being single, but women who have suffered disappointments, loss, and other deprivations as children may feel that being single is yet another experience of deprivation and is history repeating itself. In contrast, women who have good self-esteem, are optimistic, and have good coping skills, can enjoy the space of being single, even though they are still hoping for marriage and children. (See, for example, Marcy Cole's dissertation.)

Bella: One of the reasons I coined the term "singlism" was to put a name to all of the ways in which single people are stereotyped and stigmatized, and draw attention to what all of these inappropriate beliefs and behaviors have in common. Do you find that the stigma and stereotypes around being single are issues for the singles you work with?

Wendy: Stigmas and stereotypes about singleness are very evident in my work, and are problems not only for single people, but married people as well. Being single means "being lonely," "something is wrong with me that I am single," "desperate," "I don't have a care in the world, and I'm out having the time of my life," "I must not want a relationship," etc. Lots of stigmas, stereotypes, and assumptions exist about single life and singles, and it's difficult to avoid them. It really challenges the single woman to be strong in her own sense of who she is. One of the benefits of moving towards middle adulthood is that we are less influenced by social judgments and how we and life are supposed to look.

Stigmas and stereotypes are particularly hard to handle and shrug off when we have our own fears and doubts about ourselves. It is harder to challenge or laugh off Aunt

Mary's comments that "we better hurry up, if we want to get married" if we have our own worries. Ideally, it fosters more authentic communication (and education), when the single person can address such questions and concerns directly, and take the conversation to a deeper level. I worry about that too sometimes; but I'm also part of a growing number of women who are single and developing their lives without waiting to find the "right partner."

Source URL: http://www.psychologytoday.com/node/3396

Links:
[1] http://www.psychologytoday.com/blog/living-single/200902/living-single-are-the-early-adult-years-the-hardest-part-i[2] http://www.psychologytoday.com/blog/living-single/200902/are-the-early-years-single-life-the-hardest-part-ii-approaching-age-30[3] http://www.wendywassonphd.com/[4] http://psycnet.apa.org/index.cfm?fa=search.displayRecord&uid=1995-29052-001[5] http://arjournals.annualreviews.org/doi/abs/10.1146/annurev.psych.58.110405.085641?journalCode=psych[6] http://www.amazon.com/Singled-Out-Singles-Stereotyped-Stigmatized/dp/0312340826/ref=ed_oe_p/102-4637341-6604139[7] http://www.amazon.com/Shame-Guilt-June-Price-Tangney/dp/1572307153[8] http://www.sfsu.edu/~multsowk/title/494.htm[9] http://www.mysinglespace.org/aboutus.html[10] http://www.mysinglespace.org/

23.

Are the Early Years of Single Life the Hardest? Part IV: Single-Again and Single After 40

Feb 14 2009

This discussion with psychotherapist Wendy Wasson is the last of a four-part series exploring the question of whether the early adult years are the hardest for people who are single. Click to read Part I, Part II, and Part III.

Bella: Let's talk about women who are single-again. What are the main issues for them?

Wendy: Many women come in for therapy when they are anticipating or experiencing the break up of a marriage or partnership. There is often panic and feelings of failure as they contemplate re-entering the world of being Single-Again. And here again, it's common to hear some of the same fears we have discussed (e.g. single means lonely/disconnected/isolated; people are going to think that I'm a failure; how can I manage on my own?). In addition, women grieve the loss of what they hoped their marriage would be, and in addition have to face the loss of many of the friendships and structures that they had built during their married years. Ironically, once they get over the fear of being single-again and grieve these losses, in my experience, most of these women <u>reorganize their lives and friendships</u>, and thrive in the space of being single. They <u>savor the possibilities</u> that open up to them in shaping a life built on who they now know themselves to be.

Bella: That is such an intriguing point. It reminds me of something I remember from right after my father died. Among the many condolence notes I received were several with the same theme: They were from women who said that when their father died, after the grief period, their mothers actually thrived. At the time, I thought it was a really odd thing to find in a note in a sympathy card - and especially to see it appear out of the blue from more than one person! That was before I started studying single life.

Wendy: Well, I think that speaks to how we gain and give up certain possibilities in the life paths we choose. Many widows who have been happily married say that they are not interested in marrying again, not because they didn't enjoy marriage, but they appreciate that now they don't have to consult a partner about decisions, or cook dinner every night. While they miss their partner, they can explore other ways of living life. Similarly, women who have enjoyed being single for many years and then marry, may miss the adventures and freedom they had, but enjoy some of the comforts that come from being with a partner who will pick up the dry-cleaning. There are pros and cons in the choices we make.

Bella: What you said about the widows underscores something else that surprised me when I first started talking to other single people and reading their life stories. I heard the same thing you just mentioned - that among the women who were single and wanted to stay that way were people who were previously married, and HAPPILY so. At the time, that was news to me. I thought that people who liked being married would want to remarry after their marriage ended.

Finally, let's talk about the over-40 singles. Tell us about your experiences working with them.

Wendy: For whatever reason, I see fewer single women over forty, and when they do seek help it is to work on a particular area of their life where there is a problem (e.g. work, difficulty with a child), or they are coping with some kind of change or crisis that has befallen them. Although content in being single, some women who really long for partnership continue to work on removing any barriers they have blocking intimacy while also accepting that they may not meet an appropriate partner to marry. They learn to live more comfortably with the ambiguity of "will I meet someone or not." (See Karen Gail Lewis, <u>With or Without a Man</u>, p. 137, for an important discussion of "ambiguous loss.") Finally, if a serious health crisis occurs, some single women who have highly valued independence and self reliance may need help overcoming barriers to accepting or seeking help.

But "being single" is rarely a primary focus of concern. Indeed, several women I have worked with evidence humor and acceptance about being Always Single, or Single-Again..."I don't actually think much about being single, I'm just living my life."

It also seems that the feeling of being "out of step" as "the" single woman in the group fades as the reference group for older single women swells to include Always Single women, Single-Again women, and widows. In addition, it may be that the Always Single woman's strengths (e.g. confidence, autonomy, social abilities) are valued (especially among women who are on their own for the first time).

Indeed, Carol Anderson and Susan Stewart in Flying Solo (1994) wrote of "Midlife's Gifts to Single Women." Based on 90 intensive interviews of single women from age 40 to 55, they found that these women described an increase in clarity, vitality, and agency. "No longer bound by societal prescriptions of how their lives should be lived, they are finally free to write their own stories" (p.39). Similarly, E.Kay Trimberger (The New Single Woman, 2005) found that the 27 Always Single and Single-Again women over the age of 40 in her study had created satisfying and fulfilling lives. Women in both these studies appeared to have found effective ways to meet their needs and express who they are in the structure of their single life. For example, women who might have wanted children had found ways to nurture nieces and nephews or nurture future generations through their work.

Many thanks, Wendy, for your generosity in talking to us in such detail about single life across the adult years. Readers, you can click the relevant links to learn more about Wendy Wasson and her website, My Single Space.

To those who are interested in reading more about SINGLE MEN, Wendy's website now includes a special section on that topic. I will also write more about single men in future posts.

Source URL: http://www.psychologytoday.com/node/3420
Links:
[1] http://www.wendywassonphd.com/ [2] http://www.psychologytoday.com/blog/living-single/200902/living-single-are-the-early-adult-years-the-hardest-part-i [3] http://www.psychologytoday.com/blog/living-single/200902/are-the-early-years-single-life-the-hardest-part-ii-approaching-age-30 [4] http://www.psychologytoday.com/blog/living-single/200902/are-the-early-years-single-life-the-hardest-part-iii-fears-and-mispercepti [5] http://www.psychologytoday.com/blog/living-single/200902/step-away-spouse-another-take-the-value-friends [6] http://www.amazon.com/Singled-Out-Singles-Stereotyped-Stigmatized/dp/0312340826/ref=ed_oe_p/102-4637341-6604139 [7] http://www.amazon.com/Without-Man-Single-Taking-Control/dp/092352150X/ref=sr_1_1?ie=UTF8&s=books&qid=1234427796&sr=1-1 [8] http://www.amazon.com/Flying-Solo-Single-Women-Midlife/dp/0393313476/ref=sr_1_1?ie=UTF8&s=books&qid=1234428012&sr=1-1[9] http://www.amazon.com/New-Single-Woman-Kay-Trimberger/dp/0807065234/ref=sr_1_1?ie=UTF8&s=books&qid=1234428072&sr=1-1[10] http://www.mysinglespace.org/aboutus.html[11] http://www.mysinglespace.org/[12] http://www.psychologytoday.com/blog/living-single/200806/but-what-about-single-men[13] http://www.mysinglespace.org/themensroom.html

24.

I Never Knew His Name

Dec 14 2008

Every Tuesday afternoon, just blocks from the Pacific Ocean, the wooden horses come out, and Santa Barbara's lower State Street is closed to all but the shopkeepers and restauranteurs on the sidewalks, and the farmers and pedestrians in the street. Then, onto the makeshift wooden tables tumble the cherries and lemons and berries, the eggplant and green beans and carrots, in a cascade of colors.

I feel right at home here. I grew up in an Italian family, where there was always someone imploring me to "try this - eat! eat!" Now the children of the farmers hold out their trays, and a bit more meekly than my relatives, offer samples from the earth's tasting menu. At some stands, all I want is one small red onion or a slender serrano chile pepper. As I reach into my pocket for some coins, I get waved away; like the samples and sunshine and the scents of the tuberose, the small stuff is free.

The misshapen heirloom tomatoes appeared and disappeared with the seasons, but I could count on the talk dark troubadour to be there always. With his guitar, big black stetson, and wide smile, he caught the eyes of the tots and the tweens, the grown-ups and the grown-olds, as he serenaded them. Some said he didn't have much family that anyone knew of. But when he died, they streamed into the Plaza Del Mar - the tots and the tweens, the grown-ups and the grown-olds - to smile back up at him and say good-bye.

Source URL: http://www.psychologytoday.com/node/2662

25.

The Ultimate Threat to Single People: You'll Die Alone

Jan 23 2009

I'm not a regular viewer of the TV show, Private Practice, but I watched it last night. One of the storylines was about a man who was in the final stages of pancreatic cancer, in pain, and wanting to die. Two of the regular doctors on the show, Sam and Pete - described in the episode preview as old friends and colleagues of the dying man - clash over the ethics of facilitating the man's death.

On another matter, though, the two share an understanding that is so deep that it never occurs to either to question it: that the man, because he has no spouse, is "dying alone." They consider this tragic, and horribly unsettling, because they, too, are single. They are stricken with the fear that their own death could be akin to that of their long-time friend and colleague.

As the man lays dying, at home in his own bed, the two friends are sitting there near him. By the time his last breath is about to be drawn, Pete has climbed into bed with him, cradling him in his arms. That's where he dies.

This is *Private Practice*'s definition of "dying alone." It is many other people's as well. The usual perversion of the "alone" word is in play: If you have two old friends with you, one actually in bed with you and holding you in his arms, you have died alone. By this taken-for-granted definition, friends are not people. Unless there is a spouse present, you have died alone.

There is something stunningly clueless about the belief that if you marry, you will not die alone. First, a point that should be obvious: Unless both partners die simultaneously, someone is left "alone" (according to the dopey definition of "alone").

My parents were married for 42 years, and had four kids. My father died first. He was hospitalized because of some pain that had not yet been properly diagnosed. The cause turned out to be an abdominal aneurysm. It left him lying dead on the bathroom floor of his hospital room late at night, after my mother had gone home for the evening. All of us grown kids were by then living in other parts of the country. He really did die alone.

My mother, in the popular parlance, was then "alone." During the last five days of her life, as she was dying from cancer, all four of us kids were there with her, often sleeping in chairs or on the floor in the same room, leaving only occasionally to grab a quick shower or a bag of bagels to pass around. Her brother and a lifetime of relatives and friends wanted to be there, too, and they had visited many times before; during the last days, though, my sibs and I did not want to share.

It is true that some single people really do die alone, in the true sense of the word and not the sense that discounts everyone who is not a spouse. But as the example of my own father shows, so, too, do some people who are in the fifth decade of their only marriage, and have four grown children.

As Kay Trimberger has noted, marital status may not be as powerful a predictor of whether you will die alone as whether you have maintained a circle of friends. In fact, the intensive coupling that some married partners practice (whereby all of the once-important people in their lives are moved to the back burner as the marital relationship becomes all-consuming) may be what leaves people particularly vulnerable to loneliness and dying alone when the marriage ends.

I have another challenge to the "Horrors: You'll Die Alone!" threat: Some people actually prefer to be alone, even in death. For a beautifully written example, read the afterword in the book Party of One, by fellow *Psych Today* blogger Anneli Rufus.

Suppose, though, that you are not one of those people. Suppose you really do want people around you when you die. I'll even up the ante: Suppose you want a spouse there with you when you die. Still, I have to wonder: Should you let that wish for your final hours determine the fate of the rest of your life? Should you find someone to marry, even if you are not sure you really want to marry? Even if you do want to marry but have never found a person you truly want to spend your life with, should you marry someone who is a "good enough" partner just to have a spouse there with you at the end?

Answer any of these questions any way you like. Just don't accept the "die alone" threat unthinkingly. Let your life decisions be governed by your own beliefs and values and feelings, your sense of who you really are and who you want to be, and not by the mindless myths designed to scare or shame you out of your single state.

Source URL: http://www.psychologytoday.com/node/3090

Links:
[1] http://www.buddytv.com/articles/private-practice/private-practice-preview-episo-25865.aspx [2] http://www.amazon.com/New-Single-Woman-Kay-Trimberger/dp/0807065234/ref=sr_1_1?ie=UTF8&s=books&qid=1232705815&sr=1-1 [3] http://www.amazon.com/Party-One-Manifesto-Anneli-Rufus/dp/1569245134/ref=sr_1_1?ie=UTF8&s=books&qid=1232705689&sr=1-1[4] http://www.psychologytoday.com/authors/anneli-rufus [5] http://www.amazon.com/Singled-Out-Singles-Stereotyped-Stigmatized/dp/0312340826/ref=ed_oe_p/102-4637341-6604139

26.

The Fragile Spouse and the Resilient Single Person

Nov 17 2008

Who are the people who are important to you now? That was the key question that motivated a significant study of the personal communities of people in contemporary Britain.

Think about the question as it applies to your life. The people can be from any categories – family, friends, spouse/partner, coworkers, neighbors, and so forth. You get to define what "important" means.

Using a series of concentric circles, put yourself in the innermost circle, then put the people who are the very most important to you in that same inner circle. Add more people to the other circles in order of their importance to you. Use as many or as few of the circles as you consider relevant.

That's what <u>Liz Spencer and Ray Pahl</u> did in their study. They interviewed, in depth, 60 people in their own homes. The participants ranged in age from 18 to 75, and they were diverse in race, sexual orientation, employment status, marital status, parental status, health, mobility, and living arrangements.

The concentric circles correspond to "personal communities." Most of them fit into one of 7 types. Here's a description of one of the types that may sound familiar, a **partner (spouse)-based personal community**:

"The partner is the focal point of the person's social world, acting as confidant, provider of emotional and practical support, and constant companion."

Not everyone in the study who had a spouse (partner) had a partner-based personal community. For those who did, their partner was in that innermost circle, and no one else shared that space (except, sometimes, for other members of the immediate family). People with partner-based communities often had other family members and friends sprinkled throughout the circles. However, they were not close to their family members and their friendships were narrow (limited, for example, to socializing and not confiding).

I found this partner-based personal community particularly intriguing because it seems to correspond to the type of coupled-relationship that is celebrated, even swooned over, in our society. Consider, for instance, the many songs with lyrics that all sound so similar:

- "You're my everything;"
- "I just want to be your everything;"
- "How can I live without you? You're my world, my heart, my soul."

To many loving listeners, these lyrics are truly romantic. They describe the soulmate they yearn for, or would like to think they already have.

Popular culture is rarely so enthralled by the other 6 types of personal communities. **Family-based** personal communities, in which family is deeply and broadly valued beyond just the nuclear family, do get respect, but not too many chart-topping tunes. **Friend-based** communities are good <u>dramatic television and movie material</u>, until the writers marry off all of the main characters. (Spencer and Pahl describe two different family-based personal communities, and two friend-based communities, varying in the extent to which the family members or friends monopolize the inner circles.)

The other personal community types are **neighbor-based**, in which neighbors have valued places in the inner circles, and the less familiar **professional-based** communities, in which people put their professional helpers (such as therapists or social workers) in their inner circle and friends or family are missing or peripheral.

Does it matter what kinds of personal communities people have? Spencer and Pahl looked at one other important aspect of people's lives: their mental health. During the interview, participants completed a standardized questionnaire assessing a range of indicators such as difficulty concentrating or sleeping, feeling worthless or depressed, and losing interest in everyday activities.

People in two of the 7 types of personal communities were especially likely to have poor mental health. One of the types was the professional-based personal community. Not too surprising.

The other was the partner-based personal community.

People with partner-based personal communities are vulnerable, the authors believe, because "they lack diverse sources of support." If you look to your spouse to be your everything, you have no back-up.

The authors were quick to point out that people with the other types of personal communities sometimes had poor mental health, too, and not everyone in a partner-based personal community had problems. But as a general rule, the person with a partner-based personal community was a fragile and vulnerable spouse.

Here I want to add my two favorite caveats. First, we can't draw causal conclusions from this type of study; it is not experimental (ethically, it can't be) and it is not longitudinal. Second, there are always individual differences. The type of personal community that is best for many persons is not best for every person.

When I wrote Singled Out, the Spencer and Pahl book had not yet been published and I didn't know about partner-based personal communities. I made up my own clunky phrase for partners who were expected to fulfill all of their spouse's hopes and wishes and dreams (and also pick up the laundry): "**S**ex and **E**verything **E**lse Partners." In the first draft of the book manuscript, I called them "seepies" for short, but some readers really hated that word so I dropped it.

The point I was trying to make was that Seepie relationships could be great during untroubled times for some people, but they were risky. The personal communities study provides some data in support of that formulation.

There's another more important reason why I wanted to tell you about the fragility of the partner-based personal communities (which single people do not have) and the relative resilience of friend-based personal communities that many single people do have. When I hear from other singles, sometimes in comments posted to this blog and more often in personal communications, there is a theme that comes up all too frequently. Single people feel hurt by their once-single friends who ditch them as soon as they marry or become involved in a serious romantic relationship. I can relate.

I can also tend to my relationships with the people who remain important to me, and pursue my passions, and live happily ever after.

Links:
[1] http://www.amazon.com/Rethinking-Friendship-Hidden-Solidarities-Today/dp/0691127425/ref=sr_1_1?ie=UTF8&s=books&qid=1226919789&sr=1-1[2] http://www.psychologytoday.com/blog/living-single/200806/sex-and-the-city-the-magic-show[3] http://www.amazon.com/Singled-Out-Singles-Stereotyped-Stigmatized/dp/0312340826/ref=ed_oe_p/102-4637341-6604139

27.

Step Away from that Spouse! Another Take on the Value of Friends

Feb 9 2009

A few days ago, a post to this *Psychology Today* website was teased with this preview: "Dr. Bill Cloke on the perils of romance and the value of friendship." I was SO happy! I thought the message was going to be that couples should not get so sucked into the treacly romantic sentimentality of Valentine's Day that they forget the value of their close friends.

Wrong! The real message of that post was that couples should not be just romantic partners to one another - they should also be friends. Now, there's nothing wrong with that message. In fact, it is probably wise. What's not wise is if your spouse or romantic partner is your ONLY close friend.

Why is that relevant in a blog on Living Single? Because when couples decide that their romantic partner is going to be their everything, often the other people in their lives who are getting ditched are their single friends. I hear stories like this fairly regularly, but there seems to be an uptick in this theme recently in the e-mails I'm receiving from single people.

There's a name that scholars have given to the shedding of friends as a coupled relationship becomes more serious - dyadic withdrawal. The members of the couple become more focused on each other, and less likely to maintain separate friends.

I was reminded of the importance of friends, even to people who are coupled and see their partner as a friend, as I watched Katie Couric's story on Captain Chesley "Sully" Sullenberger last night on *60 Minutes*. Sully is the pilot who landed a flailing plane into the Hudson River, making survivors out of 155 near-fatalities.

Couric asked Sullenberger's wife Lorrie how she reacted when she first heard the news. Here's what Lorrie said: "I was just in shock, really shaking hard. I called an old best friend and said, 'Sully has just crashed an airplane and I don't know what to do.'"

At what was perhaps the most frightening moment in her life, she reached for the phone and called her best friend. Imagine if the news she received was not just that her husband had crash-landed the plane, but that she had become widowed. That best friend would have become even more important.

I'm not just guessing about that. A study of more than 1,500 older couples found that, compared to married people, widowed people receive more support from friends.

There is evidence that friends are important to coupled people at many different phases of their relationship. They are important conversational partners, even with regard to matters concerning the marriage. In one study, for example, more than 50 wives were asked how often they discussed each of 10 marriage-relevant topics with their close friends and with their spouse. There was only one topic that they discussed more often with their spouse: finances. They discussed in-laws more often with their friends. For the other eight topics (family decision-making, division of chores, spouse's childrearing philosophy, etc.), the wives were just as likely to discuss them with their friends as with their spouse.

Friends are also important when couples make the transition to parenting, which can be a trying and even depressing time. In one study, more than 100 couples were asked about their social networks both before their first child was born, and three more times in the two years after the child was born. The new parents who reported greater satisfaction with their friends also reported feeling less depressed. What's more, that link - between feeling good about your friendships and feeling less depressed yourself - got even stronger over time (i.e., from before the child was born until 2 years after).

Still another study looked at the place of friends in the lives of both heterosexual couples and lesbian couples waiting to adopt their first child. Perhaps it is not surprising that the lesbian women reported receiving at least as much support from friends as from family. But so did the heterosexual women. (In both cases, the support scores were actually higher from the friends than from family, but the results may not have been statistically significant - tests were not reported. For the men, the means were identical.)

Think again about Valentine's Day iconography - and indeed, about all the matrimaniacal imagery that never totally disappears, even after Valentine's Day is long gone. The uber-romantic image is of the couple, leaning toward each other over a candlelight dinner, or walking hand-in-hand on the beach, with no one else in the picture.

Question: What's the appeal of that image?
Answer: There's no one else there.

Question: What's the risk?
Answer: There's no one else there.

28.

Deleting a Friend to Spotlight a Spouse

Oct 1 2008

In "A Mighty Heart," the movie about the kidnapping and beheading of *Wall Street Journal* reporter Danny Pearl, there is a portentous scene early on. Angelina Jolie, playing Danny's wife Mariane Pearl, stands alone outside a home in Karachi, Pakistan, and waves goodbye to Danny as he ducks into a taxi. Danny was investigating the infamous shoe-bomber Richard Reid; on that fateful day, he thought he was off to an interview with Reid's al-Qaeda handler.

Viewers already know what the real Mariane Pearl did not: She would never see Danny again. Now, the visuals proclaim, Mariane is really alone.

Only she wasn't.

In the real-life version of the scene, there was another person standing there with Mariane, smiling, waving, and calling out "Good luck, Dude" as Danny departed. She was Asra Nomani, a fellow reporter of Danny's at the *Wall Street Journal* and a close friend of his for nearly a decade.

The true story of Asra and Danny's quirky and touching friendship could have added depth and dignity to the Hollywood script. Asra is Muslim; Danny was Jewish. She's a single mom; he was married and about to be a parent. Their shared experiences as children of immigrants contributed to the bond that transcended their superficial

82

differences; so did their like-minded penchant for trying to push the stodgy *Journal* toward the unconventional.

Asra taught Danny to say "Do I look like a fool?" in Urdu so he had a rejoinder for the cab drivers in Mumbai who proposed preposterous fares. He, the star reporter, sent her materials for a book she was writing, with a handwritten note, "From your assistant, Danny."

Does the name Asra Nomani sound familiar? If so, maybe it is because she is an activist and educator as well as a reporter and an author. Her interest in the circumstances of Danny's death did not begin or end with the movie. She is a director of The Pearl Project, mentoring a group of Georgetown University journalism students as they try to learn what really did happen.

The home featured in that scene from the movie was Nomani's rented home in Karachi. In the film, she was cast not as the world-class reporter, writer, and friend that she was in fact, but as Mariane Pearl's "charming assistant."

"A Mighty Heart" does not just trivialize friendship; it erases it. It does so, in the myth-addled logic of movie-making, to make the relationship between husband Danny and wife Mariane all the more romantic, and the ending of Danny's life that much more tragic.

Of course, matrimania (the over-the-top hyping of all things marriage-related) is rampant in the movie industry. What makes this instance particularly exasperating and offensive is that "A Mighty Heart" pretended to be telling a true story.

***

Source URL: http://www.psychologytoday.com/node/1943

Links:
[1] http://www.washingtonpost.com/wp-dyn/content/article/2007/06/22/AR2007062201673.html [2] http://lifestyle.msn.com/your-life/bigger-picture/articlemc.aspx?cp-documentid=9845384 [3] http://www.asranomani.com/[4] http://explore.georgetown.edu/news/?ID=24573 [5] http://www.amazon.com/Singled-Out-Singles-Stereotyped-Stigmatized/dp/0312340826/ref=ed_oe_p/102-4637341-6604139

***

29.

Sex and the City: The Magic Show

Jun 12 2008

No spoilers, I promise. But really, do you have to see the "Sex and the City" (SATC) movie, or read any of the reviews, to forecast the plotlines?

How about these possibilities:

> Will he stay or will he go?
> Will their relationship survive?
> Who will end up together?

Ask someone who has seen the movie what it was about, and most likely, she (the appropriate pronoun here) will provide answers to these kinds of questions. Push for more detail, and maybe you will hear, also predictably, about the shoes, the sex, the fashion, the apartments, and the drinks.

There's plenty of all of those themes in the movie, but they are the distractions. They are signs of the movie-maker as magician, coaxing and tricking the audience to gaze away from the real action: "Hey, look at this guy! Look at that glitz! Can you believe the size of that closet! Can you believe the size of that..." (Oh, never mind; I never did identify with Samantha.)

SATC - the TV series and the movie - has been unabashed, unconventional, and explicit about sex. By equal measure, though, it has been reticent, conventional, and indirect about the real emotional power of the show.

There was a point in the movie when I thought that one of the women would dare to say, clearly and unambiguously, what she really did care about. Samantha was standing on the sands of the Pacific, outside of her spectacular beach house she shared with the guy who adored her, pondering all that she had in her life in L.A. But, we learn in the voice-over, something was missing.

This was the point at which I thought the show would bare its emotional soul. I thought Samantha would say that despite all that she had in L.A., her life was not the same without those three women who had meant so much to her for so many years. I thought she would say that she yearned for her friends.

Instead, Samantha's eyes alighted on the naked hunk next door.

No matter what these four women faced, in the end, they were always there for each other. The crises in the TV series went beyond the break-up by post-it note, to include the decision to have a child, a diagnosis of cancer, the death of a parent, and more. We, the audience, saw the women drawn toward one another, in sickness and in health. But we were rarely treated to storylines powered by the dynamics of their friendships (or their careers - but that's another topic). Somehow, the explicit narrative was almost always about The Guy.

So it is in our society, our customs, our conversations and our laws. The sex-based couple is privileged and protected; to some extent, so are parents and children. In the Terri Schaivo case, the sparring was between Terri's spouse and her parents. But if Carrie Bradshaw were a real person and stricken with Terri's fate, who would be most likely to know her true wishes? I don't think it would be her parents or Mr. Big. I think it would be Miranda.

I was born in 1953, and that's long enough ago to seem like another era. I was one of four children. My father had just one sibling, but my mother had six. I had cousins, aunts, and uncles who lived within a few miles, and I treated that as walking distance, so I could spend time with them without always asking for a ride. Just about every holiday or minor celebration was cause for an extended family gathering.

Those days are mostly gone. As family size decreases, people grow up with fewer siblings. As grown children criss-cross the country (and the world) in pursuit of whatever attracts them, fewer people can walk to the front door of the relatives they grew up with. Now that <u>Americans spend more years of their adult lives unmarried than married</u>, a spouse is not so reliably the person who is there for you, always. I think that all of these trends point to the growing importance of friends in contemporary society.

SATC is not the only popular show that is frivolous on the outside and deep on the inside. In the soap-opera silly <u>Desperate Housewives</u> (which offers much to dislike, including heaping dollops of singlism), the friendship among the four women is its emotional force. The theme song of the <u>Golden Girls</u> was "Thank You for Being a Friend." The show was broadcast from 1985 until 1992 and is still attracting enough viewers to continue airing in reruns.

Source URL: http://www.psychologytoday.com/node/981
Links:
[1] http://sexandthecitymovie.org/ [2] http://news.findlaw.com/legalnews/lit/schiavo/ [3] http://www.amazon.com/Singled-Out-Singles-Stereotyped-Stigmatized/dp/0312340826/ref=ed_oe_p/102-4637341-6604139 [4] http://abc.go.com/primetime/desperate/index?pn=index [5] http://www.goldengirlscentral.com/show.html

30.

First Friends

Jul 24 2009

It was past midnight on Inauguration Day, after the balls and all of the other events had ended. It had been an exhilarating and exhausting day. Michelle and the kids headed to bed. Barack Obama, the new President, was still up. Right there with him were the people who for years had been such a big part of his life. <u>He was with his friends</u>. His time with them was the capstone of this personally profound and historically significant day.

Back when Obama was a state senator, the next wish on his list - becoming a United States senator - seemed highly unlikely to come true. (He had just lost an election.) But Barack thought he could do it, and he knew whom he had to persuade. He called his closest friend Valerie Jarrett, invited himself to her place, and asked her to invite his closest friends. That, in a way, is how Obama's ascension to the United States Senate, and then the Presidency, began.

Years later, as the Presidential primary season would drag on longer than anyone had anticipated, Obama's friends were concerned about him. Three of the closest among them - Jarrett, Martin Nesbitt, and Eric Whitaker - decided that one of them should try to be with him on the road as often as possible until the Democrats finally had a candidate.

Of course, what the Democrats also had was a winner. Between the day of the election and the day of the inauguration, meetings about policy, planning, and personnel piled up, one atop another atop still another. Psychologically, one of the most significant meetings, I suspect, was not about any of those matters. In early December, those three close friends met with Obama in Nesbitt's Chicago home to draft "an elaborate visiting schedule that will bring Hyde Park to Washington."

In those last days of the transition between President-Elect and just plain President, Barack and his family headed for a Hawaiian vacation. This wasn't an inward-looking, just-the-four (or five, counting Grandma)-of-us sort of event. With them, once again, were those three closest friends - Valerie Jarrett (who is single - no ditching of single friends by the First Couple), Martin Nesbitt, Eric Whitaker, and their families.

The Obama friends did not attach themselves to him to bask in his reflected glory. Initially, Barack wasn't even the most eminent among them. Looking ahead, it is possible that Obama will eventually develop new and close friendships, but "newcomers are unlikely to replicate the intensity of this group's ties, formed over more than a decade by births and deaths, Scrabble games, barbecues and vacations, but also by shared beliefs about race, success and responsibility."

Friendship Writ Large

Barack and Michelle don't just attend to their own friends - they recognize the value of friends in other people's lives, too. When Michelle Obama gave the commencement address at UC Merced, she encouraged the graduates to

> "think about the friends who never got the chance to go to college but were still invested in your success -- friends who talked you out of dropping out, friends who kept you out of trouble so that you could graduate on time, friends who forced you to study when you wanted to procrastinate."

The decision made by Michelle's mother, Marian Robinson, to move from her settled life in Chicago to join the First Family in the White House, was not an easy one. Among the people she would miss was one of her closest friends, Yvonne Davila, who has two daughters. So the three of them decided that they would visit. Said Davila of Barack and Michelle's attitude, "They've made it abundantly clear that we're welcome."

Sasha and Malia are also making new friends and keeping the old. Their Chicago friends visit, and so do the kids from their new school. Commenting about her kids' social schedule back in May, the First Lady noted, "Slumber parties - we had about seven girls over, screaming and yelling."

Even the Closest of Friends Aren't the Same as Family - and Maybe that's a Good Thing

It is easy to be smitten by the First Family. They're smart, they're affectionate, they're fun. After decades of sober tomes and talk about the low rates of marriage among blacks - including, most recently, a segment on CNN's Black in America 2 - the picture of that close and happy family must seem all the more remarkable.

What's more impressive to me is the way that Obama practices friendship. It is not just among Blacks that the number of years that adults spend married has declined - it is a national, and even international trend. What is likely to become increasingly important in all of our lives is the place of friends. As the life story of Barack Obama illustrates, friendships do not have to compete with marriage or traditional family. They can stand right alongside both, enriching them, and giving them a break from carrying all of the emotional load.

Maybe friendship is beginning to garner greater recognition. This Sunday's cover story in the *New York Times Magazine* is about Valerie Jarrett, "the ultimate Obama insider."

Throughout the lengthy story, Jarrett is described repeatedly - both by Obama and the reporter - as "family," a "sibling," a "sister." These are the analogies we reach for first when we want to describe a friend who is especially close and dear. They are meant as high compliments. They are compliments. But they miss something important about friendship.

Friends are not siblings - not even the closest ones are. Siblings can become indifferent, hostile, or even estranged, but they are still siblings. Friends who feel so little warmth toward one another typically cease to be friends at all.

Obama's friends did not need to rearrange their lives to be with him during the grueling Presidential primaries - they chose to. Obama did not have to invite his friends to be there with him on Inauguration evening or on the last vacation he took before stepping into the most powerful position on the planet - he chose to.

Obama chose friendship. He values it. May that legacy live as long as all of his others.

Source URL: http://www.psychologytoday.com/node/31294
Links:
[1] http://www.washingtonpost.com/wp-dyn/content/story/2009/01/31/ST2009013102074.html [2] http://www.nytimes.com/2009/07/26/magazine/26jarrett-t.html?hp [3]

http://www.nytimes.com/2008/12/14/us/politics/14friends.html [4]
http://www.psychologytoday.com/blog/living-single/200905/michelle-obama-and-justice-david-souter-stand-singles [5]
http://www.nytimes.com/2009/05/04/us/politics/04robinson.html [6]
http://www.examiner.com/x-11484-Boston-TV-Examiner~y2009m7d24-CNNs-Black-in-America-2-review-A [7] http://www.amazon.com/Singled-Out-Singles-Stereotyped-Stigmatized/dp/0312340826/ref=ed_oe_p/102-4637341-6604139 [8]
http://www.psychologytoday.com/blog/living-single/200811/living-single-longer-its-global-phenomenon

31.

How Do You Make Friends When You Are Single?

Apr 19 2009

Part 1: Posing the Question and Asking for Your Suggestions

I once taught an extension course on living single. Of the dozen who signed up for the course, many were retired. They ranged in age all the way into the 80s. When I asked them, on the first day, to introduce themselves by talking about their single lives, I didn't know what to expect.

One after another, the first 11 students mostly described how proud they were to be single and how much they valued their independence. A few even gently mocked some of the people they knew who would never travel or even step into a casual restaurant on their own. Most of them had important people in their lives whom they enjoyed seeing (two of the men in the class already seemed to be good friends), and they also appreciated the time they had to themselves. Sure, they also expressed some ambivalences and pointed to some challenges. For the most part, though, they seemed to have settled comfortably into their single lives.

Then it was the last person's turn to speak. She said she HATED being single. No, she DESPISED it. Why? Because she was bored.

She wasn't one of the older people in the class, and she seemed to be in excellent health, but she no longer worked - didn't need the money. She also didn't like TV. She loved reading, and did a lot of that, but it was not enough. She also signed up for a number of volunteer activities, and she didn't mind those, but did not find them all that meaningful.

I thought a lot about her in the intervening week, and was very eager to see her again. For starters, I wanted to thank her for her honesty. It must have been difficult for her to say how much she hated her single life after the professor and 11 other people had effused about their own. But she never did come back to class.

She saw her problem as being single, and maybe it really was. My guess, though, was that regardless of whether she ever became seriously involved with a romantic partner, she would have been much happier with her life if she had some close friends. I also wondered if she just wasn't quite sure how to go about making friends.

That was a few years ago, but I've been thinking about her lately because of an e-mail I got from Karl, a "Living Single" reader. Karl said that his mother, who is 55, would love to have some close friends. In most ways, she is very different from the woman in my class. Karl described her as someone who "works in an office, is extremely popular, does a great job, and also writes and enjoys movies, sports, books, etc." She has many acquaintances, but what she craves are "really good friends."

So how do you make close friends when you are single, especially when you are no longer 19 years old?

I have to admit that this isn't an easy question for me to answer. I don't like to think of making friends as something you strategize about. Seems like it should just happen naturally. But of course, it doesn't always.

I've read stacks of academic papers on friendship. I can (and perhaps will, in the next post) tell you about the kinds of conditions that make friendships more likely to develop. I can also tell you about some of my own experiences, and about the books I've read about other people's close friendships. But I'm not sure that any of that will add up to a totally satisfying set of answers.

So as Step One in trying to answer this question, let me throw it open to you. What are your suggestions for making friends? Not just casual friends, but close ones.

Source URL: http://www.psychologytoday.com/node/4393
Links:
[1] http://www.sololady.com/ [2] http://blogs.psychologytoday.com/blog/living-single/200804/if-you-dine-alone-what-will-people-think-you-part-1-see-if-you-can-predict [3] http://blogs.psychologytoday.com/blog/living-single/200811/the-fragile-spouse-and-the-resilient-single-person [4] http://blogs.psychologytoday.com/blog/living-single/200808/the-american-psyche-tipping-toward-solitude [5] http://www.amazon.com/Singled-Out-Singles-Stereotyped-Stigmatized/dp/0312340826/ref=ed_oe_p/102-4637341-6604139 [6] http://blogs.psychologytoday.com/blog/living-single/200904/susan-boyle-the-new-face-and-voice-the-spinster-cat-lady [7] http://blogs.psychologytoday.com/blog/beautiful-minds/200904/susan-boyle-not-hot

---

32.

Finding a Friend: The Social Psychological Detective Leads the Way

Apr 23 2009

Part 2 of Making Friends

As I started writing this post, a story published in the *New York Times* on Monday (April 20) was sitting atop the list of most e-mailed articles at the paper. "What are friends for? A longer life," was the title of reporter Tara Parker-Pope's story. Longevity is just one of the benefits; friendships can also be good for health, happiness, confidence, and feeling good about yourself.

Judging from the response to my last post, "Living Single" readers do not need to be persuaded. They already get it about the appeal of friendship, and are interested in discussing the topic of making friends.

To say that some singles sometimes want advice about making friends is NOT to say that singles are generally deficient in friendship skills or in the giving spirit that friendship can entail. Quite the contrary! Data from two national surveys have shown that single people are more likely than married people to provide emotional support and practical help to friends, and to spend time with them.

Still, in a matrimaniacal society in which so many social events are organized by the couple, making friends can present some special challenges to singles. At the same time, some of the time-tested truths about friendship (for example: if you want a friend, be one) care not a wit about marital status.

Readers posted many wonderful suggestions about how to make friends, including the one about being a friend. If you are interested, I hope you will read them all and enjoy them. (Personally, I was especially gratified to see how adept "Living Single" readers are at recognizing singlism and responding to it.)

There's a lot to say about making friends, so there will be more posts to come. In this one, I'll start with a consideration that is paramount to social psychologists: The situation. In what contexts are you most likely to figure out real friend-potential?

Be a psychology detective: What's the potential friend really like?

The question we are grappling with is not just how to make any friend but how to make a CLOSE friend. For that, you may need to put on your psychologist's hat and figure out the best settings for finding clues. Here in Santa Barbara, there is an annual writers' conference, featuring workshops in which students take turns reading their own work and critiquing the other students' work. If you have any interest in writing, I think that's a great context for scoping out potential friends. You get to listen to their writing voice, and that can tell you a great deal about how they think and feel, about their sensibilities and maybe their sense of humor. You can also see how they interact with others in a delicate situation. (Giving other people feedback about their writing can be very touchy.) The downside, for me, was that a lot of the participants came from out-of-town, and I prefer to have in-person possibilities for my closest friendships, at least at first.

I liked Kristen's story (from the comments section of my last post) of how she found friends when she moved to a new town. She went to the animal shelter to get a cat, watched the other people there, and felt drawn to them. She started volunteering there and now has close friends.

Groups such as book clubs and hiking clubs (mentioned by several people who commented) can also be terrific. For about a decade, I was in a cooking club with about 7-10 other people. We had our core group, and in addition, we took turns inviting mystery guests. Conversing all evening over a leisurely meal is another way of getting a good sense of whether you might like someone as a friend and whether that person might be open to a new friendship.

Just about any activity that brings you together with another person for an extended period of time can be a great way of developing a friendship if there is any potential there. A long car trip is one example. A colleague once told me about driving cross-country with someone he did not know all that well at the start of the trip. He asked the person to tell him all about his life, starting at the very beginning. Within an hour or so, the person telling his life story was totally into it. Every time he had to stop his narration (for a pit stop or whatever other reason), he couldn't wait to get back in the car and start up again. (The risk here is obvious - you might soon realize that you can't stand the person, and now you have countless hours to spend in the car with him!)

Source URL: http://www.psychologytoday.com/node/4445
Links:
[1] http://www.nytimes.com/2009/04/21/health/21well.html?em [2] http://blogs.psychologytoday.com/blog/living-single/200904/how-do-you-make-friends-when-you-are-single [3] http://caliber.ucpress.net/doi/abs/10.1525/ctx.2006.5.4.16 [4] http://www.amazon.com/Singled-Out-Singles-Stereotyped-Stigmatized/dp/0312340826/ref=ed_oe_p/102-4637341-6604139 [5] http://www.sbwriters.com/

33.

About Making Friends: Suggestion from an Overheard Conversation

May 7 2009

I'm still been thinking about friendship, and the many comments left on my recent posts on the topic (here and here). Eventually, I'll write more on the topic of making friends. For now, I'll just tell you about a conversation I overheard the Saturday before last, at the Los Angeles Book Festival. As a friend and I were waiting in line for one of the three panels we never did get into, a woman behind us was telling the person next to her about a group she meets with regularly. The people in the group are all writers. The listener, assuming this was the typical writers group, asked if the participants took turns reading their work and discussing the reactions. Oh, no, the story-teller explained. The group is not about work at all. They all gather together once a month or so just to socialize, cheer successes and commiserate about disappointments.

The part of this story that is pertinent to our ongoing discussion is how this group got started. One person, wanting to make friends with other authors, posted on Craigslist, asking whether there were writers in the area interested in getting together and getting to know each other. (I know, Craigslist has had some bad press these days.) Years later they are still meeting, not just as fellow writers, but as friends.

Source URL: http://www.psychologytoday.com/node/4659

Links:
[1] http://blogs.psychologytoday.com/blog/living-single/200904/how-do-you-make-friends-when-you-are-single [2] http://blogs.psychologytoday.com/blog/living-single/200904/finding-friend-the-social-psychological-detective-leads-the-way [3] http://www.latimes.com/extras/festivalofbooks/ [4] http://www.craigslist.org/

34.

Magical Friendship-Making Moments

Jun 1 2009

A while back, a "Living Single" reader asked me to write about how to make friends when you are single. I started addressing the question here, here, and here, but there is so much to say that I want to continue coming back to the topic now and then.

I've been reading accounts of great friendships, and noticing that the beginnings of those friendships often have something striking in common. The friends come together at a time that is emotionally consequential; they are experiencing the same big change in their lives.

Journalists Ellen Goodman and Patricia O'Brien wrote about their decades-long friendship in I Know Just What You Mean: The Power of Friendship in Women's Lives. They met in 1974 as winners of the highly prestigious Nieman Fellowship in journalism. They would spend the year together at Harvard.

Ellen describes her first impression of Pat this way: "perky California cheerleader. Suburban mom. Smiling, pretty, very Little League, station wagon driving. Verrrrry straight." Pat, in turn, said this about her first impression of Ellen: "Craftsy orange earrings; no makeup. An in-charge, what's-it-to-you type."

They both agree that if they had met under other circumstances - say, during a brief chat at some random cocktail party - they probably would never have become friends. But this was different. Living as a Neiman fellow for a year was a big change for both of them, and prestige comes with pressure. In their Neiman class, there were few women, and of those, they were the only two who had children. So what if they had little else in common in their backgrounds, upbringings, biographies, or hippie/homemaker leanings? They were on the cusp of a year in their lives that could be momentous; it was one of those magical friendship-making moments.

Same for the intense friendship between Ann Patchett and Lucy Grealy, described in Patchett's bestselling book, Truth & Beauty: A Friendship. Ann and Lucy were at Sarah Lawrence at the same time, but did not become friends there. Once they were both accepted into the same class of the wildly competitive Iowa Writers' Workshop, though, a fast friendship was born.

Recently, one of my East Coast friends was out here visiting, and we started discussing special friendship-making moments. She said she thought that many more close friendships are formed during the first year of college than during subsequent years. I don't know of any systematic research on the topic, but if she's right, it would fit with my sense that times of important changes, and times of emotional significance, are great moments for making friends.

It has been that way for me. The person I met as my roommate on the first day of college and the new Assistant Professor hired the same time as me at my first job are among the friendships I've made that lasted for years.

Of course, these life-changing crucibles are not the only vats that cook up a good stew of friendship, but I think they have their place. So if you are thinking of making a major life change, consider the possibility that a new and lasting friendship may be one of the rewards for all of your effort and anxiety. (No guarantees.)

Links:
[1] http://blogs.psychologytoday.com/blog/living-single/200904/how-do-you-make-friends-when-you-are-single [2] http://blogs.psychologytoday.com/blog/living-single/200904/finding-friend-the-social-psychological-detective-leads-the-way [3] http://blogs.psychologytoday.com/blog/living-single/200905/watching-the-fire-thinking-about-friends [4] http://www.amazon.com/Know-Just-What-You-Mean/dp/074320171X/ref=sr_1_1?ie=UTF8&s=books&qid=1243851171&sr=1-1 [5] http://www.nieman.harvard.edu/NiemanFoundation.aspx [6] http://www.amazon.com/Truth-Beauty-Friendship-Ann-Patchett/dp/0060572159/ref=sr_1_1?ie=UTF8&s=books&qid=1243851117&sr=1-1 [7] http://at-lamp.its.uiowa.edu/virtualwu/index.php/main/category/C36/ [8] http://www.elle.com/Living/Society-Culture/Love-thy-frenemy [9] http://www.amazon.com/Singled-Out-Singles-Stereotyped-Stigmatized/dp/0312340826/ref=ed_oe_p/102-4637341-6604139)

35.

What Matters is Whether You Matter to Others

Mar 22 2009

Do you think you matter to other people? Two inquiring sociologists wanted to know, because they thought the answer would be important in explaining the answer to another question: Are you depressed?

Here are the questions they used to see who thought they mattered:

1. How important are you to others?
2. How much do others pay attention to you?
3. How much would you be missed if you went away?
4. How interested are others in what you have to say?
5. How much do other people depend on you?

The authors predicted that people who believed that they mattered to others would be less depressed. That sounded right to me (almost too obvious). What interested me even more were the correlates of feeling that you matter to other people. What goes along with feeling that way?

Here's a conventional wisdom prediction (an immediate tip-off that it is not MY prediction): the people who are most likely to believe that they matter to someone are those who have a supportive relationship with a spouse.

The authors asked about that. All of the married participants were asked questions such as how close they felt to their spouse and whether they could talk to their spouse about problems. Importantly, they also asked everyone (married or not) comparable questions about closeness to other categories of people, including

94

friends, relatives, and coworkers. About 1,300 Canadians answered all of these questions (and more) one year, then again a year later.

Here are the correlations, for men and for women, between believing that you matter and believing that you have close, supportive relationships with these different categories of people:

Correlations with the Belief that You Matter

	For WOMEN	For MEN
Having support from FRIENDS	.34	.43
Having support from FAMILY	.22	.29
Having support from CO-WORKERS	.21	.32
Having support from SPOUSE	.20	.34

For both women and men, it is support from FRIENDS, more so than support from a spouse, from family, or from co-workers, that is most likely to be linked to the feeling that you matter.

That made me wonder whether people who had always been single, to whom friends may be particularly important, would be especially likely to believe that they mattered to other people (which would put quite a dent in the conventional wisdom). I'd also like to see how the feeling of mattering changed as people got married or divorced or widowed, or stayed single.

Unfortunately, the authors did not report the answers to any of those questions. Instead, they just compared the people who were currently married with all of the people who were unmarried (the widowed, divorced, and the always-single). On a 1 to 4 scale (where 1 means you don't think you matter at all and 4 means you think you matter a lot), the currently married averaged 3.4, and the widowed, divorced, and ever-single, taken together, averaged 3.3. My guess is that if you looked at the four groups separately, you would find the same pattern that emerged for so many of the other outcomes that I reviewed in Singled Out: the always-single and the currently-married look similar, and the previously married do a bit less well (especially if the divorce or the death of the partner was recent).

What about the question that motivated the authors to conduct their study? I thought that the answer to their question was obvious: Of course, people who believed that they mattered would be less depressed. Also, people who felt that they mattered when they were first asked would be less depressed when they were asked again a year later.

It turns out that the prediction was obvious and accurate only as a description of how things worked for women. For men, another factor had to be added to the equation. Men's feelings of mattering were also linked to their feelings of mastery - the belief that their actions are consequential.

I'll end with what, for me, is the take-away message of the study: Friendship matters. (Not a new theme for me; see here and here and here and here.) Having supportive friendships is linked to the feeling that you matter, too. In fact, supportive friends are more reliably linked to feelings of mattering than are supportive spouses or family members or coworkers.

Source URL: http://www.psychologytoday.com/node/3964

Links:
[1] http://www.jstor.org/pss/3090217 [2] http://www.amazon.com/Singled-Out-Singles-Stereotyped-Stigmatized/dp/0312340826/ref=ed_oe_p/102-4637341-6604139 [3] http://blogs.psychologytoday.com/blog/living-single/200902/step-away-spouse-another-take-the-value-friends [4] http://blogs.psychologytoday.com/blog/living-single/200811/the-fragile-spouse-and-the-resilient-single-person [5] http://blogs.psychologytoday.com/blog/living-single/200810/deleting-a-friend-spotlight-a-spouse [6] http://blogs.psychologytoday.com/blog/living-single/200808/the-real-mystery-why-dont-friendships-get-what-they-deserve

36.

Bigger, Broader Meanings of Love and Romance

May 11 2008

A few weeks ago, Ted Sorensen - husband, father, and renowned speechwriter for President John F. Kennedy - was interviewed by the *New York Times*. Consider this excerpt:

NY Times: "Was your working relationship with J.F.K. the great love affair of your life?"
Sorensen: "Yes, of course."

A public figure, a married man, says to the paper of record that the great love affair of his life was not with his wife but with his boss, the President.

Ted Sorensen is not listening to the music. Lyrics such as "You're my everything;" "I just want to be your everything;" and "How do I live without you?...You're my world, my heart, my soul" express the myth of modern marriage: Find "The One" and your whole life falls into place. No pursuit, no passion, no love could be any greater than the love you feel when you finally embrace your soulmate - not music, not scientific discovery, and surely not speechwriting.

To many Americans, the soulmate interpretation of love is not an interpretation, it is not a myth, and it is not modern. Rather, it is The Way It Is, and the way it always has been. I think I believed something like that myself, before I started doing the research for Singled Out. It didn't make any sense for me to believe in the soulmate mythology, since I have always been single, I've always loved my single life (well, except for the singlism and the matrimania), and I have never had any desire to become unsingle. Still, I figured I was the exception.

In my high school, history was taught by the athletic coaches, so we learned mostly about the history of the scoring that took place in the game the night before. I realized how woefully unprepared I was to take a real history course when I got to college, so I didn't. Those were the days when there were hardly any requirements. I took 19 psychology courses.

Once I started reading social history, all these years later, I was amazed at what I had missed. From Francesca Cancian's Love in America, I learned that less than a century before the married couple and their feelings for each other had become so glorified, "intimacy and sexual relations between spouses were NOT central and both spouses had important ties with relatives and friends of their own sex."

In Marriage, A History, Stephanie Coontz noted that during the 1800s, Westerners believed that "love developed slowly out of admiration, respect, and appreciation;" therefore, "the love one felt for a sweetheart was not seen as qualitatively different from the feeling one might have for a sister, a friend, or even an idea."

I don't think Americans have lost the bigger, broader senses of love and romance and passion and meaning that have probably been part of the human experience through the ages. Rather, I think that contemporary American society has been slow to give those experiences their due. It is ordinary, nowadays, to express one's love and devotion to a life partner. It is far from ordinary to do as Sorensen did and proclaim his life's work to be the great love affair of his life.

I've taken to gathering unabashed expressions of dedication to something or someone other than a soulmate. Here's a sampling from my collection.

In 2004, singer and songwriter John Mayer told Newsweek: "I really might just be the guy who loves playing music so much that [even] if I'm on a date with somebody, I can't wait to go home and play guitar. If I even seal the deal, I can't wait for them to leave so I can play the guitar."

Sometimes book titles say it all. The Man Who Loved Only Numbers, for instance, is about the brilliant mathematician Paul Erdos, who spend decades "crisscrossing four continents, chasing mathematical problems in pursuit of lasting beauty and ultimate truth."

The title Liberty, A Better Husband comes from the diary of Louisa May Alcott. The author was writing about the single woman of antebellum America, who "envisioned her liberty as both autonomy and affiliation...Her freedom enabled her to commit her life and her capacities to the betterment of her sex, her community, or her kin."

For generations of women and men devoted to the cause of social justice, the meanings of love and passion have always transcended diamond rings and limestone altars.

97

Of course, Ted Sorensen, John Mayer, Paul Erdos, and Louisa May Alcott are in the stratospheres of their fields. That's not a requirement. Love and romance and meaning can be found in everyday life. In her book, The New Single Woman, Kay Trimberger described one woman's passion for flamenco dancing. A whole book full of tributes to big, broad meanings of love is what you will find in Isn't It Romantic? Finding the Magic in Everyday Life. Examples range from the love of nature and architecture to the "the romance of perfect solitude" and the weaving and cherishing of a "web of silver strings" between a Juilliard teacher of song and her vulnerable students.

There's a special place in my collection for the pairs of people who have said the following about one another: "We fell in love." "We are planning a future together." "We use the exact same expressions, sighs, and body language without realizing it, often at the same time." We are "memory banks for each other." All are quotes from friends, not lovers.

Here's one last example. This one comes from a woman writing about the appeal of working alone in her office at home:

"There I am drawn to the warm southern exposure, the familiarity of my papers strewn everywhere, piles on the bed, the floor, the desk. Mostly, I'm drawn to the stillness. The only sound is the muted hum of the computer. I've dreamed of a room like this for years but never imagined how comforting it would feel to walk in every day."

The person who wrote this was married, but was craving a sabbatical from her marriage. What she really wanted, at least for a while, was to be single. Now THAT's romantic!

Source URL: http://www.psychologytoday.com/node/671
Links:
[1] http://www.nytimes.com/2008/04/27/magazine/27wwln-Q4-t.html [2] http://www.amazon.com/Singled-Out-Singles-Stereotyped-Stigmatized/dp/0312340826/ref=ed_oe_p [3] http://www.amazon.com/Love-America-Self-Development-Francesca-Cancian/dp/0521396913/ref=sr_1_1?ie=UTF8&s=books&qid=1210555469&sr=1-1[4] http://www.amazon.com/Marriage-History-How-Love-Conquered/dp/014303667X/ref=sr_1_1?ie=UTF8&s=books&qid=1210555502&sr=1-1 [5] http://www.newsweek.com/ [6] http://www.amazon.com/MAN-WHO-LOVED-ONLY-NUMBERS/dp/0786884061/ref=pd_bbs_sr_1?ie=UTF8&s=books&qid=1210555544&sr=1-1 [7] http://www.amazon.com/Liberty-Better-Husband-Generations-1780-1840/dp/0300039220/ref=sr_1_1?ie=UTF8&s=books&qid=1210555578&sr=1-1 [8] http://www.amazon.com/New-Single-Woman-Kay-Trimberger/dp/0807065234/ref=sr_1_1?ie=UTF8&s=books&qid=1210555616&sr=1-1 [9] http://www.amazon.com/Isnt-Romantic-Finding-Magic-Everyday/dp/0060932473/ref=sr_1_1?ie=UTF8&s=books&qid=1210555690&sr=1-1 [10] http://www.amazon.com/Marriage-Sabbatical-Journey-That-Brings/dp/0767910028/ref=sr_1_2?ie=UTF8&s=books&qid=1210555732&sr=1-2

37.

Is It Better to Have Loved and Lost Than Never to Have Loved at All?

Aug 17 2008

Even if poetry is not your thing, you probably know by heart the words of Alfred Lord Tennyson:

> 'Tis better to have loved and lost
> Than never to have loved at all.

If you define love narrowly as romantic love, operationalized as marriage (though I surely don't), then Tennyson has been felled by science - the data show that it's just not true. In happiness, health, longevity, and just about everything else that has been studied (except maybe wealth), people who have always been single do better than people who were previously married (divorced or widowed).

As is often the case in marital status comparisons, the differences can be small. But they are quite consistently in the opposite direction than Tennyson would have led us to believe. (I provide a critical overview of the research in the science chapter of Singled Out. Karen Rook and Laura Zettel reviewed studies of physical health here.)

The question is why: Why do people who have always been single do better than people who are divorced or widowed?

Scholars of marriage have a ready response. It even has its own name, with three variations: the "stress" or "crisis" or "loss" hypothesis. People who have always been single have not experienced the same depth of stress (or crisis or loss) as people who have divorced or become widowed.

The explanation has an intuitive appeal, and charts of relevant data often seem consistent. For example, if you look at graphs of people's happiness over time, as they get married and then divorced or widowed, you can see happiness plunging as the year of the divorce approaches, or during the year of the partner's death, and then you can see it slowly start to rebound as the dissolution of the marriage recedes further into the past. (The graphs are on pages 38 and 39 of Singled Out.)

Studies of marital status take a fine-grained view of people who have gotten married. They separate out of that group the people who eventually divorce or become widowed. Then they find that the divorced and widowed people sometimes do worse than the currently-married people. (In other studies, married people are divided by the quality of their marriage, or their economic or class status, or any of a wide array of other variables.) Now consider what happens when people who have always been single are included in studies: This "never-married" group is one big undifferentiated blob. It is as if people who study marriage have an attitude of "they all look alike" when it comes to their views of single people.

My point is hardly earth-shattering but I have rarely seen it acknowledged in the scientific literature: People who have always been single also experience intense stress, acute crises, and devastating losses. If you were to ask single people about such experiences and plot the lifelines of their happiness the same way the lifelines of the once-married are typically plotted, I think you would see something similar. Single people also experience stress and sadness and grief when someone they love dies or when a profoundly important relationship falls apart (and it doesn't have to be a romantic relationship). You can't see it in the results of the published studies because the singles who have experienced great losses are not separated out the way divorced and widowed people are separated from the still-married.

There is something else important about the published literature on marital status. When people who have always been single fare better than some other group (such as the previously married), scholars rarely propose an explanation that assumes that single people may actually have some special skills and strengths.

Think of all the tasks that married people divide between them. The splits are a little less likely to be traditional than they once were (she takes care of the kids and the cooking, he pays the bills and mows the lawn), but they are often apportioned in some way. While the marriage lasts, this can be useful and efficient. When it is over, though, the newly uncoupled individuals are left with mastery of only those tasks that were once in their domain. Even memory is implicated, as when one person in the couple took charge of remembering the birthdays and the other kept track of the times for the oil changes.

People who have always been single, though, are likely to find some way of accomplishing all of the tasks of everyday life. Maybe they master some, tap a network of friends for others, and hire people to do the rest. One way or another, they get things done. I think that's a strength.

Maybe, too, the network is part of the answer. Perhaps people who have always been single maintain a more diversified relationship portfolio than the married people who invest all of their relationship capital into just one person. Maybe single people have friendships that have endured longer than many marriages. Maybe they attend to those friendships consistently, rather than stowing them on the back burner while focusing on The One. Maybe that's why they do better than people who were previously married.

I'm generating hypotheses. They could be wrong. What is important - and, I think, stunning - is that my suggestions are mostly new. Scholarly research on marriage dates back more than half a century. It has been supported by journals, conferences, degree programs, and piles and piles of funding. For all that, there have been hardly any scholars who have been able or willing to step outside the conventional ways of thinking and pursue the kinds of possibilities I'm suggesting here.

My argument is in the spirit of diversity. Just as there were many ways of thinking that never did get much notice when psychological (or medical) research focused mainly on men, or primarily on white people, or overwhelmingly on heterosexuals, so too has the absence of a singles perspective left us intellectually poorer. Fortunately, that is starting to change (here and here).

Finally, going back to the initial question that motivated this post (is it better to have loved and lost...): Of course, my point is not that we should steer clear of love. As I've said before in this space, I think we should embrace big, broad meanings of love. What we should steer clear of are narrow ways of thinking that leave us all locked in small, stifling ideological boxes.

Source URL: http://www.psychologytoday.com/node/1568
Links:
[1] http://www.phrases.org.uk/meanings/62650.html [2] http://www.amazon.com/Singled-Out-Singles-Stereotyped-Stigmatized/dp/0312340826/ref=ed_oe_p [3] http://www.informaworld.com/smpp/content~content=a785830591~db=all~order=page [4] http://psycnet.apa.org/index.cfm?fa=search.displayRecord&id=D2D6C65C-B9AA-258C-9524-8DA18FD6925E&resultID=71&page=1&dbTab=all [5] http://www.eric.ed.gov/ERICWebPortal/Home.portal;jsessionid=HvNDtvLVlwTTksBYQS1j5Rw28TPDDxxG2T8htPngYbQxnJ4r3Wpy!-1229935084?_nfpb=true&_pageLabel=ERICSearchResult&_urlType=action&newSearch=true&ERICExtSearch_SearchType_0=au&ERICExtSearch_SearchValue_0="Trimberger E. Kay" [6] http://www.psychologytoday.com/blog/living-single/200807/singles-doc-stars [7] http://www.psychologytoday.com/blog/living-single/200805/bigger-broader-meanings-love-and-romance

38.

Sex and the Single Person

May 25 2009

Over the course of history, the "shoulds" and "should-nots" of sex have changed dramatically. There have been times when sex was not discussed in polite company, times when women were believed merely to tolerate the experience, times when engaging in sex before marriage was considered scandalous, and many other permutations as well. Now the should-scale has tipped in another direction. We are all - women and men, both - expected to want and crave sex, lots of it, whether we are married or single or in some unclassifiable state in between. During each historical era, the prevailing view seemed natural and true.

In her widely-read essay, "Sex is not a natural act," Leonore Tiefer put it this way:

> "The modern view of sexuality as a fundamental drive that is very individualized, deeply gendered, central to personality and intimate

relationships, separate from reproduction, and lifelong (literally womb-to-tomb) would be quite unrecognizable to people living in different civilizations."

The desires of many contemporaries do, in fact, conform to today's new sex-suffused norm. Theirs is not a forced fit but a genuine one. For those who not only like lots of sex but can readily find compatible partners, these are the best of times. (Although, with AIDS still unconquered, these are also among the riskiest of times.)

The dark side of the new norms, though, is that they leave little room for people with different sexual profiles or opportunities. For those would like to have a sexual relationship but don't, the relentless celebration of all things sexual must be particularly painful. (Thanks to commenter Incel for reminding me to acknowledge the community of Involuntary Celibates. You can read more in Chapter 9 of A History of Celibacy.) Those who simply care less - or not at all - about sex are marginalized by contemporary sexual norms, too. In other eras, they may have felt virtuous. Now, even the most contented among them must wonder at times whether there is something wrong with them.

The relentless feting of sex and the implacable sexualizing of society has shaped and strengthened a particular stereotype of singles - that their lives, more than those of married people - are driven by sex. Singles, it is believed, are always looking for sex but not finding it, or indulging in too much of it for their own good, or they are spectacularly bad at it, or they are such cold fish that they could never enjoy it, or - well, think of something damning, and it has probably been said about singles. All of those criticisms really are true of some singles. But here's the point: They are also true of some married people. And as a generalization, mindlessly applied to a whole swath of people, not one of the caricatures is accurate.

When it comes to sex, people who are single have been set up. The group to whom they are compared does not consist of real married people but idealized ones. In the matrimaniacal picture in our minds, married people - simply because they are married - have magical access to perfect sex. One spouse's wish is the other's desire. A partner is always there, willing and able, never too tired, never not in the mood. Each spouse wants just the same amount and kind of sex as the other, and at exactly the same times.

Of course, if that were true, a lot of marriage counselors would be out of a job.

So yes, there are challenges around sex for people who are single. But do not believe for a split second that getting married will make all of your sexual dreams come true. Sure, there can be tremendous rewards for partners who are sexually compatible and who stay that way for the duration. But if and when things fall apart - as one person wants more sex and the other wants less, as one wants to experiment and the other is appalled by the mere thought of it, as one or both become bored or even hostile - being married can be even more daunting than being single. Especially if there are children involved. Any two people, married or not, can work on their relationship and their sex, and get counseling if they are so inclined, but when all efforts prove futile, married people are entangled in a way that singles are not.

It is not even true that getting married means that your sexual experiences will become less risky. A review of all available research, including studies of people of different races and sexual orientations, came to this conclusion: "practicing unprotected sexual intercourse with a committed relationship partner who is not tested for HIV appears to be a major and unrecognized source of HIV risk." When a relationship becomes close and committed, partners seem to believe that it is therefore safe. People whose relationships are just beginning are more cautious. Counter-intuitively, they end up better protected.

I'll end with my usual disclaimer. I'm not saying that you shouldn't get married if that's what you want to do. I'm not saying that marriage can never succeed. But I am cautioning you to beware of the marital mythology and the baseless stigmatizing of people who are single. Don't believe that singles are more self-centered than married people - they're not. Don't believe that you should be governed by other people's ideas of how you should live your sexual life (or any other aspect of your life). Live the life that feels authentic and fulfilling to you. No matter what it is, there will be challenges and rewards.

Source URL: http://www.psychologytoday.com/node/4912

Links:
[1] http://www.amazon.com/Intimate-Matters-History-Sexuality-America/dp/0226142647/ref=sr_1_1?ie=UTF8&s=books&qid=1243236016&sr=1-1 [2] http://www.amazon.com/Sex-Not-Natural-Other-Essays/dp/081334185X/ref=sr_1_1?ie=UTF8&s=books&qid=1243236114&sr=1-1 [3] http://www.kaytrimberger.com/chron-oped.php.html [4] http://www.amazon.com/History-Celibacy-Elizabeth-Abbott/dp/0306810417/ref=sr_1_3?ie=UTF8&s=books&qid=1243154098&sr=1-3 [5] http://psycnet.apa.org/index.cfm?fa=main.doiLanding&uid=1997-04867-004 [6] http://www.amazon.com/Singled-Out-Singles-Stereotyped-Stigmatized/dp/0312340826/ref=ed_oe_p/102-4637341-6604139

39.

It Takes a Single Person to Create a Village

Apr 21 2008

There are some studies you will probably never read about in the mainstream media. They may have been published in the most selective and prestigious professional journals. The findings may be important, even provocative. Still, they stay in their place, nestled in pages read only by people to whom phrases such as "ordinary least square regression" are, well, ordinary.

The problem is that the findings do not fit the conventional wisdom of our time. We have no mental hooks on which to hang them. Take, for instance, a study about single parenting and reading performance published in the *Journal of Marriage and Family*. The author, Hyunjoon Park, compared the reading scores of 15-year olds in single-parent vs 2 biological parent households, in five Asian countries. In only one of them, Japan, did the children in 2-parent families read significantly better than the children in single-parent families. In fact, in two of the countries, Thailand and Indonesia, the children from single-parent households were actually BETTER readers than the children from 2-parent households.

To many Americans, it seems nonsensical that children from single-parent families could ever outperform children from 2-parent families. After all, don't the children living with two parents have twice the love, attention, resources, and help with their homework as the children of single parents?

Traditional nuclear families have been so sentimentalized in American society that when we think of them, we immediately leap to a fantasy of two fully engaged and available adults who lavish their love and attention on one another and the children in a home free of anger, conflict, or recriminations.

In contrast, we imagine the children of single parents trudging home after school, latchkey in hand, glumly tossing a backpack into a tiny, wretched apartment. In the movie in our minds, the kids then plop on the couch to watch TV until a harried mom finally makes it home from work, way too exhausted and too poor to put a decent dinner on the table.

Both images are caricatures, and in my book, SINGLED OUT, I explain the many misrepresentations and misunderstandings that stand in the way of a more informed and enlightened view of different family forms. Here, I want to focus on just one myth about the children of single parents - that they have only one adult in their life who pays attention to them, cares about them, and loves them.

Park posed an intriguing explanation for why children of single parents are such good readers in Indonesia and Thailand - they have an extended family network of people who help them and care about them. Sociologists in the United States who have studied single mothers (such as Rosanna Hertz and Faith Ferguson) have also found that single parents are rarely raising their children single-handedly. Instead, they have a whole ensemble of friends, relatives, and neighbors who are invested in their lives and the lives of their children.

I've been thinking about these issues lately because of an e-mail I received from Paula Otero, who hosts "Women and Success," an online magazine and blog. Paula is a single woman with no children who would love to bring her 12-year old niece to work this Thursday (April 24), the annual "Take Our Daughters and Sons to Work" day. She is a true believer in the importance of expanding children's horizons and in the power of mentoring. Paula also adores her niece, and believes the child would greatly appreciate and benefit from a day at work with her aunt.

The problem is that in Paula's workplace, only mothers and their daughters are welcome to participate in the day's activities. It is true that when the Ms. Foundation initiated the event in 1993, it was called "Take Our Daughters to Work." Since 1993, though, the program has been expanded to include boys as well.

Even more important - especially in a blog about Living Single - is this note that I found on the website of the Take Our Daughters and Sons to Work Foundation:

> "When we say 'Our Daughters and Sons,' we mean more than our own children. [The Foundation] encourages workplaces and individuals to ensure all our nation's daughters and sons participate in the program by inviting children from housing authorities and shelters, nieces and nephews, neighbors and friends, and more, to join them."

Although I have been focusing on the children of single parents, it is not just those kids who are likely to benefit from the nurturing and attention and love of adults other than their parents. I, a lifelong single person, grew up in an Italian Catholic home with two parents who married in 1949 and stayed that way until my dad died more than forty years later. Every occasion, from Thanksgiving and Christmas and Easter, through birthdays and First Holy Communions and Confirmations and graduations, was marked by a gathering of aunts and uncles and cousins and grandparents and neighbors and friends. (On New Years Eve, party hats were also included, as were rum cookies that were more rum than cookie.) I don't think it ever occurred to me that the sleepovers at the homes of favorite relatives - occasions that my three siblings and I found so exciting - were probably special events for our parents as well.

So this Thursday, if your own workplace planners have not yet caught up with the new American spirit, let them in on it (ever so politely, of course). Tell them that you value the contemporary version of the Day, in which all children (and not just biological offspring) are welcome at work, and all of the workers who love children (and not just the parents) are encouraged to bring a special little guest. Sometimes it takes a single person, without children of his or her own, to create a village.

One more thing. Let's not forget that there are many people, both single and coupled, who are not so enamored of children. In the spirit of Bill Maher, let me suggest a New Rule: You do not need to bring any children to work, and you only need to give that "oh, how cute!" look once, then you are covered for the entire day.

Source URL: http://www.psychologytoday.com/node/468

Links:
[1]
http://eric.ed.gov/ERICWebPortal/custom/portlets/recordDetails/detailmini.jsp?_nfpb=true&_&ERICExtSearch_SearchValue_0=EJ768661&ERICExtSearch_SearchType_0=no&accno=EJ768661 [2] http://www.amazon.com/Singled-Out-Singles-Stereotyped-Stigmatized/dp/0312340826/ref=ed_oe_p/102-4637341-6604139 [3] http://www.springerlink.com/content/q525812276602356/ [4] http://www.mujerescaminoalexito.com/home-page/ [5] http://www.daughtersandsonstowork.org/wmspage.cfm?parm1=164 [6] http://www.hbo.com/billmaher/new_rules/

40.

Children of Single Mothers: How Do They Really Fare?

Jan 16 2009

There is one social commentator, all too visible in the media, who is so vile that I make a point of not ever watching her or mentioning her name. I've been getting some e-mails about her in the past week. Apparently, she's been bashing single mothers. Her latest claim, according to the "Living Single" readers who have gotten in touch with me, is that single mothers, together with liberals, are responsible for all of the nation's ills.

I haven't heard her version and I'm not going to look it up. I'm totally open to other points of view but I don't want to encourage hateful expressions of them. So regardless of what she actually did say, I thought that readers might like to see my take on single mothers. Here is what I wrote for the Huffington Post on Mother's Day in 2007 (before I started blogging here at *Psychology Today*).

****

"Mom and Dad." In our cultural fantasies, that team will always be #1 when it comes to raising happy and healthy kids. As for single moms, well maybe some of them are trying hard, but they are up against it, forever trying to lure their children back from the brink of addiction, aggression, and crime.

Before I read reams of scientific papers comparing children who grew up in different kinds of homes, I probably bought what both political parties were selling - the belief in the supposedly overwhelming superiority of two-parent homes. There is a certain logic to the arguments. Don't children raised by two parents have twice the love, attention, and resources than children raised by just one parent? And isn't each of the parents in a married couple all the better at parenting for having the love and support of each other?

So I wasn't surprised when the results of a national substance abuse survey, based on 22,000 adolescents, found more substance abuse among the children of single mothers than among the children of two biological parents. But, considering the rhetoric about single parenting, I was struck by how few of the children of single mothers had substance problems - 5.7% -- and how similar the number was for the children of two biological parents - 4.5%. A difference of about one percentage point is not a very big return on twice the love, attention, and resources.

It's not that two was a magical number of parents - on the average, the kids did better living with a single mom than they did with a dad who was married to a stepmother. The best living arrangement of all (with regard to substance abuse) included three adults - typically, mom, dad, and a grandparent.

What about grades? Relationships with siblings and friends? There's research on those questions, too. In a nationally representative sample of many different kinds of households - two-parent biological households, single-mother households, adoptive households, stepmother, and stepfather households - there were no differences at all. What mattered was NOT how many parents there were, or whether the parents were biologically related to the children. Instead, whether children had problems with their grades or with their siblings or friends depended on whether there was a lot of conflict within families, high levels of disagreements between parents, or endless arguments between parents and kids.

Sometimes children of single parents do better than children of married parents. For example, a study of hundreds of 10- to 14-year olds and their parents showed that in their day-to-day lives, single parents were friendlier to their children than were married parents. The children of single parents also spent more time with people in their extended families than did the children of married parents.

But if two-parent households have twice of everything that adults have to offer children, then why don't the children in those households do far better than the children in single-parent households? And why would they ever do the same or even worse?

Here's how I answered those questions in the chapter on single parents in my book, SINGLED OUT: "I think there are several ways around this dilemma. The first is to let go of the fantasy that all children living in nuclear families have two totally engaged parents who lavish their love and attention on all their children, and on each other, in a home free of anger, conflict, and recriminations. The second is to grab onto a different sort of possibility - that many children living with single mothers have other important adults in their lives, too. I don't mean just kids who have Grandma living with them. I also mean all of the kids who have grandparents, aunts, uncles, neighbors, teachers, family friends, and others who care about them and make sure they know it."

Sociologists who have studied single mothers of different races, classes, and sexual orientations have found that those mothers are rarely raising their children single-handedly. Instead, they have networks of friends and relatives and neighbors who care about them and their children, and have been part of their lives for years.

I agree with the traditionalists about stability: It is good for kids. So is the comfort of knowing that you can walk outside the door of your family home and have other adults who believe in you. Adults who have cared about you for as long as you can remember. Many children of single parents have the stability and security of a loving parent and a supportive network.

Source URL: http://www.psychologytoday.com/node/2999

Links:
[1] http://www.amazon.com/Singled-Out-Singles-Stereotyped-Stigmatized/dp/0312340826/ref=ed_oe_p/102-4637341-6604139

41.

The Marriage-Promotion Claim that Is Right – for All the Wrong Reasons

Apr 2 2008

Law professor Nancy Polikoff, author of the important new book, Beyond (Straight and Gay) Marriage: Valuing All Families under the Law, left this comment on one of my previous blogs:

> Last week, I blogged about a bus shelter poster campaign in Washington, DC. (www.beyondstraightandgaymarriage.blogspot.com) The posters have a bride and a groom and a statement. This "marriage promotion" campaign comes from a group that received almost $5 million in GOVERNMENT funding in 2006. (The group also supports abstinence-only sex education.) One of the posters reads: "Married people earn more money." Can you tell us what's wrong with that statement as an encouragement to marry?

I've looked into all sorts of claims about the joys and rewards that will be yours if only you wed - for example, that getting married makes you happier, healthier, sexier, lengthens your life, and saves your children from the doom that would befall them if they were raised by a single parent. When I assessed these vaunted benefits of getting married for my book, Singled Out, I found that just about all of them were myths. The supposed "evidence" in support of most of these claims is typically misrepresented, exaggerated, or just not there.

Here's the exception. The link between getting married and having more money really is there - and for all the wrong reasons. People who marry are rewarded with a treasure trove of economic goodies withheld from people who stay single.

Consider, for example, the issue of such prominence in the Democratic presidential campaign: health insurance. In many workplaces, married employees can include their spouse on their health plan at a reduced rate. Their single co-workers - who may have been doing the same job at the same level of competence for the same number of years - cannot include another adult (such as a sibling, parent, or close friend) on their plan. Analogously, no other workers can include those single people on their plans. That amounts to unequal compensation for the same work.

Same for Social Security. After married workers die, the benefits they earned go to their spouse. The same benefits earned by single workers go back into the system. Singles cannot give their benefits to other people who are important to them, nor can other workers leave their Social Security benefits to adults who are single.

It is not even necessary to look at benefits to find workplace discrimination against people who are single. A stack of studies has shown that married men are paid more than single men - even when the two are comparable in their seniority and accomplishments. (The references are in Singled Out.) In fact, in one study of identical male twins, the married twin was paid an average of 26% more than the single twin.

There is a supposed "penalty" for getting married that may well be the most notorious of them all. You may even have it on your mind around this time - the purported "marriage penalty." Just how bad is it? If a single person's taxable income were exactly the same as that of a married couple filing jointly, how much more would the married couple pay in federal taxes? It differs at different levels of income, but one part of the answer never changes: It is the single person who ALWAYS pays more. That's a singles penalty, not a marriage penalty.

Those who fret about the "marriage penalty" are not comparing married couples to single people. They are comparing two kinds of couples: those who are married, and those who pool their income but are not married. Under some conditions, the couples who marry do pay more in federal taxes than the couples who do not. Still, getting married more often results in a perk than a penalty.

Income taxes are just one of the domains in which the federal government favors people who get married. There are many other tax advantages and legal protections. In fact, as of 2004, there were 1,138 federal provisions in which marital status was a factor in the allocation of benefits, rights, and privileges. That's just the feds - states can pile on their rewards as well.

The marketplace is more generous to married people, too. Whenever people who are married pay less per person than people who are single, they are being subsidized by the single people who are paying full price. The list of examples begins with car insurance, club memberships, and travel packages; continues through restaurant coupons and grocery discounts for those who buy the jumbo sizes; and never ends.

Adults can access all of these legal benefits and protections and all of the economic perks simply by getting married. No child-rearing needs to be involved. In fact, married people can behave badly toward their spouse, dishonor their vows, move into a hotel room, and still remain recipients of the government's largesse.

Back to those posters that Professor Polikoff mentioned. "Married people earn more money," they claim. (The money is not really "earned," but never mind.) So why not get married for the money?

Remember that the posters are in bus shelters, not yacht clubs. The people who are targeted by the marriage-promotion campaigns are primarily those who are poor. Unwed mothers are of particular interest to the leaders of the marriage movement. So, "Is Marriage a Panacea?" That was the question posed by a study published in the journal *Social Problems* in 2003. The researchers found that unwed mothers from economically disadvantaged backgrounds who married did in fact, on the average, do better financially - but only if they stayed married. To quote the authors, "for women who marry, but later divorce, poverty rates exceed those of never-married women."

Now, finally, for the psychology. I'm no sappy romantic, but seriously - do you really want to marry for money?

Suppose you do. Ethics and values and fairness aside, would there be anything wrong with that?

Psychology students and fans may be familiar with a simple study from long ago, one that touched off decades of intriguing research. The participants in the study were children who loved playing with magic markers. Some of the kids (randomly assigned) were rewarded for doing what they already loved to do; the others were not. The rewarded children subsequently liked playing with the markers less than they had before! When the kids saw their drawing as something they did in order to get rewarded, their intrinsic motivation was undermined.

What if adults come to see the act of getting married as something to do in order to get more money? That's what the marriage-promotion posters seem, in a way, to be suggesting. Would the couples come to love one another less than if they had not been tempted by the promise of financial gains? Fortunately, scientists do not set ethics and values and fairness aside, so the relevant experimental research will never will be done. All we can do is guess. What do you think would be the consequences of marrying for money?

Source URL: http://www.psychologytoday.com/node/321

Links:
[1] http://www.amazon.com/Beyond-Straight-Gay-Marriage-Families/dp/0807044326/ref=pd_bbs_sr_1?ie=UTF8&s=books&qid=1207128974&sr=1-1
[2] http://www.beyondstraightandgaymarriage.blogspot.com [3] http://www.amazon.com/Singled-Out-Singles-Stereotyped-Stigmatized/dp/0312340826/ref=ed_oe_p

42

The Economy: A Single Person's Vulnerability that is Real

Oct 7 2008

A week or so ago, I was a featured guest on a radio call-in show. The host invited listeners to ask me anything about singles, singlism, or single life. I was scheduled to take calls for a half-hour.

One of the first calls was about workplace and economic issues facing people who are single, and off we went. Callers said they were asked to cover for married co-workers. They noted that they got last dibs on vacation dates. They described married co-workers and bosses who expected the single people to work during holidays so married people could spend those special times with their spouse and family.

Then they started in on issues of pay and perks and benefits. An enlightened married man called in and said that when he got married, his boss, in a private conversation, told him that he was going to increase his pay because he was now married. The reason I describe this man enlightened is because of the point he made on the air - that he was not any less valuable, motivated, or talented a worker when he was single.

The host was surprised when I told him that the married caller's experience was not unusual. In researching Singled Out, I found study after study showing that married men are paid more than single men, even when they have the same seniority and achievements. In fact, in one study in which the participants were identical twins, the married twin made an average of 26% more in pay than the single twin.

The calls kept coming. The producer asked me to stay for another segment.

Callers wanted to talk about disparities in benefits - married workers, for example, can often put their spouse on their health care plan at a reduced rate, while single people doing the same work side-by-side with the married person cannot put a sibling or a parent or a nephew or a close friend on their plan. They weren't happy that their married colleagues' Social Security benefits go to their spouse after they die, whereas the single workers' benefits go back into the system.

The phone lines continued to light up. The producer asked if I could continue with the show. We started in on all the many ways in which married people pay less than single people and get more - as with the auto insurance rates, health club memberships, professional subscriptions, vacation packages, and all the rest of the deals for which two married people each pay less than one single person. (In my book, I describe these in a section titled "Cheaper by the Couple.")

Then there are the little things. Supermarkets, for example, reward super-sizers, as when shoppers get to pay less per unit the more they buy. For perishable items, this can be a complete-lose situation for singles - they are just not going to use all that food before it goes bad. Even for non-perishables, these deals are no deal at all if you don't have the extra space to store the stuff. (There is an interesting public-health irony to these pricing practices. At a time when Americans probably weigh more than they ever have before, the buy-more, pay-less promotions encourage them to keep piling on the pounds.)

Finally, the producer ended my part of the show, even though callers were still lined up waiting to talk. I don't think we got through all the relevant economic issues that I described in <u>Singled Out</u> or in <u>another post</u> on this blog, but it was clear that the topic had struck a nerve.

I've done many, many radio call-in shows over the years, and, with one exception, the topic of singles has always drawn listeners to their phones. (In the one dud, the host mistakenly introduced me as a therapist - not sure if that was the reason.) This time seemed different. The host was surprised, too - he said he never expected so many calls.

Of course, any individual event like this can just be something random, but my guess is that something else was involved. Tough economic times are difficult for almost everyone, but they can be especially challenging for people who are single.

There are lots of reasons for this. Most obviously, single people do not have a spouse's job or income to fall back on if their own financial situation falters. Singles who live alone cannot take advantage of the "economies of scale" enjoyed by those who live with others and can draw from several paychecks to pay one rent or mortgage and one set of utility bills. Also, single people are targets of economic discrimination that is legal - it is written right into our laws and public policies (as I've described in Chapter 12 of <u>Singled Out</u>).

So what's a single person - or any person concerned with fairness - to do? One possibility is to speak up. A graduate student (someone I don't know) e-mailed me yesterday to say that reading my book motivated her to complain to her local grocery store about sales practices that favored married people. Another student in a Lifelong Learning course that I taught sent me a hand-written note telling me about her experience challenging a restaurant deal that singled out people who are single.

I also hear from single people who tell me about their experiences of singlism in the workplace, and their efforts to deal with them. From those people - as well as from published <u>research</u> - I've become very attuned to the risks of speaking out. People who hear such complaints about singlism, even when stated very politely, are not often receptive to them. In fact, they can be downright hostile.

I've been especially intrigued by nasty reactions I've gotten from people in academia, many of whom seem, in other ways, to be on the forefront of fairness. Some even study topics related to discrimination. The problem, I think, is that they also see themselves as especially fair and just people. When first faced with the suggestion that they may be treating single people inappropriately, they are startled - and angry.

I think the way around this involves education and consciousness-raising. Most people just don't know much about the real discriminations faced by single Americans. Once the topic becomes part of our public conversation - in the media, in the classroom, in political discourse, and in our everyday lives - then individual experiences will not be so personal. They will be part of a societal issue, a matter of what we want to be as a people and a nation.

Source URL: http://www.psychologytoday.com/node/2018

Links:
[1] http://www.amazon.com/Singled-Out-Singles-Stereotyped-Stigmatized/dp/0312340826/ref=ed_oe_p/102-4637341-6604139 [2] http://www.psychologytoday.com/blog/living-single/200804/the-marriage-promotion-claim-is-right-all-the-wrong-reasons [3] http://www.psychologytoday.com/blog/living-single/200805/is-it-bad-notice-discrimination [4] http://www.unmarried.org/ [5] http://www.psychologytoday.com/blog/living-single/200808/cracking-the-code-how-think-critically-about-reports-the-alleged-superiori [6] http://chronicle.com/free/v54/i05/05b04401.htm [7] http://www.psychologytoday.com/blog/living-single/200805/single-voters-should-rule-will-they

43.

Hey, Singles: Do Co-Workers and Bosses Expect You to Cover for Everyone Else Over the Holidays?

Dec 1 2008

It's that time! The holidays are here, and along with all of the possible joy, bustle, and stress of the season, there is sometimes a special indignity thrust upon single people in the workplace. Their co-workers and bosses, believing that they "don't have anyone" or "don't have a life," expect them to cover for the holidays.

Of course, the notion that single people don't have anyone, or don't have a life, is complete and utter bull. I've mocked it mercilessly on this blog and in Singled Out. There was already evidence aplenty when I wrote my book. Since then, the results of several national surveys have been published showing that single people are more likely than married people to contact, visit, advise, and support their parents and siblings. They are also more likely to encourage, help, and socialize with their friends and neighbors. It is also single people who do more of the work - emotional, practical, and financial - of maintaining intergenerational ties.

One of the reasons why people persist in their misperceptions that single people "don't have anyone" or "don't have a life" is that many of the people who are so important to singles are <u>culturally invisible</u> in our nation of matrimaniacs. Spouses and romantic partners are celebrated endlessly, but <u>friends</u> are considered "just friends" (even when the <u>friendships have outlasted many marriages</u>), siblings are nothing but grist for rivalry, and inspiring mentors and other significant figures are not even on society's relationship map. And, as I've discussed before, many people cherish time to themselves, but the <u>value of solitude</u> is too rarely acknowledged in our cultural conversations, especially in comparison to its evil twin, loneliness.

In everyday life in the workplace, singles are sometimes asked to cover while others leave early or beg off weekend work or unappealing travel. During holiday season, this expectation can get ramped up. Most everyone is busy, even frazzled, and so people put on their stereotyped-colored glasses and "see" that surely singles can pick up the slack.

I don't think singles should refuse to cover for the holidays - I think they should share, along with everyone else. Each worker should have an equal obligation to put in holiday time, no questions asked. So if you are single and a co-worker or boss asks you to work on a holiday, you could perhaps say something like, "Sure, I'll cover this one and you can take the next." Or, "That won't work for me this time but I'm happy to cover next time." Other suggestions?

In a <u>previous post</u>, I've explained the risks of speaking up for yourself about these issues. I also proposed that one step toward a more just workplace is consciousness-raising about these issues. We all need to understand that issues of singlism are pervasive - they are not just about specific individual workers.

Source URL: <u>http://www.psychologytoday.com/node/2539</u>

Links:
[1] <u>http://www.amazon.com/Singled-Out-Singles-Stereotyped-Stigmatized/dp/0312340826/ref=ed_oe_p/102-4637341-6604139</u> [2] http://caliber.ucpress.net/toc/ctx/5/4?cookieSet=1 <u>http://www.boston.com/news/globe/ideas/articles/2007/09/16/the_greedy_marriage/</u> [3] <u>http://www3.interscience.wiley.com/journal/119393014/abstract?CRETRY=1&SRETRY=0</u> [4] <u>http://www.psychologytoday.com/blog/living-single/200810/deleting-a-friend-spotlight-a-spouse</u> [5] <u>http://www.fracturedfriendships.com/</u> [6] <u>http://www.psychologytoday.com/blog/living-single/200808/the-real-mystery-why-dont-friendships-get-what-they-deserve</u> [7] <u>http://www.psychologytoday.com/blog/living-single/200808/the-american-psyche-tipping-toward-solitude</u> [8] <u>http://www.psychologytoday.com/blog/living-single/200810/the-economy-a-single-persons-vulnerability-is-real</u> [9] <u>http://www.belladepaulo.com/contact.htm</u>

44

Changing Careers: Is It Different for Singles?

Jan 27 2009

Recently, I received a book in the mail with a request that I review it for this blog. Hallie Crawford's <u>Flying Solo: Career Transition Tips for Singles</u> may be of interest to some singles for what it offers at face value. I'll describe that in Section I of this post.

What I find even more intriguing, though, is the worldview that is conveyed between the lines. Crawford is an author who wants to send a positive message to singles. She is not a deliberate practitioner of singlism. So I read the book closely to see what assumptions about single and married life were woven throughout her text. That's in Section II. As always, my hope is that from my analysis, you can get more than just a sense of the implicit messages in this particular book. I hope you can also hone your skills at recognizing and challenging <u>implicit assumptions about singlehood</u> and marriage, wherever you find them.

Finally, in Section III, I'll pose some bigger questions, at the societal level, about what it is like for single people to pursue major career changes, and what it could be like in a more idyllic world.

I. About the Book: Face Value

The book is what the subtitle says it is: a compendium of "career transition tips for singles." There are pieces of advice for all phases of the transition process, from figuring out whether it really is time to leave your current career, to coming up with your dream career, to marshalling the financial and emotional resources you will need along the way. There are sections on interviewing, networking, and writing a resume, as well as a list of resources.

The author, Hallie Crawford, is a career coach, and the book also functions as an advertisement for her services. Flying Solo is a quick and easy read, and I think you can get from it some sense of what it would be like to have Crawford as your coach.

Crawford strikes me as a motivated, talented, and gracious person who would be fun to work with, if having a coach is your thing. Personally, I don't agree with her general approach. She takes too seriously "The Secret" and "The Law of Attraction," whereby we become magnets for anything we want (health, wealth, and all the rest) by thinking positive thoughts. Here's a sample sentence from <u>The Secret</u> book: "Food cannot cause you to put on weight, unless you think it can." By my reckoning, that's not a secret, it's a hoax.

Millions of people are Secret fans, so I don't presume my own skepticism to be widely shared. More importantly, I don't think the magical thinking subtext of Crawford's book takes away from the potential usefulness of some of her tips.

I don't agree with all of the tips. Still, if I were considering a big career change right now, I think I'd appreciate the opportunity to read through a discussion of so many of the issues that come up, especially from someone who has coached many other people through the process.

I like Crawford's recognition that employers will sometimes expect single people to work longer and harder than everyone else, and her recommendation that singles be prepared to set boundaries. She also raises the issue of friends who are not supportive of your plans to make a big career change, and suggests that you don't bring up the topic with them until you are farther along in the process. I like that a lot better than what I've seen in some other self-help books - that is, if your friends don't like your goal, ditch them.

II. More about the Book: Between the Lines

Although Crawford's book is specifically about single people's career transitions, her assumptions about what single and married life are like are implicit throughout. That's what interests me most.

Here is a non-random sampling of quotes from the book. Consider what you think of each point.

> • As a single person, you can "go anywhere and do anything you want because you have no personal obligations or responsibilities to anyone else."

> • Being single "can be a lonely place."

> • One of the emotional obstacles that singles face: "My friends aren't being supportive."

> • As a single person, you might "start comparing yourself to your attached friends, wondering if and when you'll be on that path."

> • For singles, when you are down, "there is no immediate partner who can pat you on the back and tell you everything will work out all right."

> • Here's a quote from one of the author's clients: "As a single person, I feel that my friends and family support my career transitions. But that's not the same as a husband creating a life vision with me, or supporting me so I can take chances, or being there whether or not my risks pay off."

What these quotes add up to is a conventional view of what it means to be single or married: Single people have their independence, because they do not have any obligations or responsibilities to anyone else. Single life can be lonely, and friends can be unsupportive. Even when your friends are supportive, that's not the same as having a spouse who is always there for you. As a single person, you don't have a partner to pat you on the back and tell you everything will be okay. You start looking at your "attached" friends and wondering when you will be on that path.

Not all of these statements are untrue. Sure, single people can be lonely. Sometimes their friends are unsupportive. Sometimes married people have partners who share their vision and help and encourage them through their career transitions and everything else.

What's Missing from this Conventional View?

What's missing is the other side of the picture. Like so many other authors and journalists and scientists and pundits and people on the street, Crawford underscores what is potentially problematic about being single and what is potentially great about being married. The parallel advantages of being single and disadvantages of being married go mostly unacknowledged.

I say that even though some of her observations about single people were offered up as pros rather than cons. Take the first quote, for example: As a single person, you can "go anywhere and do anything you want because you have no personal obligations or responsibilities to anyone else."

A. The Missing Persons

This is the view of a single person as an untethered free agent, with no obligations to any other humans. (Never mind that there are nearly 13 million single parents.) It is true that with regard to other adults, single people do not have the legal obligations (or protections) that come with official marriage. In fact, though, they are often the ones doing the work of keeping families and friends and communities together. They maintain intergenerational ties, and provide plenty of care for aging or ill relatives and friends.

When my mother was gravely ill, she was in Dunmore, Pennsylvania, and I was living in Charlottesville, Virginia, the university town where I taught. Ever chance I could get, I made the 377 mile trip to see her. A few years later, I made my big career transition and moved to the West Coast. I would not have done so while she was so sick - not because she would have guilted me into staying, or because I had an official legal obligation to stay. It was what I wanted to do.

To say that single people have no obligations or responsibilities to others also dismisses or devalues or simply fails to recognize all of the important people in their lives. Again, it is true that single people have no official requirements to care for friends or siblings or any other category of person who has no standing in the law. But they may value deeply their relationships with those people, and that can be an emotional constraint to moving, though one that is rarely acknowledged or accommodated.

In Virginia, I had friends who had a significant place in my life. I had what I thought of as concentric circles of friends, some very close, others not as close, but all geographically accessible. It took me years, if not decades, to develop that network. I wasn't legally "responsible" for any of those people, but moving 3,000 miles away from them was one of the few serious downsides of making my life-changing

117

transition. They are still emotionally important to me, but I no longer get to meet them regularly for dinner at an outdoor table on the downtown mall.

B. The Missing Marriages

Consider again how the author's single client described the picture in her mind of what it means to be married. Having supportive friends, she said, is "not the same as a husband creating a life vision with me, or supporting me so I can take chances, or being there whether or not my risks pay off."

To her, getting married is like stepping into a fairy tale, where the handsome prince is forever holding you, carrying you over rough waters and rocky streams and toward the rainbow. I think there really are some princely and princessly spouses, but if they were all that way, the divorce rate would not be so high.

I would have liked the book better if it seemed to instill a more balanced view of single and married life. It is fine to acknowledge that some single people are lonely, but not without cautioning that marriage can be lonely, too. It is fine to list unsupportive friends as a possible emotional obstacle, but not without admitting that spouses can also be unsupportive. The tip that Crawford offered about unsupportive friends - just don't bring up the topic of your big move - may be harder to implement if the nagging naysayer is sharing your home and your bed.

My concern is that readers could come away from this book thinking that they need career tips because they are single, and if only they got married, many of the apparent challenges of making a big move would simply vanish. I don't think the author actually believes that, and I know she is trying to be encouraging to singles. But there's just too much talk, for my tastes, of the lonely, free-standing single people and the comforted and cushioned married people.

C. The Missing Perspectives

When I made my big career change, it was true (as Crawford notes) that as a single person I did not have the salary of a spouse to fall back on if my big plans did not turn out so great. I was taking a financial risk, and I was taking it myself. For me, though, that made it easier to go ahead with my move than if I had been married. Even with a supportive spouse, I would have been uncomfortable contributing less than my share to our collective finances, and taking an economic risk that would make my partner vulnerable, too. I liked the fact that the risk was my own.

As for having no one to encourage me all through my career transition because I was single - that wasn't my experience. I still remember the friend who first suggested that I try to create a career as an independent scholar, at a time when that seemed far too fanciful a possibility. I have a flashbulb memory of walking along the beach with another friend, at a time when I was due to pack up and return back to the East Coast after a 1-year sabbatical; she suggested that I try to extend my sabbatical for another year. A third friend was creating her own career out of the aspects of her training and expertise that she enjoyed the most; we exchanged stories all along the way. Still do.

III. Thoughts toward a Fantasy World for Singles Making Career Changes

The world of work, like so much of the rest of society, has not yet caught up with how we actually live our lives in the 21st century. Couples and nuclear families are still at the center of policies and procedures, but they are no longer the actual demographic center of American life. There are now more single-person households than nuclear family households. Most of those people who are living alone are not emotionally or socially isolated; there are important people in their lives - they just don't live under the same roof.

Now consider how employers treat their new recruits or the employees they are asking to make major moves. Do they offer to pay more in moving expenses if the employee is married than if the employee is single? Do they pull out all the stops to find employment for the spouse of the person they are hiring, without making any comparable efforts on behalf of the single worker? If so, maybe that should change.

My suggestions are motivated in part by simple fairness. A company hiring two workers, one married and one single, for the same position should not compensate one of them more than the other. That's the same reason I think that employers should offer all employees a menu of benefits from which each worker can choose the benefits they need most, adding up to the same dollar amount.

The other motivation behind my suggestion is the more radical notion that it is time to recognize the most important people in everyone's lives. If a company is willing to pay to move a spouse, why not do the same for a sibling or a close friend? (I know, it costs more - but the benefit is shared by all employees, and not just the married ones.) If a company is willing to look for employment opportunities for a spouse, why not also help find living arrangements for an aging parent?

Those are just a few of my fantasies. What are yours?

Source URL: http://www.psychologytoday.com/node/3156

Links:
[1] http://www.amazon.com/Flying-Solo-Career-Transition-Singles/dp/0615175570/ref=sr_1_1?ie=UTF8&s=books&qid=1233020613&sr=1-1 [2] http://www.amazon.com/Singled-Out-Singles-Stereotyped-Stigmatized/dp/0312340826/ref=ed_oe_p/102-4637341-6604139 [3] http://www.amazon.com/Secret-Rhonda-Byrne/dp/1582701709/ref=sr_1_1?ie=UTF8&s=books&qid=1233020997&sr=1-1 [4] http://caliber.ucpress.net/doi/abs/10.1525/ctx.2006.5.4.16 [5] http://www3.interscience.wiley.com/journal/119393014/abstract?CRETRY=1&SRETRY=0 [6] http://www.psychologytoday.com/blog/living-single/200811/my-previous-life-a-deception-researcher [7] http://www.psychologytoday.com/blog/living-single/200811/the-fragile-spouse-and-the-resilient-single-person

45.

Marriage Penalty? I Don't Think So

Apr 13 2009

Before I started studying singlism, I thought I knew what the "marriage penalty" was: On the same taxable income, married people pay more taxes than single people do. What I wondered was just how much more the married couples paid. So I used the handy tax calculator at the Money Chimp website to see. (Here, I'll use the most recent tax figures, for 2008, so they will differ from the numbers on p. 227 of Singled Out.)

What if I had a taxable income of **$50,000** and a married couple filing jointly had the same $50,000 of taxable income? I'd pay $8,844. How much more would the married couple pay? Their tax bill would be $6,698. Hey, that's less! $2,146 less!

Hmm, well what if the married couple and I both report taxable incomes of **$100,000**? I owe $21,978. The married couple owes $17,688. Wait, there's still no "marriage penalty" - the couple is paying less! ($4,290 less)

Let's try **a million dollars**. I pay $328,597. A married couple pays about $7,000 LESS.

I kept at this for a while. No matter how giant or how tiny a taxable income I entered into the calculator, the answer was the same: Single people always pay more taxes.

Does it seem unfair to compare the taxes paid by one person to the taxes paid by two? Then remember that the married couple does not need to have two wage-earners and they also do not have to have any children to qualify for the break. So one spouse can go to work, the other can stay home and watch TV, and the couple will still get tax breaks that are subsidized by single people.

In any case, it is clear that I hadn't understood what the so-called "marriage penalty" really was. Now I've read up on it and learned that when Americans rail against the marriage penalty, what they usually mean is this: If two people marry, their total taxes are sometimes higher than if they stayed unmarried. But even this is misleading, because more than half the time, the twosome reaps a tax **bonus** when they marry, not a penalty. What's more, the comparison is only about couples - married ones and unmarried ones. It is not as if a single person could file jointly with a sibling, friend, or parent - even if the two of them vowed to care for each other as long as they lived, and actually honored that vow.

Tax rates around the world: Do singles always pay more?

David from Chicago, a Living Single reader, sent me this mind-expanding link documenting tax rates across the globe. The numbers, from 30 different countries, were compiled by the Organization for Economic Cooperation and Development (OECD).

I'm going to unveil some mighty big numbers, so before you gasp, keep this important qualifier in mind: These aren't just income taxes. They include payroll taxes, social security contributions, and cash benefits as well.

Of all the nations in the study, the most tax-burdensome to singles is Belgium, where singles (with no kids) pay a rate of 55%! Married couples with 2 kids pay 40%. (That's the only other category in the table; the more appropriate comparison would be married without kids.)

Germany is the next most onerous place for singles. There, they pay 52%, compared to 36% for married with kids.

The lightest tax rate for singles is in Korea, at 17% (compared to 16% for marrieds). Mexico's rates are nearly as low, at 18%. Here's something else interesting about Mexico: It is one of only 3 countries, out of the 30, in which singles do NOT pay higher rates than marrieds. In Mexico, as well as in Turkey (where the rate is 43%), singles and marrieds pay the same rates. Greece really stands out from all the rest - singles actually pay less than marrieds (a shade under 39%, compared to a tad over).

At this time of year it can be hard to think kindly about taxes, but they actually can be put to good use. As a general rule, nations that have higher tax rates also offer more services and protections, such as health care and pensions. So I'm not going to take to the streets (or seaports) to protest taxation. But I don't think married people should get a tax break just because they are married. (Kids are a separate question.) And they surely should not get a tax break and call it a penalty. That, I will protest.

Source URL: http://www.psychologytoday.com/node/4286

Links:
[1] http://www.moneychimp.com/features/tax_brackets.htm [2] http://www.amazon.com/Singled-Out-Singles-Stereotyped-Stigmatized/dp/0312340826/ref=ed_oe_p/102-4637341-6604139 [3] http://articles.moneycentral.msn.com/CollegeAndFamily/LoveAndMoney/TheMythOfTheMarriagePenalty.aspx [4] http://moneycentral.msn.com/content/Taxes/P148855.asp?GT1=8011

46.

Single Boomers: Marketing Myths and Mistakes

June 13, 2008

One of the most significant demographic trends over the past half-century is the ascendence of people who are single. They have the power of numbers -- as a proportion of the adult population, they are closing in on people who are married. As householders, their place is dramatically different than it was a few decades ago: There are now more households consisting of single people living solo than of households comprised of mom, dad, and the kids. (And -- further attesting to their numbers -- most single people do not live alone.) Perhaps the most significant of all of these new demographic realities is the place of singlehood in our individual life stories -- Americans now spend more years of their adult lives unmarried than married.

Marketers -- like much of the rest of society -- have not caught up with the changes that have made single life vastly different than it was before. They have yet to realize the implications of those changes for their portrayals of singles and their pitches to them.

At last, though, the topic is on the table. Last week, the marketing firm JWT Boom hosted a two-day conference on marketing to boomers, including a panel on single boomers. I joined Sarah Zapolsky of AARP, Deborah Blake of Pulte Homes, and journalist and moderator Jane Ganahl to discuss the real lives of 21st century boomers who are single.

I focused on six mistakes that marketers sometimes make in their appeals:

MARKETING MYTH AND MISTAKE #1: What single people want, more than any particular product, is a soul mate. Because (some) marketers believe this, they try to sell their products by selling the fantasy of getting married.

A telling example of this came from a television ad that Coldwell Banker ran over and over again a few summers ago. In it, the narrator, a realtor, said this:

> "When Sylvia Maxwell was single again, she came to me at Coldwell Banker to find a new home. I searched high and low and when I found one she loved, she made a proposal to buy it. Larry was a single professor who lived next door, until one day he made a proposal of another kind. Gives a whole new meaning to 'love thy neighbor.' For almost a century, Coldwell Banker has known that real estate is only part of the story."

Visually, the ad introduces us to Sylvia and Larry. By the end, the two of them are holding hands, skipping, and frolicking through the yards of their homes, she in full bridal attire and he in his groom-ware. The bridesmaids and groomsmen follow gleefully behind them.

But never mind the visuals. What really got to me was that last line, about how Coldwell has always known that real estate is only part of the story. So I, a single woman, might go to a Coldwell Banker realtor in search of a home. The realtor, though, will just know that what I really want is a husband.

I started keeping track of all of the ads that feature weddings or brides. Setting aside the totally understandable products such as jewelry, catering, photography, and tuxedos, I also found wedding themes in ads for:

- Cereal, soft drinks, ice cream, chocolate, and cheese
- Dentistry, headache medication, body lotion, and eye drops
- Cars, clothes, and credit cards
- Beer, cigarettes, and wine coolers
- Hotels and life insurance
- Lottery tickets and motor oil. (Motor oil!)

Advertising is matrimaniacal. And yet, consider these results of a <u>Pew Research Survey</u>. Single people (divorced, widowed, always single) were asked:

- Whether they were already in a committed relationship, and
- Whether they were looking for a partner.

The most common answer, given by 55%, was that they were *not* in a committed relationship and that they were *not* looking for one.

Related to the mistake of seeing singles as more concerned about getting married than anything else is the vision of singles as living a narrow, constricted life, as if they were waiting to find "The One" before buying homes or traveling the world or pursuing their passions. That's **MARKETING MYTH AND MISTAKE #2**.

An example comes from advice offered by a boomer woman who is most certainly not leading a stunted or timid life. I'm talking about Suze Orman. In <u>The Road to Wealth</u>, she began a sentence like this:

"If you are a single person, a one-bedroom condo may seem ideal now."

I was excited. I thought she was going to continue by saying that I would soon discover how much I would love having more space, so I should just go for it right from the beginning!

But no. Instead, she continued the sentence this way:

"but if you hope to get married and start a family in the next few years, you'll need more space pretty quickly."

Suze Orman was thinking like the realtor who tried to sell me a town house or condo, after I had come to an open house because I wanted a house. Many singles have told me similar stories. When realtors lead their single clients to smaller and cheaper places than the clients were seeking, they are doing something extraordinarily rare in the business world -- working against their own self-interest.

MARKETING MISTAKE #3 is to portray singles in demeaning and dismissive ways. Here I think single men have it at least as bad, if not worse, than single women.

Remember the "lost another loan to Ditech" campaign? That ad featured a doughy man with ill-fitting suits and pudgy ringless fingers who worked for Ditech's competitor. So pathetic was the guy that even his therapist got his loan from Ditech. One of the ads ends with the hapless bachelor emitting a plaintive wail, "Mommmm!" He's a mama's boy, but even his mother has gotten her loan from Ditech instead of from her own son.

MARKETING MISTAKE #4 is to act as if single people do not even exist.

> • Think of all the ads that list prices "per couple."
> • Think of all of the greeting cards that express "our" congratulations or "our" condolences.
> • Or consider the Magellan catalog. It tries to tempt me to buy a colorful luggage strap with the promise of solving that pesky problem, "Which bag is ours?"

Again, by assuming that people come packaged in couples, these businesses talk past the very people who may be interested in their products. There are millions of us, and those numbers just keep growing.

MARKETING MISTAKE #5: Peddling insecurities.

Insecurities are for kids. Many single boomers are living their lives fully and unapologetically. Unless you want to alienate them, speak to their strengths and their real life needs and interests.

MARKETING MYTH AND MISTAKE #6: Assuming that single people "don't have anyone."

The belief that single people are "alone" and "don't have anyone" has been battered by one sociological and marketing study after another. Many single boomers may live alone but they have important people in their lives. Singles are more likely than married people to help, encourage, and spend time with their neighbors and friends. They are also the ones who more often visit, support, advise, and contact their siblings and parents.

Results of the Boomer Heartbeat study, recently reported by JWT and C & R Research, also demonstrated the important places of friends in the lives of single boomers. Whereas married couples with kids spend only 16% of their time with friends, single boomers without kids spend 28% of their time with friends. This is not because kids take up so much time. Boomers whose kids are no longer at home (the empty nesters) still spend only 15% of their time with friends. Even more strikingly, single boomers with kids at home spend about the same amount of time with their friends as do single boomers without kids (29%). The explanation that spending time with friends "compensates" for not having a spouse also won't fly (even apart from the fact that it is insulting). Married couples without kids also spend 27% of their time with friends.

The difference, I think, is that people who are single (along with married couples without kids) are not taking their cues about how to live their lives from advertisers or from conventional wisdom. Single boomers are myth-busters. They know that friends are not "just" friends. Single boomer women, in particular, will reward those who recognize the important place of friends in their lives. (What do *Sex and the City*, the *Golden Girls*, and even the "Desperate Housewives" - who spend a lot of their time out of their houses and their marriages - have in common? The friendship among the women is the emotional core of the shows.)

Single boomers, though, are often alone in one important way: They alone control the purse strings.

Can you hear me now?

Source URL: http://www.huffingtonpost.com/bella-depaulo/single-boomers-marketing_b_106897.html

---

47.

Do We Need Magazines for Singles?

May 15 2009

The first time I taught a course on singles ("Singles in Society"), all except one of the students were graduate students. The sole undergrad had a suggestion I loved - there should be an enlightened magazine for singles. Enlightened as in NOT about dating or make-up or becoming unsingle. Enlightened as in living single, fully and unapologetically.

Fast forward a decade, and we now have a magazine for singles, based out of Los Angeles, called Singular. When an editor at Forbes magazine first perused a copy of the magazine, she wrote an article saying, basically, who needs it?

That set me off, and I wrote an impassioned response. Much to my surprise and delight, *Forbes* immediately agreed to publish it. Here it is.

My Response to *Forbes*' Dismissal of *Singular* Magazine

(This article by Bella DePaulo was first published on *Forbes*.com on December 22, 2008.)

Death to *Singular* magazine! And deservedly so. That's not my opinion; it came from *Forbes*.com columnist Elisabeth Eaves, who asked, "Does the world really need a magazine for single people?"

As a lifelong single person, and an author and social scientist with expertise in singlehood, I was hoping for a different prediction. Still, I was intrigued by the arguments marshaled by Eaves to back her bet on *Singular*'s premature demise. Here they are:

- Single people are just too broad a category. They are like people with brown hair. How do you market to people with brown hair?
- Unmarried Americans are a diverse group who share no interests, except, of course, mate hunting.
- Single people do not define themselves as single.
- Marital status doesn't stand still. Who's going to identify with that?
- Singlehood is "not a state people aspire to--not, at least, in the same way they desire to be stylish or wealthy." What's more, "there's no reason to aspire to singlehood, because it's easy to get there."

The 93 million Americans who are divorced, widowed or have always been single are an extraordinarily diverse group. Eaves is right about that. We are women and men of all ages, social and economic categories, races, religions, sexual orientations, living arrangements and, yes, hair colors. Officially, we have but one defining characteristic: We are not legally married.

Yet, in staking her claims that singles share only an interest in mate seeking and that singlehood is not something people aspire to, Eaves is already demonstrating that we singles actually do have some experiences in common. That is that we know what other people think of us: that no one would want to be what we are (single), and that what we long for, more than anything else, is to become unsingle.

Eaves' view is an accurate description of the conventional wisdom about singlehood. My colleagues and I have surveyed thousands of people; many of them see singles in much the same way she does. But they--and she--are wrong.

In a Pew survey, unmarried Americans were asked whether they were in a committed relationship and whether they were looking for a partner. Twenty-six percent said they already had a committed relationship. The biggest group, 55%, said they were not in such a relationship *and* that they were not looking for a partner. The category Eaves assumed to be the most commonplace--not in a relationship but looking for one--amounted to a skimpy 16%. (The other 3% did not answer.)

While the conventional wisdom insists that singles are yearning to escape their supposedly sorry state, we real single people are living our lives fully. We are buying homes and furnishing them (well, as much as anyone can these days), traveling, supporting ourselves and sometimes some children, tending to our friendships and kinships, and pursuing our passions. We're not putting our lives on hold, marking time until we find The One.

And why should we? Although it is true, as Eaves states, that marital status is something that can change, singlehood is not the transitional period it once was. In fact, Americans now spend more years of their adult lives unmarried than married. That means that it is marriage that is transitional--separating one state of singlehood from the next--and only for those who do marry.

We are living in interesting times, historically and sociologically. What it means to live single has changed dramatically over the last several decades, but our perceptions have not caught up.

The place of singles in today's society is similar to the place of women before the women's movement of the 1970s. Back then, most people either did not recognize, or did not question, the degree to which the male point of view was the standard in the workplace, the media, in popular culture and even in science. Studies of heart disease based solely on men, the pervasive use of male pronouns to refer to all people, the separate and unequal want ads for men and women, and all of the other now-familiar examples--well, at the time, that's just the way it was. The initial challenges to those practices rocked the nation. Some felt threatened by the challenges, others liberated and enlightened.

Now, it is singlism that seeps into the nooks and crevices and crannies of the contemporary landscape, unnoticed and unchallenged. Singlism (my term for the stereotyping and stigmatizing of people who are single) and matrimania (the over-the-top hyping of weddings and couples) make up our cultural wallpaper. That's just the way it is.

Millions of single people dine with friends, colleagues or family and pay their own way; still, ads routinely list prices "per couple." Greeting cards convey "our" condolences or birthday wishes. In many workplaces, married workers can add their spouse to their health care plan at a reduced rate; singles cannot add the most important person in their lives to their plans. Most soldiers are single, but in televised clips of returning warriors, it seems that most are rushing toward the open arms of a spouse. Promotional materials from retirement services are adorned with pictures of older couples walking hand in hand, when most women that age are single.

What's more, hardly anyone thinks there is anything wrong with any of this. We're all locked in the conventional marriage and nuclear family box. We've been there so long, with so few missives from beyond, that we don't even realize that we're trapped. We need a magazine for singles because it is time for some unconventional wisdom.

So what might such a magazine (or blog or Web site or any other media) look like?

I would like to see a magazine that is for single people, for living single and not for becoming unsingle. Want to tell me about those Best Cities for Singles, as *Forbes*.com does every year? I'd love that. But I'm not so interested in some of the *Forbes*.com criteria, such as the number of online dating profiles or the number of bars and nightclubs per capita. You wouldn't list the number of divorce attorneys per capita as a criterion for the "Best Cities for Couples."

Tell me about the cities that are the most friend-friendly. I value my friendships, and I want to feel just as welcome in restaurants and public events and informal gatherings when I walk in with a friend or two than when I arrive hand in hand with a mate or a date.

Don't know how to measure friend-friendliness? Isn't that interesting? More people have friends than have romantic partners, and single people often have friendships

127

that have outlasted many marriages. Yet we don't know how to recognize places that support and value friendships. Let's discuss that.

I want to know about travel packages that are not tarred with single supplements. I'd like to know about car insurance and health insurance companies that do not charge me more than a same-aged married person. Tell me about the health clubs that are not cheaper by the couple, and the restaurant deals that are just as valuable to me when I'm dining solo as when I show up with friends or family.

I'd love to hear from and about authors who write compellingly--not condescendingly or pityingly--about singles, whether in novels or memoirs or other nonfiction.

I'd like to see a book review feature, where I can learn about works of fiction in which the characters are as unblinkered by the mythologies of marriage as so many of us happily single people are. All too often, I've started reading a novel that seemed poised to take me along on a soulful psychological journey. Ultimately, though, it takes a turn toward the hackneyed. When the protagonists are up against all that challenges them in their lives, they decide that conventional romantic love is the answer. I don't live in that box. Let me out.

I want to read the latest from the front lines of psychology, sociology and medicine. But I want fair renderings. I've been checking out matrimaniacal headlines for years. Almost without fail, all of those "get married, and you'll get happy and healthy and live longer" claims are misrepresented, exaggerated or just plain wrong.

I'd like to hear from singles who have dealt with bosses or co-workers who expect them to cover for everyone else, on the assumption that if you are single, you don't have anyone and you don't have a life. I also appreciate the everyday tales of funny looks, awkward questions and strange situations.

My own preferences are not all that quirky. I write the "Living Single" blog for *Psychology Today*, and when I blog about solitude or friendship, or what's wrong with the latest claims about getting married, or why no single person should ever have to answer the question "So why have you never been married," or why we need a National Singles Week, or about dining solo, or about singlism and matrimania in everyday life, thousands of people vote their interest with their clicks.

The topics that might appeal to singles like me are many and varied. What a joy it would be to read about them in a publication that is gloriously free of singlism and matrimania, and that recognizes that we are not defined by a desire to be coupled.

But do we define ourselves as single? Eaves thinks not. Actually, some singles do and some don't. Perhaps more important, other people regard our singlehood as definitional. They see it as a sign of what's inside us (the sadness, the loneliness, the tragic flaw that has left us stuck in our single state--myths, all). Sometimes they use it as grounds for exclusion, as when social events are planned for couples only.

Eaves also said it is easy to get to the state of singlehood. That one is true. I can (and I do) choose to be single. Anyone can. But I cannot be single in the same way that you can be married. My status as a single person is suspect in a way that a married person's never is. I get asked why I'm single; you don't get asked why you're married. I cannot be single with the same presumption of a life well lived. I cannot be single with the same material benefits and protections as you can. In the federal statutes alone (never mind state or local), there are 1,138 provisions and privileges accorded only to people who are legally married.

It is not at all like brown hair.

I don't know if the new magazine for singles will be successful. At a time when so many different kinds of magazines are folding, I wouldn't be too quick to attribute any downfall to its dedication to people who are single. Whatever its eventual fate, though, I think it has made a contribution. A buzz is in the air; we're talking about singles and their lives. Even the dismissive reactions, such as Eaves', have their place; they invite counterarguments, and let some light shine in. Now that *Singular* has made its debut, it's a little less unusual to think of singles as a group than it was before. Maybe, because of that, the next publication for singles will be even more likely to succeed.

Source URL: http://www.psychologytoday.com/node/4770

Links:
[1] http://singularcity.com/magazine [2] http://www.forbes.com/ [3] http://www.forbes.com/2008/12/11/single-magazine-marketing-oped-cx_ee_1212eaves.html [4] http://singularcity.com/web-articles/48-web-articles/322-yes-there-is-a-singles-demographic [5] http://www.singularcity.com [6] http://www.thenation.com/ [7] http://www.forbes.com/2008/12/22/unmarrieds-singles-magazine-oped-cx_bd_1223depaulo.html [8] http://www.amazon.com/Singled-Out-Singles-Stereotyped-Stigmatized/dp/0312340826/ref=ed_oe_p/102-4637341-6604139 [9] http://www.pewinternet.org/Reports/2006/Romance-in-America.aspx [10] http://www.forbes.com/2008/09/04/best-cities-singles-forbeslife-singles08-cx_ee_0904singles_land.html [11] http://blogs.psychologytoday.com/blog/living-single [12] http://blogs.psychologytoday.com/blog/living-single/200808/the-american-psyche-tipping-toward-solitude [13] http://blogs.psychologytoday.com/blog/living-single/200811/the-fragile-spouse-and-the-resilient-single-person [14] http://blogs.psychologytoday.com/blog/living-single/200803/are-singles-doomed-high-blood-pressure-only-if-they-read-the-media-reports [15] http://blogs.psychologytoday.com/blog/living-single/200807/so-why-have-you-never-been-married-a-case-study-in-accidental-singlism [16] http://blogs.psychologytoday.com/blog/living-single/200809/its-national-singles-week-here-are-14-reasons-why-we-need-it [17] http://blogs.psychologytoday.com/blog/living-single/200804/dining-alone-part-2-here-s-what-people-really-do-think-you [18] http://blogs.psychologytoday.com/blog/living-single/200804/singlism-and-matrimania-in-everyday-life

48.

The American Psyche: Tipping Toward Solitude?

Aug 21 2008

I live in the most ordinary American household - I live alone. Knock on any door in the nation and you are more likely to find a household like mine than a household with mom, dad, and the kids, or a household with a married couple and no kids, or a single-parent household, or any other kind.

There has been a surge in the number of single-person households, and a decline in the number of married-with-kids households. This is not a fad - it is a decades-long demographic juggernaut. It has many pundits and prognosticators plenty worried.

One of their fears is that we may be on the cusp of an epidemic of loneliness. Interventions, they say, may be in order. Some even present statistics in support of the link between living alone and feeling lonely. Not bogus statistics but real ones. For example, a recent report about the well-being of older people in the UK noted that 17% of older people living alone say that they are often lonely, compared to only 2% of those living with others.

That's a meaningful difference. I do believe that many older people are isolated, lonely, and depressed (though not as many as our stereotypes would lead us to believe). Their problems should be taken seriously. But let's not make a pathology out of a preference.

Think again about the statistic that 17% of older people living alone report that they often feel lonely. What strikes me about this finding is that 83% of older people living alone do NOT often feel lonely. Remember that they are old, some may have health problems that limit their mobility, others may have close friends and family who have died, and they are living without anyone under the same roof readily available for small talk or interesting excursions. Yet 83% say that they are not often lonely.

When I was writing Singled Out, I read voraciously about demographic patterns (such as the increase in 1-person households) and about loneliness, and thought a lot about my own life. I live alone and I am almost never lonely. I am also rarely bored. Then I realized something that seemed startling at first: During those atypical times when I am bored, I am almost always with other people. I'm never bored when I'm alone.

I don't consider myself an introvert. I love to socialize (with people who do not bore me), I love the visits (time-limited) from friends and family who come to catch up with me and soak up the sun from my deck, and I love to entertain. But I also cherish my solitude.

Introverts and loners: They are not apologizing anymore

Jonathan Rauch does consider himself an introvert. In 2003, he wrote an essay for the *Atlantic* magazine that began like this:

> Do you know someone who needs hours alone every day? Who loves quiet conversations about feelings or ideas, and can give a dynamite presentation to a big audience, but seems awkward in groups and maladroit at small talk? Who has to be dragged to parties and then needs the rest of the day to recuperate? Who growls or scowls or grunts or winces when accosted with pleasantries by people who are just trying to be nice?

> If so, do you tell this person he is 'too serious,' or ask if he is okay? Regard him as aloof, arrogant, rude? Redouble your efforts to draw him out?

> If you answered yes to these questions, chances are that you have an introvert on your hands - and that you aren't caring for him properly.

Rauch, a prolific writer, got more enthusiastic responses to that essay than to anything else he had ever written. Three years later, the *Atlantic* reported that readers were still clicking their approval: Online, no other piece had drawn more traffic than Rauch's "Caring for Your Introvert."

The same year that Rauch's essay appeared, the witty and wonderful Party of One: The Loners' Manifesto was also published. Loners, notes author Anneli Rufus, are people who prefer to be alone. They are not sad, lonely, or deranged.

Contrary to stereotypes and TV-punditry, loners are not serial murderers and they are not school shooters, either. True, there are criminals who look like loners, in that they spend lots of time alone. Typically, though, they are just pseudo-loners, who never craved all that time to themselves. They wanted to be included but were instead rejected.

True loners do not withdraw in order to stew in misery or plot violent revenge. Instead, Rufus reminds us, loners "know better than anyone how to entertain themselves...They have a knack for imagination, concentration, inner discipline, and invention."

Not all introverts or loners live alone. Their experiences, though, should give pause to those whose thoughts leap to loneliness when imagining the experiences of solo-dwellers, and to those who are tempted to swoop in with their interventions to rescue people who may be perfectly content exactly as they are.

Togetherness can also breed loneliness

The same report that underscored a link between living alone and feeling lonely also implicated divorce in the mix. As one headline put it, "Easy divorce has left elderly lonely and depressed."

The logic is that people who are divorced, and who also feel lonely, are lonely because they are divorced. Probably a good number really are.

The reverse sequence, though, should not be discounted. Some people divorce because they are lonely in their marriages. In the anthology, Women on Divorce, several contributors described such experiences. Ann Hood, for example, said, "I wanted my old pre-marriage back...I remembered how at night I used to sleep well. How being alone felt fine because there was no one down the hall not talking to me." Daphne Merkin added, "I, for instance, married a man who left me feeling lonely not because he wasn't home but because he was."

Preferences for togetherness can change over the course of your life

When I arrived at my first academic job at the age of 26, I considered it my great good fortune to have colleagues who wanted to go out to lunch every day. Now, 28 years later, if I had to go out to lunch every day - even with people I really like - I would go stark raving mad.

Early theorists of aging believed that with age came isolation. Some thought that older people were socially marginalized by a society preoccupied with youth. Others believed that older people wanted to withdraw from society, so they isolated themselves on purpose.

Then along came Laura Carstensen and her colleagues, who actually studied the social interaction preferences of people of different ages. Carstensen found that older people socialize more selectively. They still spend time with the people to whom they feel closest. They don't bother as much, though, with people they do not know so well, or with people who annoy them. That's by choice.

Tipping toward solitude

If there is such a thing as a national psyche, then I think the American version is showing signs of change. Think of trends such as the growing number of people who live alone, the growing preference for working from home, the increasing inclination for families (who have the means to do so) to give their kids rooms of their own, and the preference for older people to live independently as long as possible (instead of moving in with other family members, as they once did). There are many possible reasons for each of these trends, but perhaps at least some of the people in each of the categories have one thing in common: They like their time alone.

In all of our lives, we negotiate a balance between the time we spend with others and the time we spend alone. There are, and always will be, big individual differences.

Some love the constant give-and-take of the company of other people, and others prefer more alone time.

Of course, humans are social beings. Meaningful relationships with other people, and time spent with others, will always be important. Still, if there were a national average of the solitude-sociability balance, and if that average were computed over time, I bet it would show that the American scales are tipping toward solitude.

Source URL: http://www.psychologytoday.com/node/1594

Links:
[1] http://findarticles.com/p/articles/mi_m4021/is_9_25/ai_109384501 [2] http://www.mailonsunday.co.uk/health/article-1038109/Easy-divorce-left-elderly-lonely-depressed.html# [3] http://www.amazon.com/Singled-Out-Singles-Stereotyped-Stigmatized/dp/0312340826/ref=ed_oe_p/102-4637341-6604139 [4] http://www.theatlantic.com/doc/200303/rauch [5] http://www.theatlantic.com/doc/200602u/introverts [6] http://www.amazon.com/Party-One-Manifesto-Anneli-Rufus/dp/1569245134/ref=sr_1_1?ie=UTF8&s=books&qid=1217413964&sr=1-1 [7] http://www.amazon.com/Women-Divorce-Companion-Penny-Kaganoff/dp/0156004623/ref=sr_1_1?ie=UTF8&s=books&qid=1219312199&sr=1-1 [8] http://www-psych.stanford.edu/~lifespan/llc.htm

49.

Supreme Court Justice David Souter Stands Up for Singles

May 17 2009

David Souter's contribution to the place of singles in society may seem self-evident - he is a Supreme Court Justice and he has been single all his life. That's not the only reason I like him. It is amusing (if sad) to watch writers and pundits get tangled in singlism as they try to figure out this unusual guy who has never been married. In Singled Out, I made fun of what was written about him when he was first nominated for his position. Now, as he prepares to retire, they're at it again.

Souter really is unusual, and not because he has been single all his life. When court is not in session, he lives in a centuries-old New Hampshire farmhouse where he watches no television and has no access to e-mail. Every day, he has the same thing for lunch - a yogurt and an apple. Plus, as the *New York Times* noted, "he's leaving one of the most powerful positions on earth because he wants more time to hike in his beloved New Hampshire mountains."

I see two singles-relevant contributions here. First, "work-life balance" has all to often been interpreted as the juggling that married people do - especially wives who are also mothers. In Justice Souter's decision to step down at the tender (for a Supreme Court Justice) age of 69, there is a statement about the importance of balance in the lives of single people, too. Souter loves hiking and reading books next to the fireplace in his cabin, and he's not too enamored of Washington, D.C.

Second, Souter doesn't need a TV or an internet connection to realize that people find him odd. He seems to care not a wit. Anyone who wants to live single - fully and unapologetically - in this society of ours that still can't seem to get its collective head around such an aspiration, could use a bit of Souter's bite-me attitude.

Source URL: http://www.psychologytoday.com/node/4779

Links:
[1] http://www.amazon.com/Singled-Out-Singles-Stereotyped-Stigmatized/dp/0312340826/ref=ed_oe_p/102-4637341-6604139 [2] http://egan.blogs.nytimes.com/2009/05/13/souters-summits/ [3] http://abcnews.go.com/Politics/SCOTUS/story?id=7483045&page=1

50.

What's With the Cat, and Other Questions about Singles and Their Pets

Oct 22 2008

One time, a publication that interviewed me about Singled Out sent someone to take a picture of me at home. The photographer asked what my book was about, then stopped for a moment to think about how to set up the shot. Looking like he had just been struck by a bolt of inspiration, he asked, "Where's your cat?"

Well, I don't have a cat. I have nothing against cats - or any other pets for that matter - I just don't happen to have any.

Recently, I heard from a student planning to do some research on singles and their pets, and that got me thinking about the stereotypes. I wonder why it is that single people - women especially - are so often cast as cat-crazy. Is it a way of attributing a cat-like caricature to singles - say, aloof and unsociable? Or maybe even a more flattering portrait of cool and unruffled independence?

I don't know if single people really are any more likely than married people to have cats or any other pets. As far as I know, there is no research on the matter. That means we are reduced to anecdotes. The only real-life cat lady I ever knew was married to the dean of a major university. I think her cat count always exceeded 30. Her husband was rumored to enjoy his time away from home.

Is the cat-stereotype an American thing? I don't know that either. I do remember, though, that one of the most infamous quotes from one of the most famous British singletons was about a dog. According to Bridget Jones (okay, so she's not real), all of her single friends were convinced that they would "end up dying alone and found three weeks later half-eaten by an Alsatian."

By itself, the perception of singles as cat-people (or pet-people) doesn't bother me. What does rub me the wrong way is the interpretation that is sometimes offered for the supposed link between being single and having a pet - that singles have pets as "compensation" for not having a spouse.

Now maybe that interpretation actually is true of some single people, just as some married people have a pet as practice for having a kid. (This is not hypothetical. I knew a couple who admitted to this. The two of them also liked to quip that they hoped the kid they planned to have would like the dog they already did have, because it would be a shame to have to get rid of the kid. I'm pretty sure they meant that as a joke.)

But why do I so rarely hear an entirely different and (I think) more plausible explanation - that single people who have cats have them because they like them? Because they are caring people who love animals and would want to have pets in their lives regardless of their marital status?

The compensation interpretation is not limited to pets. Single people's close relationships with siblings, parents, and friends have also been described as compensation for not having a spouse, sometimes even by academics.

That, to me, is a way of saying that unless you have a spouse, none of your other adult relationships count as genuine or as valuable in and of themselves. A similarly dismissive explanation dogs (sorry) single people who are devoted to their jobs or to some cause or interest that they pursue passionately - they are just compensating for not having a spouse.

The most fundamental problem, I think, is that too many Americans simply cannot believe that any adult would actually like being single and choose to stay that way. Until that nut is cracked, deluded amateur and professional psychologists will continue to see compensation under every single person's cat dish.

Source URL: http://www.psychologytoday.com/node/2131

Links:
[1] http://www.amazon.com/Singled-Out-Singles-Stereotyped-Stigmatized/dp/0312340826/ref=ed_oe_p/102-4637341-6604139 [2] http://www.amazon.com/Bridget-Joness-Diary-Helen-Fielding/dp/014028009X

51.

Is It Bad to be "Set in Your Ways"?

Apr 7 2009

There is something that is often said of older single men, and it is not meant kindly: They are "set in their ways." Usually I make fun of this by pointing out that younger single men are taunted with the admonition that they need to "settle down." The two jabs at single men amuse me because, as with so many other instances of singlism, they get you coming and going. If your life has a lot of spontaneity, then you need to settle down; if you have a stable routine, then you are "set in your ways." (Single women contend with their own version - for example, they are sometimes seen either as promiscuous or as poor things who don't get any.)

Today, though, I have a different take on the "set in your ways" rebuke: What's wrong with having a routine and liking it?

I've been thinking about this because I just got back from a cross-country trip in which many of my usual routines were disrupted. There are times when I love that about traveling - ending up in a whole different place on a different schedule with different people, vistas, foods, cultures, and customs.

The recent trip wasn't one of those times. I was at a meeting of a working group in Cambridge, Massachusetts. The intellectual content of the meeting was terrific, as were many of the participants, but we were holed up in a windowless conference room for more than a dozen hours over two days. We were not even let loose into the natural light for our lunch break. I missed the sunlight and the fresh air.

I'm a late-night person. Always have been. (Really, from infancy, according to my parents' reports.) But our meetings started at 8 a.m. East Coast time, which is 5 a.m. "my" time, and now start counting backwards for the time it takes to get up and get to the meeting...

I did my graduate work in Cambridge. Parts of the city are charming and I usually delight in my return visits. But the meetings were in the numbered-buildings section, with no character and no green leafy things anywhere in sight. Dreary, dreary, dreary. Cambridge also has some wonderful restaurants but I was too wiped out after the first full day of meetings to do any hunting or gathering, and too economically-challenged to spring for the extra night of a hotel room so I could take the Red Line to the vibrant and savory parts of the city later on.

One of the joys of single life - especially for people like me who are not only single but also live solo - is that you have a lot of room to arrange your life the way you like it. That could mean a lot of routine or a lot of spontaneity or anything in between. For me, it's a bit of both. Take dinner, for example. Unless I have plans to meet someone, the timing is totally unpredictable. But the beginning of the day is something else entirely. I always want to check my e-mail, first thing. Then I check out the New York Times online, then the Huffington Post, and often the *Psych Today* blogs, too. Some of that will lead me elsewhere. What I'm doing is getting a sense of what's going on in my world, and in the world-at-large. Only then am I ready to settle comfortably and happily into my work and all the rest.

My trip disrupted that routine, too. I didn't bring a laptop because I was trying to fit everything into carry-on's, and I wasn't going to get up any earlier than I already had to in order to access the public computer at the hotel.

I don't mean to imply that any of what I experienced amounted to a hardship. It was all minor stuff. Plus, I'm grateful to have been invited to the meeting; it was a valuable and enlightening experience. My point is simply this: What's so bad about having a routine and liking it? What's wrong with being "set in your ways"?

One of my uncles was bereft at first when his wife died. The two of them were married for a lifetime and did everything together. But they were very different. He was easygoing and calm. His wife - not so much. He followed her lead while she was well, going wherever she wanted whenever she wanted, as often as she wanted. I remember asking him, sometime into his widowhood, how he was doing. He began to describe his day - how he'd take his time making breakfast, reading the paper, and making his way through the rest of the day on his own schedule.

I knew he still grieved for his wife, and missed her every day. But now he was set in his ways. They were *his* ways. And there was a real comfort to that.

Source URL: http://www.psychologytoday.com/node/4197

Links:
[1] http://www.amazon.com/Singled-Out-Singles-Stereotyped-Stigmatized/dp/0312340826/ref=ed_oe_p/102-4637341-6604139 [2] http://travel.yahoo.com/p-travelguide-476504-cambridge_vacations-i [3] http://www.nytimes.com/ [4] http://www.huffingtonpost.com/

52.

If You Dine Alone, What Will People Think of You? PART 1: See If You Can Predict the Results

Apr 8 2008

On a beautiful summer evening at Baltimore's Inner Harbor, back when I lived on the East Coast, I stopped for dinner at an outdoor café. My server lingered a while each time she appeared, offering conversation along with the refills of my iced tea. I wondered - did she think I was uncomfortable dining alone?

In fact, I was feeling serene. I had spent a busy, boisterous day with three guys I adore - one of my brothers and his two sons. They had already left. I wanted to stay and savor in solitude the warm breezes, fresh seafood, and the parade of people passing by.

It wasn't just my server who seemed surprised and a bit protective of her lone diner. The hostess who seated me also did the solo-diner double take, glancing an extra time or two to see whether there really was someone else with me, who had just wandered off for a moment. At least she did not ask the "just one?" question. (Nor did a spotlight follow me to my table, as happened to Steve Martin in The Lonely Guy.)

While people-watching, it struck me that no one else seemed to be at the Inner Harbor on their own. I observed intently for 20 minutes, and never spotted even one person who seemed to be there without another person or group alongside them. Wasn't there anyone else within driving distance of the Inner Harbor who would have enjoyed heading off on their own to saunter around on such a perfect evening?

I have always thought it odd that in a nation supposedly known for its rugged individualists and daring adventurers, so many people seem reluctant to venture on their own into safe and comfortable places such as restaurants and movie theaters. When I first looked for research on the topic, I didn't find much. There was a study published in 1981 that reported that people seem more distressed at the prospect of walking into a restaurant alone than walking into an empty room alone, staying home alone, or living alone.

Why the hesitation? The celebrated sociologist, Erving Goffman, offered one explanation: "To attend alone is to expose oneself as possibly not being able to muster up companionship."

Yeah, I know. You didn't need a sociologist to tell you that if you go out to dinner on your own, other people will think you are a loser.

I'm a social psychologist, though, and a numbers-loving one at that. No matter how strong my intuition may be, and how many others may seem to agree with me, I want to see the relevant research. What do other people really think when they see someone dining alone?

Because there were no relevant studies out there, I decided to do my own. My collaborators (Wendy Morris and Cathy Popp) and I took pictures of pairs of heterosexual couples dining together - one couple on each side of a table in a restaurant. Some of the couples were in their 20s or 30s, and others were a decade or two older.

Then we took each of the pictures and used some computer wizardry to make people disappear. Erase one of the men, and now a woman appears to be dining with a couple. Erase the other man, and she appears to be dining with another woman. Erase the other woman instead of the man, and she appears to be dining with a man.

Erase all of the other people, and now she is dining alone. (We did the same thing with each of the diners - male and female, younger and older.)

We thought it was important to do the study this way so that each of the people we photographed (with their permission) would have the exact same posture and expression regardless of whether she or he appeared to be with other people or alone. If our intuitions were correct, the diners would be perceived (for example) as sadder when seated alone than with others - even though they actually had identical expressions each time.

We brought our pictures to a shopping mall, and asked adults to tell us why a designated person in the picture went out to dinner that evening. When the picture was of a person dining solo, we asked them to tell us why they thought the person went out to dinner alone.

Now we had hundreds of responses and comments made by the shoppers. What do you think they said? Focus especially on the solo diners. Can you guess what the shoppers said about the people who appeared to be dining on their own, compared to when the same people were pictured with others? In my next post, I'll describe the results of the study.

53.

Dining Alone, PART 2: Here's What People Really Do Think of You

Apr 9 2008

Thanks to all who predicted the results of the study that asked, "If you dine alone, what will people think of you?" A variety of suggestions were offered. My colleagues and I - before we actually conducted the study - thought all of your predictions seemed plausible. Well, all except one: the one that was correct! "Adora" nailed it when she said, "It is probably no big deal if you dine alone."

I don't mean that no one ever has a snide thought about a person who is dining solo. The shoppers who commented on our photos did have some unkind things to say about the solo diners, including the very remarks that some of you predicted. But, they also made many neutral and positive observations. Most importantly, the people who commented on the pictures were no more likely to say anything negative (and no less likely to say anything positive) when the person in the picture was dining solo than when the same person was with other people.

We looked at all sorts of factors to see if they mattered - for example, was the person in the picture a male or a female? A younger adult or an older one? Were the people making the comments male or female? Single or married? No matter what we included in the analyses, the answer was always the same - there were no consistent differences in how a person was judged depending on whether that person was dining solo vs. with one or more other people.

Let me explain. Some negative comments were made about the solo diners, as we anticipated. For example, people said things like, "He is lonely," "Doesn't have many friends," "She looks depressed."

But look at some of the other comments we got:

"Enjoying a few good peaceful moments."
"She just wanted to eat by herself."
"Wanted to relax."
"Traveling."
"He seems to be enjoying his dinner."
"Wanted time to ponder."
And my favorite: "He is secure."

For comparison, let me tell you about some of the comments that were made about the pictures that showed one man and one woman dining together. We expected those pictures to elicit mostly kind words. We did get some positive comments. For example, people said that the man was out to "dinner with his wife for fun;" or that the two are having a "fine, quiet conversation." Others said that "they are very close," or that "they enjoy spending time together."

But now look at some of the other comments that were made about the male-female pairs:

They went to dinner "to have a talk because their relationship needs some mending."
"She is upset."
"He thought he liked her."
They wanted to "get away from the children."
She went out to dinner with him "out of obligation - she's married to him."

We found the same mix of some positive, some negative, some neutral comments for all of the different sets of diners we studied - same-sex pairs, one person sitting across from a male and a female, or a male and a female on each side of the table.

Two of the people who commented on Part 1 of my post made an important observation. "Terry" and "Ladyexpat" said that by showing people photos of solo diners and asking for comments, we were creating a focus on the solo diners that may not occur naturally. Maybe when people go out to dinner, they just pay attention to their own dinner (or dinner companions), and hardly even notice the other people in the restaurant.

There is some great research relevant to Terry and Ladyexpat's point. I think that work may also help to explain why people are reluctant to go out to dinner on their own, even though they are probably not going to be judged any more or less harshly than if they were went out to dinner with other people.

The studies were conducted by Thomas Gilovich and his colleagues to document what they call "the spotlight effect" - "people's tendency to overestimate the extent to which their behavior and appearance are noticed and evaluated by others."

Here's an example of one of the studies. College students were assigned to wear a t-shirt with a picture of Barry Manilow - how embarrassing! Then they had to knock on a door of another room, where students were filling out a questionnaire, and speak briefly to the experimenter in that room. Subsequently, they were asked to estimate how many of the students had noticed that they were sporting a Barry Manilow t-shirt. They were far more mortified than they needed to be - only half as many students had noticed and remembered their t-shirt than they feared.

I'll end, as I began, with the words of "adora":

> "I also used to think that if I dine alone, people will think I'm a loser - until I notice other people dining alone and I actually think they are very cool."

So here's to all the cool solo diners out there!

Source URL: http://www.psychologytoday.com/node/384

54.

Holiday Spirit, 21st Century Style

Nov 23 2008

[Previously, I posted an interview with Kay Trimberger, author of The New Single Woman, about single women in India. That post generated a lot of interest, so I thought readers might also enjoy our latest musings about how singles spend the holidays. We wrote this post together.]

We are both single women, so we are not at all surprised when the phone starts ringing around the holidays. We're talking reporters, not suitors. That's because we are also scholars of singlehood. We listen closely as the callers, often with a hint of pity, pose their predictable questions. How can singles survive the holidays? Can we offer advice for fending off desperation and despair?

In the minds of the questioners, single people are on the outside looking longingly into the windows of the American hearth-land. In every other household, they think, mom, dad, and the kids - and maybe other family and friends as well - are gathered around a fireplace, a dining room table, or a tree. Single people, they just know, are sad and alone.

Some really are. They wish that others would think to include them on the holidays, and they are deeply grateful when that happens (though they would prefer not to be regarded as doleful orphans rescued by the married heroes). Yet in the hundreds of conversations we have had with single people over the years, the conventional tale of yearning is not the one we hear most often.

Some single people love to celebrate holidays in blissful solitude. One single woman, a Drama professor and extraordinarily sociable person, described an idyllic Christmas spent in a big overstuffed chair with a good book and a glass of wine; the only sounds were the crackling timbers of the fire. One of us waxed rhapsodic about the joys of solitude to a reporter seeking suggestions for singletons. "Oh, I could never go to my editor with that!" she exclaimed.

Other single people organize their holiday celebrations around friendship rather than family. Dorothy, another woman one of us interviewed, should have known better than to look to marriage as her ticket to the holiday spirit. Growing up, she dreaded the holidays - too much family tension. Her second husband (the one she really loved) refused to recognize the holidays at all. Now a vibrant middle-aged single woman with no children of her own, Dorothy spends the holidays surrounded. Single friends and coupled friends, with and without children, gather round - sometimes at her place, sometimes at someone else's. This is holiday "tradition," 21st century style.

It is not just single people who set aside the familiar to try out a path less traveled. Julia and Michael, a married couple in their fifties, used to fly to Oregon to be with Julia's grown daughter from an earlier marriage, or jet to Arizona to join Michael's family, or drive 150 miles round trip to celebrate with Julia's mother, brother and his family. About ten years ago, however, exhausted from crowded airports and clogged highways, and from their demanding jobs that also involved commuting, they tried something new. Ever since, they have set aside at least one holiday a year to hike the ethereal, isolated trails of Point Reyes National Seashore.

Last Thanksgiving, when the hike was on their calendar, some friends invited the couple to go to the town's community dinner. Awesome wilderness or high school cafeteria? Out of allegiance to the ideal of fostering community ties, they headed back to high school. Only this auditorium had white tablecloths, flickering candles, and chamber music. Plus buffet tables laden with delicacies that few ninth graders could ever imagine. Singles and traditional and non-traditional couples and families intermingled. The participants differed in ethnicity and social class; they were united by community.

This Thanksgiving, Julia and Michael have accepted an invitation from a single woman friend to attend a small pot luck dinner. Now that they no longer feel guilty about separating holiday celebrations from strong and continuing ties to family, their choices have multiplied and their holidays are more likely to be joyful.

Others have talked to us about how divorce darkens the holidays, especially as children fly off to celebrate with one parent, leaving the other bereft. Yet over time, the wounds in many blended families heal, and complex combinations of extended family gather to celebrate together. The divorced couple and their new spouses and step-children assemble, perhaps inviting some or all of the multiple grandparents and other relatives, too.

So what happened to those traditional nuclear families, and their far-flung relatives who travel far and wide to join them for the holidays? They still exist, but they are in the minority. There are now more one-person American households (27%) than households consisting of a married couple and their children (23%). Households that include a married couple, with or without children, are now outnumbered by households without a married couple.

Families are smaller now, too. By the time they reach the age of 44, 20% of American women have not had any children. Those who do have children have fewer than they once did (an average of 1.9 in 2006, compared to 3.1 in 1976). Extended family gatherings, in which adult siblings find their way to a shared table for the holidays, are impossible for those who have no brothers or sisters. Friends, though, can have a place at all of our tables and in all of our lives.

Family ties are, and always will be, important. But increasingly, so are friends. Maybe our communities will also, in time, reclaim their rightful place in our hearts and our hearths. Solitude, too, may begin to get some respect.

The demographic face of the nation is changing and diversifying, and so is our holiday tableau. As Americans, we never stop re-inventing ourselves, or our holiday "traditions."

Source URL: http://www.psychologytoday.com/node/2458

Links:
[1] http://www.psychologytoday.com/blog/living-single/200810/single-women-in-india-a-conversation-with-kay-trimberger [2] http://www.amazon.com/New-Single-Woman-Kay-Trimberger/dp/0807065234/ref=ed_oe_p [3] http://www.kaytrimberger.com/ [4] http://www.census.gov/Press-Release/www/releases/archives/facts_for_features_special_editions/012246.html [5] http://www.amazon.com/Singled-Out-Singles-Stereotyped-Stigmatized/dp/0312340826/ref=ed_oe_p/102-4637341-6604139

55.

Holiday Party Game: Spot the Fake Couples

Dec 22 2008

I know that I'm supposed to feel self-conscious around the holidays, walking into all those holiday parties on my own when so many others are coupled-up. But I don't. In fact, I feel both happy and proud. Happy, because I'm a sociable person and I like some of these gatherings; and happy because I also love my solitude, and after the party is over, I can go home to some.

The proud part is more interesting: I like it that I don't grab onto someone just to try to fit in at a time of such relentless coupling.

There are people who do practice that anxiety-grab, and some of them hold on tight all the way through to Valentine's Day. Yahoo found, when they surveyed users of their Personals page, that Valentine's Day is part of "National Break-Up Season" -- a time when "people tend to 'put up' with current relationships in order to have a partner for holiday gatherings." Around then, coupled people are twice as likely to be thinking of breaking up, and once that last chocolate-covered cherry is gone, so too is their sweetheart.

A scientific approach to the same question also showed that couples are especially likely to break up during Valentine's season. Unsurprisingly, the people in relationships that were not so great were especially likely to break up. But even the people in the best relationships did not feel any better about their partners during Valentine's season than any other time of year.

So here's a little party game you can play, on your own or with any number of others. Look around you at all the different parties, through December and New Year's and Valentine's Day. See if you can spot the couples who are just faking it. Some will be rent-a-couples - they are just hanging out together as temps. Others, though, will be truly, officially, legally married.

I remember once going to an evening social event connected to a scientific conference. One very famous social psychologist arrived late to the gathering (his wife was already there) and engaged in a very public display of affection. Now I don't mean your garden-variety PDA; I mean the kind that might even make an enlightened high school student blush. I immediately thought to myself: They are doomed.

They were.

Now I'm not anti-coupling. Really, I'm not. Maybe because I love being single, I can observe couples who seem to be a great match and enjoy that, too. My favorite example comes from my own parents. They and my sibs and their kids and partners used to get together occasionally for a week at Duck beach in North Carolina. My mother, especially, seemed to love these gatherings since by then, all four of us grown "kids" were spread far and wide across the country. One night after dinner, when everyone was just relaxing and talking, my father said he was going out to put gas in the car. And my mother said she would go with him. To think that, even with all of her kids and grandkids around, she would want to go out to do errands with her husband - well, that seemed sort of bewildering and also kind of sweet. (Are you thinking up snarky ways to smash my reveries, like suggesting that maybe she wasn't so enamored of all of us as I'd like to think, or that perhaps "put gas in the car" was code for something that even grown kids try not to picture their parents doing? Well, save them! No, really, go ahead and post them.)

I said I'm not against marriage or coupling. But I am against compulsory coupling. I'm against the stigmatizing of those who are not coupled, whether by choice or by happenstance. One way to stop the stigma is to stop playing along with the game. If there is not someone you really want to be with over the holidays, then go to all those parties on your own. (Of course, I think party invitations should include friends, but that's a different topic.) Even if you do wish you were coupled and it is hard to walk in uncoupled, do it and feel proud. Embrace and enjoy your inner smug singlehood.

Don't do it just for yourself. Every time you show up as your own complete person, rather than appearing in your couple costume, you make it easier for everyone else who is also single for the holidays or for good (and I do mean good). And though they probably won't admit it, you are probably also helping the people who just can't wait for the holiday season to end, so they can return their rental partner. Maybe next year they'll show up on their own.

Happy Holidays and thank-you for reading this blog all year. I love this virtual community.

Source URL: http://www.psychologytoday.com/node/2767

Links:
[1] http://www.thefreelibrary.com/"You're Dumped!" Yahoo! Personals Research Shows National Break-Up...-a0157252925 [2] http://www.ingentaconnect.com/content/bpl/pere/2004/00000011/00000004/art00007 [3] http://www.amazon.com/Singled-Out-Singles-Stereotyped-Stigmatized/dp/0312340826/ref=ed_oe_p/102-4637341-6604139

56.

Vacationing While Single

Jul 18 2009

In my vacations, as in the rest of my life, I like some combination of <u>socializing and solitude</u>. Everyone gets the socializing part; the solitude, others often find puzzling. When I was living on the East Coast, hundreds of miles from the ocean, I'd rent a beach house for a week every summer, and invite friends to stay for the first five or six days. Then I'd want that last day to myself. I just loved having some time to be totally on my own. I remember one friend in particular who just couldn't fathom that. She'd ask, when the end of the week drew nearer, whether she could stay that last day.

Sometimes I'd go out to dinner on that final evening. I guess beach town are so much about sociability that people can have an even harder time with the solo diner in those settings than they do in others. So I'd get the solo-diner treatment, with the hostess seating me in some out-of-the-way hidden area - so as to protect me from embarrassment, I guess (or maybe to protect the reputation of the establishment as a fun place to be) - then serving me quickly, and perhaps a bit too solicitously.

When my parents were living, sometimes the entire family would share a big beach house for a week. Their kids, their grandkids - we'd all be there. Our tradition was to have dinners together every night. We would all see each other then. The rest of the time, we could head off in pairs, groups, or on our own. Perfect.

On another vacation, I coordinated with my close friend from graduate school. It was many years after the two of us had left Harvard (where we occasionally took I-Hop breaks at 3 a.m.), and she was on sabbatical with her family in Australia. I flew the 22 hours from the East Coast of the US, spent some time just with her, some time with her and her family, and some time on my own. Another version of perfect.

One other vacation started as two other single women professors and I stood shivering in the dark cold winter morning, collars up against the wind, as we waited for a shuttle to the airport. We had decided, spur of the moment, to take advantage of a great fare and head from Virginia to Cozumel, Mexico. The academic tasks we had left undone still lurked in our minds. Then hours later, as if by magic, we sat in our tees and shorts, taking in the sun and the sand and the extra whiffs of warmth blown in from the sea. Now it was visions of the good life that were dancing in our heads, as we shared margaritas and chips and a salsa so fiery that it made our ears hurt. Our time together was fabulous, and probably made the more so by the fact that at the end of the day, I could retreat to the room I had to myself. When we returned to Virginia, it was still winter of course, but we all wore our Cozumel tee shirts to the next faculty meeting.

In vacation travel, as in holiday travel, singles are at risk for being <u>treated as not fully adult</u>. You know the drill - you get the back seat of the car, and the pull-out couch in the living room instead of a room with a door that shuts. Fortunately, these examples of singlism are not universal singlehood experiences. You can have enlightened friends and family members. Or if you have the nerve, some thick skin, or a sense of humor, you can stand up for yourself. For a beautifully written example, take a look at Wendy Braitman's story, over at Huffington Post, called "How I grabbed the best bedroom in the guest house."

I like to show not a hint of defensiveness or apology about my solo traveling self, even when I'm not really traveling solo. In my book, Singled Out: How Singles Are Stereotyped, Stigmatized, and Ignored, and Still Live Happily Ever After, I mentioned the man at the beach who saw me reading on a chaise longue, with an empty one beside me, and asked whether I was "by my lonesome." I was making fun of his conflation of being alone with being lonely, and of his cluelessness in phrasing his question that way when all he really wanted to know was whether anyone was using the vacant chaise. What I didn't say in the book is that I never denied that I was on my own, even though, with all honesty, I could have. I had traveled to the Cayman Islands with a friend. I wanted to read for a while with the ocean at my feet; she wanted to head back to her room. I could have said all that - oh, I'm not alone, my friend is here, she's just in her room right now, so you can have the chaise - but I didn't. Revel in your solo spunk, and it will become easier for others to do so, too.

Source URL: http://www.psychologytoday.com/node/31047

Links:
[1] http://www.psychologytoday.com/blog/living-single/200808/the-american-psyche-tipping-toward-solitude [2] http://www.psychologytoday.com/blog/living-single/200804/if-you-dine-alone-what-will-people-think-you-part-1-see-if-you-can-predict [3] http://www.psychologytoday.com/blog/living-single/200804/dining-alone-part-2-here-s-what-people-really-do-think-you [4] http://www.amazon.com/Singled-Out-Singles-Stereotyped-Stigmatized/dp/0312340826/ref=ed_oe_p/102-4637341-6604139 [5] http://www.huffingtonpost.com/wendy-braitman/how-i-grabbed-the-best-be_b_224258.html [6] http://www.amazon.com/Singled-Out-Singles-Stereotyped-Stigmatized/dp/0312340826?SubscriptionId=AKIAIRKJRCRZW3TANMSA&tag=psychologytod-20&linkCode=xm2&camp=2025&creative=165953&creativeASIN=0312340826 [7] http://www.smartertravel.com/travel-advice/can-you-avoid-the-single-supplement.html?id=2866247

57.

Susan Boyle: The New Face – and Voice! – of the "Spinster Cat Lady"

Apr 17 2009

Count me among the multitudes of the charmed. I, too, loved the story of the woman who walked on stage to the sound of snickering, only to shock and wow them all with the sound of her music. I heart <u>Susan Boyle</u>.

I've also been intrigued by the rising tide of voices proclaiming that, thanks to Susan Boyle, we have learned our lesson: We prejudged her before we heard her sing. We should have known better, and now we do.

Or do we?

I think there are several lessons that have gone unlearned. Here are three of them.

Unlearned Lesson #1: What we still don't see in Susan Boyle's appearance

I'm flipping through my collection of clippings, looking for the descriptions of Susan Boyle's appearance. She's called dowdy, homely, matronly, frumpy, chubby, frizzy, and more. She didn't seem to mind all that much (which, for me, added to her appeal), and even offered her own assessment that she looked "<u>like a garage</u>." What I want to know is, where are the other kinds of descriptors - for example, "interesting"?

Another woman was highlighted intermittently during Susan's performance - judge Amanda Holden. No one would (or should) call Amanda dowdy, pudgy, or matronly. But I saw her as something else: Predictable. She looked like a star - blond, slim, and beautifully dressed. Just what you would expect from someone in her position. Kind of boring, in a way. Even apart from any matters of talent, I just liked watching Susan more.

Unlearned Lesson #2: The ism that slipped under the radar, still again

Letty Cottin Pogrebin, founding editor of <u>Ms. Magazine</u>, said that when Susan got the three thumbs up, "I typed 'Ageism Be Damned' into the subject line of an email and sent the YouTube link to everyone on my Women's Issues list." Pogrebin also noted that we were all "initially blinded by the entrenched stereotypes of <u>age, class, gender, and Western beauty standards</u> until her book was opened and everyone saw what was inside."

All true enough. But what about <u>singlism</u>?

Unlearned Lesson #3: We're still judging Susan Boyle's life by our values, not hers

Consider this opening paragraph in a story by an Associated Press writer:

> "Susan Boyle lives alone in a row house with her cat Pebbles, a drab existence in one of Scotland's poorest regions. She cared for her widowed mother for years, never married and sang in church and at karaoke nights at the pub."

I don't doubt that the AP writer would find that existence drab. But I don't think he's asked Susan Boyle how she views her own life. Maybe she does agree that it is drab. Or maybe she loves her life, with its space both for solitude at home and sociability at the pub. Maybe she sees her own region not as impoverished but as rich in spirit, culture, and community. Maybe her religion is important to her, and singing in church is, in her experience, not the least bit drab. Maybe she feels fortunate to have been able to be there for her mother at a time of such need. Maybe she does not feel at all sorry for herself because she is single.

Let's let Susan Boyle tell her own story. Maybe she will tell it in a song.

Source URL: http://www.psychologytoday.com/node/4367

Links:
[1] http://www.youtube.com/watch?v=9lp0IWv8QZY [2] http://www.washingtonpost.com/wp-dyn/content/article/2009/04/15/AR2009041502577.html?nav=hcmodule&sub=AR [3] http://www.msmagazine.com/ [4] http://www.huffingtonpost.com/letty-cottin-pogrebin/why-susan-boyle-makes-us_b_187790.html [5] http://www.amazon.com/Singled-Out-Singles-Stereotyped-Stigmatized/dp/0312340826/ref=ed_oe_p/102-4637341-6604139 [6] http://news.yahoo.com/s/ap/20090416/ap_on_re_eu/eu_britain_singing_sensation_5

58.

High Achievement, High Praise for a Woman Who Has Always Been Single

Nov 21 2008

"Across the spectrum, praise for Napolitano," was the headline in today's *Washington Post*. Janet Napolitano, Democratic Governor of Arizona, is likely headed to Barack Obama's cabinet, where she will serve as Secretary of Homeland Security.

The Napolitano story reminded me of Anita Hill; she was a lawyer for Hill during the Clarence Thomas nomination hearings. The story also inspired musings about some of the other women with impressive cabinet posts in both Republican and Democratic administrations - people such as Condoleezza Rice, Donna Shalala, and Janet Reno. (Shalala's appointment as Clinton's Secretary of Health and Human Services was the topic of one of my favorite *New Yorker* cartoons. It showed a little girl and a little boy at play, with the girl saying to the boy, "You be the doctor and I'll be the Secretary of Health and Human Services.")

Of course, there is another reason why people such as Janet Napolitano, Anita Hill, Condoleezza Rice, Janet Reno, and Donna Shalala are all linked in my mind and in my heart (politics aside) - all of them have been single all their lives.

As the *Post* heading suggested, the story about Napolitano was almost uniformly glowing. A collection of quotes from Republicans and Democrats, supporters and opponents, underscored the Governor's judgment, skills, intelligence, and fairness, as well as her sterling record.

There was not one word - not even an innuendo - of singlism in the article. I haven't found any hints of singlism in any of the other articles I've read about her nomination, either.

Of course, it is very early in the process (the announcement of Napolitano's appointment is not even official yet). Still, I'm hoping this initial coverage is a sign of a society that is evolving toward greater enlightenment.

How different it was when I was writing Singled Out, first published just two years ago. Then, when I researched people such as Condoleezza Rice and Ralph Nader (another political leader who has always been single), the singlism was rampant, and not just in the tabloids. Esteemed journalists such as Bob Woodward, television talking heads such as Chris Matthews, and elite publications such as the *New Yorker*, all offered dismissive commentary without apology or even awareness.

I'm a social scientist, and I love numbers and systematic research. So while individual examples of successful single people are heartening, ultimately I want more.

Here it is. A study based on a representative national sample of more than 3,000 Americans addressed the question of whether marital status mattered when it came to social well-being. There are many studies of psychological well-being (happiness, for example), and I've discussed them in this blog (here and here) and in Singled Out. Social well-being is different.

Most relevant to the high-achieving singles I've been discussing, social well-being includes a sense of contributing something important to community and society. It also encompasses as sense of belonging to a community, and perceptions of meaningfulness and progress in the world (rather than anomie).

The study compared the social well-being of people of different marital statuses at one point in time. For example, it compared people who have always been single to people who are currently married. As I've explained before, that's always a set-up. By definition, the group of people who are currently married excludes all the people who got married, found it intolerable, and got divorced. So if you compare currently married people to single people and find that the currently married people look better in some way, you can't conclude that getting married made them better. That would be like a drug company trying to persuade you to take a drug because people currently taking the drug are doing better than people not taking the drug, all the while trying to distract you from the fact that close to half of the people who took the drug had a bad reaction (so the drug company simply removed their data from the comparison).

The study in question was unusually precise about the different groups - there were people married for the first time, people who were remarried, people who had always been single, people divorced once, people divorced more than once, and people who were widowed. The authors even looked separately at people who were cohabiting, including subgroups of cohabitors who were previously married or had always been single.

In the most sophisticated analysis presented in the paper (the one that took into account variables that could have mucked up the results), the results were straightforward: Marital status just didn't matter.

So even though the currently-married group had the usual unfair advantage (people who didn't like marriage and got out of it were not included), their social well-being was still not measurably better than that of the people who were divorced or widowed or had always been single. For the always-single group, the direction of the results favored the single people - their social well-being scores were higher than those of the people who were currently married (though not significantly so). Within the group of people who had always been single, the single women reported especially high social well-being.

For one of the social well-being subscales, the women who had always been single were especially advantaged over those who were currently married - they felt that they were contributing something valuable and worthwhile to society.

Now, don't say that high-achieving single women are just compensating for not having a spouse. Bob Woodward implied something of the sort, and I made fun of him for it in *Singled Out*. I've already mocked the compensation theory as applied to singles and their pets, and check out all the witty and wise comments that were posted there by the readers of this blog. Practitioners of singlism, you're on notice!

Source URL: http://www.psychologytoday.com/node/2429

Links:
[1] http://www.washingtonpost.com/wp-dyn/content/article/2008/11/20/AR2008112001567.html [2]

http://www.amazon.com/Singled-Out-Singles-Stereotyped-Stigmatized/dp/0312340826/ref=ed_oe_p/102-4637341-6604139 [3] http://www.psychologytoday.com/blog/living-single/200806/but-what-about-single-men [4] http://www.springerlink.com/content/bj32385460402417/ [5] http://www.psychologytoday.com/blog/living-single/200808/cracking-the-code-how-think-critically-about-reports-the-alleged-superiori [6] http://www.psychologytoday.com/blog/living-single/200803/living-single-it-is-how-we-spend-the-better-part-our-adult-lives [7] http://www.psychologytoday.com/blog/living-single/200810/whats-with-the-cat-and-other-questions-about-singles-and-their-pets

59.

Ed Rendell Says Janet Napolitano Has No Life Because She Is Single!

Dec 4 2008

When the name of Arizona Governor Janet Napolitano was floated as Barack Obama's new Secretary of Homeland Security, I was exultant and said so right here in this space. It wasn't just that she was single and always had been. Tthere are plenty of accomplished single people whose values are so dissimilar from my own that I would shudder to see them in any high post. No, I was happy because in those early reports of her potential nomination, there was no trace of singlism.

Then, yesterday morning, I got a call from Gail Collins. That should have been a totally exhilarating experience. She writes for the op-ed page of the *New York Times*, and is one of my very favorite columnists. (When she gets started on Mitt Romney sticking his dog on top of his car during his vacation travels, well - empathy for the dog aside - it is ROFL hilarious.) She is, in fact, a delightful conversationalist. Unfortunately, though, she had bad news for me.

It was from her that I first learned about Pennsylvania Governor Ed Rendell's quip about Napolitano:

> "Janet's perfect for the job," he said. "Because for that job, you have to have no life. Janet has no family. Perfect. She can devote, literally, 19, 20 hours a day to it."

As humorist Dave Barry always said, I'm not making this up. In the year 2008, a state governor says of another state governor that she has no life because she is single. When I used nearly exactly those words in a Singled Out chapter subtitle, "You don't have anyone and you don't have a life," I was making fun of that belief! I was calling it a myth.

Some have mentioned that Rendell did not realize there was a live microphone beside him when he committed his act of singlism. I'm not sure it mattered. Too often, people who say these sorts of things do not even realize that they have said anything boorish. Singlism slips under the radar of our Prejudice Alert System. We really do need some consciousness-raising. Lots of it.

So here's the good news. Rendell did not get away with it this time. CNN's Campbell Brown, making good on her "no bias, no bull" promise, called him out on it. The Huffington Post report on the matter, just posted yesterday, has already drawn more than 500 comments.

And, saving the best for last.....please read this column that Gail Collins wrote. Enlightenment. (And humor, too.) Is there any better gift for the holidays?

Source URL: http://www.psychologytoday.com/node/2571

Links:
[1] http://www.governor.state.az.us/ [2] http://www.nytimes.com/2008/11/21/us/politics/21napolitano.html [3] http://www.psychologytoday.com/blog/living-single/200811/high-achievement-high-praise-a-woman-who-has-always-been-single [4] http://topics.nytimes.com/top/opinion/editorialsandoped/oped/columnists/gailcollins/index.html[5] http://www.governor.state.pa.us/portal/server.pt? [6] http://features.csmonitor.com/politics/2008/12/03/ed-rendell-on-janet-napolitano-perfect-because-she-has-no-life/ [7] http://www.amazon.com/Dave-Barry-Not-Making-This/dp/0449909735 [8] http://www.amazon.com/Singled-Out-Singles-Stereotyped-Stigmatized/dp/0312340826/ref=ed_oe_p/102-4637341-6604139 [9] http://www.cnn.com/2008/POLITICS/12/02/campbell.brown.rendell/index.html [10] http://www.huffingtonpost.com/2008/12/03/campbell-brown-hits-ed-re_n_148010.html [11] http://www.nytimes.com/2008/12/04/opinion/04collins.html

---

60.

Obama's Supreme Court Pick Is a Woman, a Latina, and...Single!

May 27 2009

One of my collaborators in the study of people who are single and the place of friendship in their lives and all of our lives is a law professor, Rachel Moran. So as soon as I heard that Sonia Sotomayor was Obama's Supreme Court nominee, I immediately sent Rachel an e-mail asking what she thought. At that moment, I had no idea that she knew Sotomayor.

What I got back was an intriguing first-person account. I then asked Rachel - a 1981 Yale Law School graduate, UC Berkeley chaired professor, and now a founding faculty member of the UC Irvine School of Law - if she would do a brief Q & A to share her impressions with others.

Bella DePaulo: *How did you get to know Sonia Sotomayor?*

Rachel Moran: Sonia was a year ahead of me at Yale. I got to know her through an organization called LANA (Latinos, Asians, and Native Americans). Believe it or not, at the time, there were so few members of these groups in the student body that we could not form separate organizations!

Bella DePaulo: *What are your impressions of her? In the flurry of initial reports in the media, is there anything you know about her that has not yet gotten much attention?*

Rachel Moran: She has a keen intellect, an articulate voice, and a sense of humor (though this is not usually mentioned in the press coverage). I think she will be a formidable presence on the Court, who will be a lively, engaging, and challenging colleague for the other Justices.

Bella DePaulo: *I recently wrote a* post about David Souter *here on my* Living Single *blog at* Psychology Today, *and when Sotomayer was introduced, reader Monica Pignotti posted this to the comments section*: "I just watched Sonia Sotomayor's speech for her Supreme Court nomination and it was wonderful! She is a currently single woman and mention was made of all her friends and family who were surrounding her and gave her so much support, and no negative mentions by anyone at all in the commentaries I heard about her civil status. It is obvious she is a happy, fulfilled and much-loved single woman. It was great to see that this was acknowledged in the way she was introduced. Looks like there really is some progress being made here." *What do you think?*

Rachel Moran: I agree. More and more Americans are spending a substantial part of their adult lives as single people. The stigma of singlehood seems to have disappeared when it comes to qualifying for high office, both for men like David Souter and women like Sonia Sotomayor. A person's marital status is considered irrelevant to the ability to do the job. [**Bella**'s aside: Still, some high-profile singles, such as Janet Napolitano, do get the Singles Treatment.] But it's still nice to have friends, including some in high places!

Bella DePaulo: *Anything else you would like to add?*

Rachel Moran: This moment is truly historic. I am sure that when we met as members of LANA all those years ago at Yale, none of us imagined that one of us someday would become the first person of Latino origin nominated to the Supreme Court. This is truly a mark of how far the legal profession has come in recognizing excellence in people with a range of backgrounds and experiences. This is definitely an occasion for celebration!

Bella DePaulo: Thanks so much, Rachel, for taking some time to share your observations. To readers who would like to know more about Rachel Moran, she is the author (with Devon Wayne Carbado) of Race Law Stories, a book about some of the most consequential legal decisions about race, and the stories behind them. She has also advocated for the return of citizen-lawyers.

Source URL: http://www.psychologytoday.com/node/4950

Links:

[1] http://chronicle.com/free/v54/i05/05b04401.htm [2] http://www.boston.com/bostonglobe/ideas/articles/2008/06/08/i_now_pronounce_you____friend_and_friend/ [3] http://www.law.uci.edu/profile_r_moran.html [4] http://www.nytimes.com/2009/05/27/us/politics/27court.html?hp [5] http://blogs.psychologytoday.com/blog/living-single/200905/michelle-obama-and-justice-david-souter-stand-singles [6] http://blogs.psychologytoday.com/blog/living-single [7] http://www.amazon.com/Singled-Out-Singles-Stereotyped-Stigmatized/dp/0312340826/ref=ed_oe_p/102-4637341-6604139 [8] http://blogs.psychologytoday.com/blog/living-single/200812/ed-rendell-says-janet-napolitano-has-no-life-because-she-is-single [9] http://www.amazon.com/Race-Law-Stories-Rachel-Moran/dp/159941001X/ref=sr_1_1?ie=UTF8&s=books&qid=1243375635&sr=1-1 [10] http://www.law.com/jsp/nlj/PubArticleNLJ.jsp?id=1202427453356&slreturn=1 [11] http://www.huffingtonpost.com/bella-depaulo/more-about-sonia-sotomayo_b_207937.html

61.

Laura Bush gives Condi Rice "The Singles Treatment," and Only Keith Olbermann Notices

December 17, 2006

I quit my day job to study singlism, the stereotyping and stigmatizing of people who are single, including even the most accomplished singles who have ascended to some of the highest posts in the land. For years, I've been writing at length about the topic. (See *SINGLED OUT: How Singles are Stereotyped, Stigmatized, and Ignored, and Still Live Happily Ever After*.) Then Laura Bush came along, and crisply captured the crux of singlism with her dismissive comment about Condoleezza Rice. Here's what the First Lady told *People* magazine:

> "Dr. Rice, who I think would be a really good candidate (for President), is not interested. Probably because she is single, her parents are no longer living, she's an only child. You need a very supportive family and supportive friends to have this job."

Laura Bush thereby gave voice to one of the fundamental myths of singlehood - that people who are single don't have anyone. Surely, Laura Bush knows that Dr. Rice has friendships that have lasted a lifetime, and that she stays in touch with those far-flung friends even as she travels the globe to meet with world leaders. Laura Bush cannot be oblivious to the gathering Dr. Rice hosts at her place, several times a month, of four other musicians. Said Rice of the foursome, "We are like family. [They are] like my best friends." And while *Newsweek* may have been using the term "friends" loosely when it claimed that 120 friends were waiting for Condoleezza Rice as she walked in the door of her surprise 50th birthday party, Laura Bush must have noticed the number of people who were there for Condi that evening. After all, she was one of them.

155

The First Lady's pity for poor friendless Condi is even more astonishing in light of the place of Condi in her own life and that of her husband. There is probably no one with whom Laura and George Bush have spent more time in the past six years than Condoleezza Rice. Dr. Rice, far more often than the first couple's own daughters, is with the Bushes at Camp David and in Crawford - and not just to work. Dr. Rice is a cabinet member and a football fan, an advisor and an athlete. She's a friend.

So why didn't Laura Bush instead express befuddlement at Dr. Rice's reluctance to run? Why didn't she point to the support that would be forthcoming from all of the people who care about Condi and would work tirelessly on her behalf - beginning, of course, with Laura and George themselves?

I do, though, see Laura Bush's point about the absence of siblings in Rice's life. If Jimmy Carter did not have the support of brother Billy, and if Bill Clinton had to govern the nation without the help and inspiration of brother Roger - well, I doubt that either of them would have dared even to fantasize about becoming President.

Here's something else that is remarkable about Laura Bush's condescending comment about Condoleezza Rice - she did not seem to think that there was anything wrong with what she was saying. And other than Keith Olbermann (and Margaret Carlson, his guest on *Countdown*), apparently no one else did, either.

That's the thing about singlism. It is practiced routinely, unselfconsciously, and unapologetically, and by people who are not known for their political blunders. Plus, they get away with it.

Laura Bush worked as a public school teacher and librarian, but she never said of those years, "I guess I could have stayed home and baked cookies." Hillary committed that quip, and she was hounded until she headed straight back to the kitchen, where she gamely played bake-off with another Bush Woman. It was Elizabeth Edwards, not Laura Bush, who was apparently misquoted as saying that her choices had made her life more joyful than Hillary's. She, too, was badgered mercilessly, until she finally called Hillary and said uncle.

But saying poor Condi doesn't have anyone? No problem there.

And still we wonder why single people do not vote in greater numbers.

Source URL: http://www.huffingtonpost.com/bella-depaulo/laura-bush-gives-condi-ri_b_36563.html

156

62.

Meghan McCain Feels Sorry for Herself Because She Is Single

Mar 5 2009

Over at the <u>Daily Beast</u> (Tina Brown's site), Meghan McCain recently blogged about her <u>post-election dating experiences</u>. Meghan is John McCain's 24-year old daughter and a Columbia University graduate. The post was one long whine.

Dating Democrats is dreary for Meghan because they get all defensive and apologetic about voting for Obama. Or, they are members of the Facebook group, "<u>I have more foreign-policy experience than Sarah Palin</u>." The ones who voted for her father can be even worse. There are the cringe-y ones, such as the dinner-date who described her selection from the menu as a "maverick choice." Then there are the creepy ones, such as the guy who declared that Meghan could be his Cindy.

Meghan McCain's point is that her father's Presidential candidacy "killed [her] personal life" (as if coupledom were the sum total of a personal life, but never mind). Personally, I don't care about her dating horror stories. But I am still shaking my head over two of the statements in her post.

First, after telling her first few tales of dating woes, she asks, "So where does that leave me?" Here's her answer: "Let's just say I'm spending a lot of time writing and even more time with my girlfriends." Think about what's wrong with that while I tell you about the second regressive statement.

That second one is the conclusion to her self-pitying post, a word of advice: "So to all the fathers out there: If you want your daughters to be single in her 20s, I can say this - run for president."

Let's go back to Sorry Statement #1. What does it say about Meghan's McCain's rank ordering of the important people in her life? Well, among her peers, all the potential dates come first. Then, when they all turn out to be losers, Meghan is left spending "even more time with [her] girlfriends." The dorks are the priority, and the friends - many of whom, perhaps, have been in her life for years - are the consolation prizes.

Among the story themes I hear repeatedly from other singles is that when their friends become seriously coupled or married, then they (the singles) get thrown under the bus. (Here I will acknowledge that married commenters to this blog sometimes claim that the ditching is not just a one-way thing.) When I hear Meghan McCain moaning about spending lots of time with friends after her dates go bust, I get a sick feeling about the kind of coupled person she is likely to be. She's already telegraphing it.

Have you been mulling over Sorry Statement #2? That's her advice to fathers to run for president if they want their daughters to be single in their 20s. Meghan is sad to be all of 24 years old and still single, and assumes that you would be, too. Now THAT'S sad. It is also breathtakingly ill-informed.

Being 20-something years old and single is not extraordinary; it's typical. In the United States, a 25.6-year old woman who has always been single shares that status with half of all other women her age. Men stay single even longer; those who reach the age of 27.4 without ever marrying have that in common with 50% of all men their age.

Even when the 20-something years are long past, people who have always been single can find plenty of others like them. For example, more than 12% of American women get all the way through their 40s without ever marrying. As I discussed in a previous post, this is not a uniquely American phenomenon; rather, staying single longer has gone global.

The Census Bureau has records of the median age at first marriage dating back to 1890. (The data are here; see Table MS-2 under Historical Times Series.) During all that time, getting married before your 20s has NEVER been typical. For the year when Americans married the youngest, 1956, the median age at first marriage was 22.5 for men and 20.1 for women. That means that even for the women, in that most marriage-crazed year, more than half were over the age of 20.0 when they first married.

So don't blame your dad, Meghan. Regardless of whether your father ran for president or for city council, whether he was in politics or in the arts, whether he was a butcher, a baker, or a candlestick maker, or whether he wasn't even in the picture, you'd probably be single in your 20s. The only thing bad about that is your attitude.

Source URL: http://www.psychologytoday.com/node/3656

Links:
[1] http://www.thedailybeast.com/[2] http://www.thedailybeast.com/blogs-and-stories/2009-03-02/looking-for-mr-far-right/[3] http://www.facebook.com/group.php?gid=36436310820[4] http://blogs.psychologytoday.com/blog/living-single/200811/living-single-longer-its-a-global-phenomenon[5] http://www.census.gov/population/www/socdemo/hh-fam.html[6] http://www.drkarengaillewis.com/[7] http://singleedition.com/[8] http://blogs.psychologytoday.com/blog/living-single/200902/are-the-early-years-single-life-the-hardest-part-ii-approaching-age-30[9] http://blogs.psychologytoday.com/blog/living-single/200902/are-the-early-years-single-life-the-hardest-part-iii-fears-and-mispercepti[10] http://blogs.psychologytoday.com/blog/living-single/200902/are-the-early-years-single-life-the-hardest-part-iv-single-again-and-singl[11] http://www.drkarengaillewis.com/8/Default.aspx

63.

Oprah, Angelina Jolie, Halle Berry, Jessica Lange...Faces of Fear?

November 4, 2007

A reporter called me recently and reeled off a list of celebrities. Oprah, Angelina Jolie, Halle Berry, and Jessica Lange were just the first few. Others in the category included Brad Pitt, Goldie Hawn, Kurt Russell, John Malkovich, Tina Turner, Susan Sarandon, and Tim Robbins. You can probably think of others. They are, of course, celebrities who are coupled but not married.

Here are the questions I was asked: Are these unmarried celebrity couples afraid of commitment? Are they afraid of the failure that would darken their reputations and their souls if they were to marry and then divorce?

So here was a bouquet of celebrities, all talented, many extraordinarily altruistic, and this reporter's first thought was to tie them all together with a ribbon of fear. Her second thought was to put them on the defensive. Like the nagging relative or the smug married friend, this inquiring mind was asking of each of these unmarried couples, "So why aren't you married?" The question is the equivalent of asking married couples when they last had sex.

When I see skilled, successful, and selfless people - whether coupled or uncoupled, famous or unknown - my first inclination is to think of them in terms of their strengths. So here, on behalf of unmarried couples (personally, I'm happily single), are some unapologetic, nondefensive answers to the clunky "why aren't you married" question that should never have been asked:

- We are secure in our relationship. Our love does not need to be propped up by a legal contract.
- We don't want Rudy or Mitt or McCain or any other government official hanging out in our bedroom. Maybe they like threesomes but we don't.
- We don't want Pat Dobson or Tony Perkins or the ghost of Jerry Falwell or any other religious representatives under our covers. We may be spiritual, we may even be religious, but we are not so sure that we are going to find divine revelations coming from the mouth of Jimmy Swaggert.
- We have our principles. If people of other sexual orientations cannot marry, then we won't either. We do not want to be part of any club that would have only us as members.
- Our principles extend beyond same-sex marriage. Even if any adult could marry any other adult, many millions of single people would still be excluded from the 1,138 federal benefits and protections awarded solely to married people.

159

- All those Bachelor reality shows, all the television dramas that build predictably to a wedding, all the cries for ever more tax breaks for married people - all this <u>matrimania</u> makes us skeptical. If marriage is so great, why does it need all these cultural and government subsidies?
- We just love it way too much when people ask us why we're not married.

So now that the cloddish question for the unmarried couples has been asked and answered, let's turn to the married celebrities. It's your turn, Larry King, Jay Leno, Ted Koppel, Chris Matthews, Michael Douglas, Catherine Zeta-Jones, and all the rest: Tell us, when did you last have sex?

Source URL: http://www.huffingtonpost.com/bella-depaulo/oprah-angelina-jolie-hall_b_71062.html

---

64.

Advice to Singles from an Editor at *Vogue* – in 1936

Jul 10 2008

When people unfamiliar with my book ask me what it is about, I like to say that <u>Singled Out</u> is a myth-busting, consciousness-raising, totally unapologetic take on singlehood. What I also think to myself, but don't say, is "and you've never seen anything like it."

Well, with regard to author "attitude," I now have to say that I HAVE seen something like *Singled Out*, and it was published 72 years ago.

When I tried to buy Marjorie Hillis's 1936 book, <u>Live Alone and Like It</u>, only used copies were available. That turned out to be fortunate, because when mine arrived, with its orange hardcover and yellowed pages coming unglued from the spine, I found a hand-written note on the inside.

With spelling and punctuation preserved, here it is:

> February 2nd 1937
>
> Happy Birthday Berenice,
>
> I found this book so amusing that I tho't you might like a copy - Now that I'm fulfilling the first part of the title I tho't I'd see how to "like it" -
>
> Anyway, its fun -

Love
Ethel

Hillis (the author) was born in 1889. When she wrote *Live Alone and Like It*, she was an editor at *Vogue*. Tired of women who whined about being single, she decided to share her own decidedly uncomplaining perspective. The book was an instant success, passed around from friend to friend and from generation to generation. Finally, in 2005, a contemporary publisher decided to print some new copies.

Here, for your entertainment and enlightenment, is a baker's dozen of my favorite quips from a book published in the same year as *Gone with the Wind*, a year when gas cost 10-cents a gallon.

From the chapter, "Solitary Refinement":

1. "This business of making your own life may sound dreary - especially if you have a dated mind."

2. About the attitude of a single woman who traveled the world: "There is an element of defiance in this attitude, but when you start to live alone, defiance is not a bad quality to have. There will be moments when you need it, especially if you've been someone's petted darling in the past. But you will soon find that independence, more truthfully than virtue, is its own reward."

3. About Miss S., a teacher in the NY public schools: "In spite of living by one of the most underpaid professions in the world, Miss S. has been to Europe three times and to Mexico once, and three years ago she paid for the care of a tubercular pupil. She feels very sorry for her friends in Maine whose lives are limited to husbands and a trip to Portland."

From the chapter, "Who Do You Think You Are?":

4. Addressing single women who live on their own and are delighted with their lives, the author warns them not to expect anyone else to share their joy. "As a matter of fact," she says, "your friends (to say nothing of your family) would find it a lot simpler if you'd acquired a husband instead of a desire to Live Your Own Life."

From the chapter, "When a Lady Needs a Friend":

5. If other people invite you to dinner, reciprocate. "The old-fashioned notion that single women are objects of social charity was killed in the War."

From the chapter, "Setting for a Solo Act":

6. "Never let the curtains go in your bedroom because 'no one sees them.'"

7. "One of the great advantages of your way of living is that you can be alone when you want to. Lots of people never discover what a pleasure this can be."

From the chapter, "Pleasures of a Single Bed":

8. "It's probably true that most people have more fun in bed than anywhere else, and we are not being vulgar. Even going to bed alone can be alluring. There are many times, in fact, when it's by far the most alluring way to go."

From the chapter, "Will You or Won't You?":

9. The question is about sex and affairs. Here's Hillis's answer:
"Hold a little mental investigation of the case - and then do exactly as you please."

10. And more about sex: "Whether or not a woman has had her Moments, if she has a grain of common sense she keeps it to herself, since, if she has, most people would be shocked, and if she hasn't, the rest would be superior."

From the chapter, "The Great Uniter":

11. "There is probably nothing that gives as much pleasure as food, not excepting love."

From the chapter on money and saving, titled, "You'd Better Skip This One":

12. "Don't worry if your scheme doesn't fit any of the books that tell you what proportion of your income should go for what. After all, that's your business and not the author's."

From the chapter, "A Lady and Her Liquor":

13. The best "advice" in this chapter? Recipes for highballs, martinis, old-fashioneds, and manhattans.

65.

A Singles Manifesto, from a Pioneer

Mar 3 2009

Optimistically, I like to think that the writing and research and public speaking that I do about living single is in the service of social change. I like to smash myths (especially the ones that purport to have scientific backing, only they don't), underscore inequities, and point to the strengths that so many singles demonstrate despite all the relentless singlism and matrimania that permeates society. You might even say that I'd like to start a revolution, or at least a singles movement.

So I was more than a little surprised when I discovered that there already was such a movement, not so very long ago. I learned this from a headline in the *Los Angeles Times* last week: "Marie Barbare Edwards dies at 89; psychologist helped pioneer a 'singles pride' movement."

Edwards had written a book, The Challenge of Being Single, in 1974. The same year, the *Los Angeles Times* wrote about her in an article titled, "A Singles' Lib Manifesto."

Of course, I immediately searched for the book. Holding it in my hands, I was both delighted at what I found and sorry that I had not known about it when I wrote Singled Out. Edwards did not write a social-science based book in the way that I did (though with her degrees from Stanford and UCLA, she could have); still, in spirit, I now consider her my intellectual godmother.

Consider just a few highlights from *The Challenge of Being Single*:

In the first chapter, she begins by gently mocking the question, "How come you're not married?" It is, she quips, the equivalent of being challenged to "prove that you're not a freak."

Among the errors and **myths** she describes are:

- Finding the one-and-only will solve all of your problems.

- All single women want to get married.
- All single men are afraid of responsibility.
- All unmarrieds are terribly lonely.
- Single life is hazardous because there will be no one around to help you if you are hurt or sick.

What, according to Edwards (and her co-author, Eleanor Hoover), is the end result of all of these stereotypes and myths? Discrimination. Again getting there before I did, she spells out the unfair costs to being single in taxes, the workplace, insurance, and housing. She does not see singles simply as victims, though, and ends with a chapter on the greatest advantage of being single and with her manifesto.

SINGLES MANIFESTO

Edwards' book includes the complete Singles Manifesto, consisting of a Preamble, three Articles (attitudes toward self, others, and society), and 17 statements. Here, for your reading pleasure, are some excerpts from this 1974 proclamation.

PREAMBLE of Marie Edwards' SINGLES MANIFESTO:

Whereas the written and spoken word about singles has been and continues to be one of gloom and doom, untruths and misinformation, we the singles of the United States - divorced, separated, and never-married - in order to bury the myths, establish the truths, uplift our spirits, promote our freedom, become cognizant of our great fortune as singles, do ordain and establish this manifesto for the singles of the United States of America.

SAMPLE STATEMENTS from Marie Edwards' 1974 SINGLES MANIFESTO:

• I will, in my deepest feelings, know that it's okay to be single and, becoming braver, know that it's even more than okay - it can be a great and untapped opportunity for continuous personal growth.

• I will stop searching for the "one-and-only," knowing that as I become more free to be myself, I will be freer to care about others, so that relationships will come to me as a natural consequence and I will feel free to accept or reject them.

• Instead of searching for the "one-and-only," I will realize the tremendous importance of friendships.

• I will no longer suffer in silence the injustices to me as a single, but will do everything I can to eradicate them.

• I will, by choosing to live a free single life, be helping to raise the status of singlehood. In doing this, I will be strengthening rather than weakening marriage, for when we truly have the option not to marry, marriage will be seen as a free choice rather than one demanded by a pairing society.

When Will Singles Awareness "Stick"?

Discovering Marie Edwards, the singles pioneer from decades past, reminded me of the experience I had while gathering materials for the first course I taught on singles in society. I found a number of academic articles, published years or even decades earlier, that all started or ended with the lament that there is just too little scholarly attention paid to people who are single. As I continued to prepare my course, I realized that the state of the scholarship had not changed much - there was still far too little serious research and thinking about the place of singles in society.

There are similar trends in the popular press. Edwards' Singles Manifesto is again a relevant example; it was published in the *Los Angeles Times* in 1974, but it did not stick.

There are no long-enduring singles advocacy groups, comparable, say, to AARP. The American Association for Single People (AASP) did some important work for a while, then got tripped up by financial challenges, and is now an informational resource. Its advocacy work is now pursued by the Alternatives to Marriage Project (AtMP).

The question now is, Will any of this stick? Will scholarship on singles gain momentum? Will the number of singles-relevant courses increase and earn a permanent place in the college curriculum? Will advocacy groups strengthen and multiply? Will awareness of singlism and matrimania take permanent hold in our society?

Source URL: http://www.psychologytoday.com/node/3628

Links:
[1] http://www.amazon.com/Singled-Out-Singles-Stereotyped-Stigmatized/dp/0312340826/ref=ed_oe_p/102-4637341-6604139 [2] http://www.belladepaulo.com/otherdepaulo.htm [3] http://www.belladepaulo.com/contact.htm [4] http://blogs.psychologytoday.com/blog/living-single/200812/singlism-should-we-just-shrug-it-off [5] http://www.latimes.com/news/obituaries/la-me-marie-edwards25-2009feb25,0,2765260.story [6] http://www.amazon.com/Challenge-Being-Single-Edwards-Hoover/dp/B000JF83I2/ref=sr_1_1?ie=UTF8&s=books&qid=1235945561&sr=1-1 [7] http://www.aarp.org/ [8] http://www.unmarriedamerica.org/ [9] http://www.unmarried.org/

66.

Meet a Brilliant, Fearless, and Funny Satirist of the Marriage Mystique

Mar 24 2009

Conversations with Jaclyn Geller: **PART 1** (of 3)

By the time I was ready to sit down and write Singled Out, the bookshelves in nearly every room of my home were stuffed with the materials I had collected. Many of those books informed and inspired me, but few were as brilliant, funny, fearless, and as historically and culturally rich as Jaclyn Geller's Here Comes the Bride: Women, Weddings, and the Marriage Mystique.

Jaclyn is an English Professor. Here Comes the Bride was published in 2001. She is also an active member of the wonderful advocacy group, The Alternatives to Marriage Project. She has contributed some thoughtful and provocative essays to the group's newsletter. I thought that "Living Single" readers would really appreciate her perspective, so I was delighted when she agreed to do this Q & A.

In preparing my questions for Jaclyn, I went back over *Here Comes the Bride*, and realized anew just how influential her ideas have been to my own thinking. Our books are different: Mine is based in social science research, and Jaclyn's is rooted in history, literature, and an analysis of the contemporary wedding industry. We sometimes make different arguments, but I owe her an important intellectual debt.

You can get a sense of some of her critiques of marriage from this quote from her book. Marriage, she says (on p. 70), "perpetuates negative hierarchical divisions such as the celebration of wives and the accompanying denigration of spinsters, the artificial distinction between good (sexually monogamous) and bad (sexually experimental) girls, the exaltation of conjugal love over platonic friendship, and the privileging of institutionalized togetherness over solitude."

That quote provides a nice lead-in to my first question.

Bella: I think I first learned that "spinster" once had a positive meaning from reading Here Comes the Bride. Want to tell us about that? Is that the word you think we should use to refer to single women?

Jaclyn: Bella, I respect your work tremendously, and I know you use the word "single," as many people do. I myself have trouble with that term, and I don't use it anymore. I don't like the "single"/ "married" binary. It implies that any unmarried person is a fragmentary half-self awaiting completion in a spouse. It suggests that all other partnerships - including the close friendships that sustain so many people - especially women - do not factor into one's self-definition. A woman who shares her life with a few long-term close partners, one of whom might be a lover, but who has no marriage license, is considered "single." If she marries a man she's known for two weeks in a Las Vegas chapel she's suddenly no longer "single; " she's married - de facto, socially complete. It's a strange way of rating people. It's very counterintuitive.

I think there are many terms that would better serve us. In her excellent book, Beyond (Straight and Gay) Marriage, Nancy D. Polikoff suggests a few different phrases: "valuing all families;" "intra-dependent." In my book I suggest reviving the term "spinster," which in England, before the onset of the modern marriage mystique, just meant a financially independent woman who supported herself by spinning - by manufacturing textiles. The term is so negative, at this point, that it's probably one few women will want to embrace, so "spinster by choice," might be better. Another term I suggest, in my most recent column for the *Alternatives to Marriage Project*, is "unconventionally partnered." That's what I write on medical forms when I visit the dentist or doctor. Despite the marriage mania that's all around us, I think we're in an interesting period of transition when many people are rejecting or at least questioning matrimony. People will experiment with new words and find the language that feels consonant with the ways they're setting up their lives.

Bella: Americans generally are not very well informed when it comes to social history (and I include myself in that indictment). My guess is that this is one of the impediments to enlightened thinking about the potential fullness of a life that does not include marriage. Our contemporaries do not recognize that our current practice of intensive coupling (the "you are my everything" approach to partnering) is not the way it has always been. I think you have a great command of social history. Want to provide an example of a different way of thinking about the relationships that should count as important?

Jaclyn: Well, I do think Americans tend to be practical and rugged and "now" oriented, and there's something great about that pragmatism. It makes us a very tough, spirited people. But it also makes us an anti-intellectual culture. The publishing industry reflects this attitude: many bestsellers are books that instruct on how to achieve results through concrete steps: seven steps to financial solvency, ten steps to spiritual enlightenment – that kind of thing. This very simplistic, ahistorical, results-oriented approach is the opposite of the one I take in my work, as an eighteenth-century scholar and a trade writer.

It's important to realize that matrimony is a fluid, ever-changing institution. It's not "natural" or "timeless," in the sense that it has an origin. If we've been around as modern human beings for, let's say 150,000 years, then marriage is actually a pretty recent phenomenon, dating from about 4,000 B.C.E. It emerges in the ancient Near East, as part of a state-sanctioned system of male dominance. The Hammurabic Code of 1750 B.C.E. and the Middle Assyrian Law Codes of the fifteenth through the eleventh centuries B.C.E. institutionalize unions arranged by men, with male controls on female sexuality and reproductivity. Husbands control all financial assets, including dowries brought into the marriage. These assets are transferred to male offspring, and producing sons is one of the main foci of the system. Men have multiple wives and concubines, but female adultery often exacts draconian punishment, as does a woman's attempt to control her own reproductive system.

Middle Assyrian Law allows a man to expose his infant child to die while punishing a pregnant woman who attempts to abort with death by impalement. So, this is the glorious origin of the institution.

Now, one thing ancient, medieval, and Renaissance marriage was not is romantic. The belief that eroticism can by institutionalized is a modern one. Historians argue fiercely about when the transition from pragmatic to "affective" -- personal -- marriage, took place in Europe. It's been placed anywhere from the fourteenth to the eighteenth century. And I'm not equipped to make that determination. But I do think it's important to access the experiences of our ancestors - to know what marriage was for millennia before perpetuating the institution. It would be interesting for many women, I think, to know that in the seventeenth century, in England, homosocial love between female friends generated some of the most beautiful lyrical poetry ever written. A woman named Katherine Philips founded a society of female friendship for like-minded women writers. They wrote extraordinary, passionate, nonsexual verse to each other. And they would have found it extremely odd - preposterous even - that one might express those sentiments to one's spouse. Matrimony was, for the most part, not the framework for those kind of emotions. Friendship was.

Source URL: http://www.psychologytoday.com/node/4011

Links:
[1] http://www.amazon.com/Here-Comes-Bride-Weddings-Marriage/dp/1568581939/ref=sr_1_1?ie=UTF8&s=books&qid=1232529547&sr=1-1 [2] http://blogs.psychologytoday.com/blog/living-single/200806/but-what-about-single-men [3] http://blogs.psychologytoday.com/blog/living-single/200902/single-men-have-good-hearts [4] http://blogs.psychologytoday.com/blog/living-single/200812/those-pitied-mocked-envied-years-between-the-late-teens-and-late-twenties- [5] http://www.amazon.com/Singled-Out-Singles-Stereotyped-Stigmatized/dp/0312340826/ref=ed_oe_p/102-4637341-6604139 [6] http://www.unmarried.org/ [7] http://www.amazon.com/Beyond-Straight-Gay-Marriage-Families/dp/0807044326/ref=sr_1_1?ie=UTF8&s=books&qid=1201544152&sr=1-1 [8] http://www.beyondstraightandgaymarriage.com/author.php [9] http://www.unmarried.org/newsletter-archives.html

---

67.

Should Newlyweds Get All the Loot, and Other Impolite Considerations

Mar 25 2009

Where else can you read about newlyweds getting all the loot and how to combat singlism, with a step in between to consider Plato and Cicero? Welcome to Part 2 of my interview of Jaclyn Geller, author of <u>Here Comes the Bride: Women, Weddings, and the Marriage Mystique</u>.

Bella: In your book, you give voice to a complaint I hear often from other single people - they are expected to subsidize all of the weddings and showers of their married friends and relatives, but the important milestones in their own lives are not similarly recognized. But what's a person to do? It seems really hard to say to another person who invites you to their wedding, "Hey, you and your partner already have two sets of linens and two salaries; why should I have to subsidize still another with my one salary?"

Jaclyn: I suggest that when every person turns 25 he or she gets a party. The celebrant can register for house wares, furniture, linen. He or she might even have a ceremony that involves committing to important people, one of whom might be a lover. But these material rewards would not be contingent upon finding "the one." There wouldn't be this mad husband-hunting mentality. It's moving that the older generation wants to help the next generation get a start in life, but reserving this support for those in amorous couples is outrageous.

As a college professor I teach 18-year old girls, Bella, and they're very aware of this system of reward and punishment. Apart from the recent economic crisis, the cost of living is high these days. Not all but many of my female students, as they near graduation, seem to get distracted from their studies as they pursue that elusive engagement ring. The anthropologists Dorothy Holland and Margaret Eisenhart tracked a group of women students at a southern college over a period of eight years. All entered school expecting to pursue careers: half said they wanted to work in the sciences. But they became increasingly invested in the matrimonial hunt: reading "how to get a man" literature and neglecting their studies. After graduation over half ended up in low paying jobs in what sociologists call "the pink ghetto" - work that's meant to supplement a husband's paychecks.

In terms of etiquette, how do we diminish the marriage mystique without insulting our friends who are tying the knot? I have two suggestions. Write a check in honor of your friends' nuptials to the Alternatives to Marriage Project, and pen a warm note expressing your happiness for your them and your determination to support diverse family structures and unconventionally partnered people's rights. Or, if you can afford it, buy a wedding gift and provide a check for matching funds to the *Alternatives to Marriage Project*. There are many wonderful causes, but AtMP is the only organization I know of that exists to fight marital status discrimination. It's a fledgling organization that really needs support.

Bella: Now I want to take advantage of your expertise in literature. I'm always looking for authors who are not matrimaniacs and do not use marriage themes as mindless shortcuts. Who can write great stories based on friendships or solitude or any of the other many experiences that make life meaningful?

Jaclyn: Where do I start? This is going to be very difficult because there's so much. There's a lot of great writing in antiquity. I would urge everyone to read Plato's The Symposium. It's a short dialogue on the meaning of love - probably the greatest piece of western literature on the subject. It does not mention marriage. I would encourage everyone to read Cicero's short essay on friendship; it's in his collection, On the Good Life. And the first century poet, Horace, has beautiful accounts of friendship in his Satires. His fifth satire, an account of a road trip he took through rural Italy with his buddies, is my favorite, and it contains the line, "For me there's nothing to compare with the joy of friendship."

Bella: Are there any other ways we can nudge society into valuing the important relationships, such as friendships, and important experiences, such as solitude, that so often go unrecognized or worse?

Jaclyn: It's hard. Marriage is a sacred cow. Married people tend to want to preserve their privileges; unmarried people often want to access those privileges by joining the conjugal club. And while we've witnessed great diversification in relationships and family structures, there's also been a terrible backlash. The past twenty years has seen the birth of a pro-marriage movement, with an agenda of preserving special rights for wedded couples. In terms of health insurance, tax breaks, immigration privileges - all sorts of benefits - they want matrimony to be the dividing line between who is "in" and who is "out," because they think wedded couples are superior. Political organizations like the Eagle Foundation, Protect the Family, and the Arlington Group assert this doctrine without apology. Their members are obsessively, hysterically pro-marriage. They blame a variety of social ills on divorce and on the large numbers of Americans now enjoying an unmarried existence. They're prone to a kind of magical thinking, laying the blame for everything from crime to disease on the doorstep of the unmarried, rather than examining deeper, more complex underlying causes. They demand even more marriage incentives and legal obstacles to divorce.

Perhaps the best thing we can do is keep the conversation alive - not let the subject of marriage status discrimination get buried among other, seemingly more urgent issues. I had an interesting recent experience. My friend Lisa Ehrlich is a certified public accountant. She's one of the really significant people in my life, and some time ago we co-authored an essay for the *Alternatives to Marriage Project Update* called "Reflections on Politics, Death, and Taxes." For those who might want to take a peek at it, it's posted in the newsletter archives of the Alternatives to Marriage Project website. Lisa's financial expertise enabled her to detail the American tax code's biases against unmarried people. For instance, a married couple doesn't have to pay capital gains tax on the first $500,000 increase in value on a house that's being sold. An unmarried person - living alone, with friends, in an unlicensed partnership that might not be monogamous - can exclude only $250,000 of the gain. That's an incredible margin.

So, we published the piece. And I got an appreciative email from my oldest friend's mom, a married social worker who lives in New York. She wrote that the essay really opened her eyes. She had not realized the kind of legal and financial privileges she was enjoying as a wife. Now, this is one of the brightest, most articulate women I know. She has worked in the area of public policy and reads the newspaper compulsively. She's been signing joint tax returns for 45 years. But she didn't have a full picture of the system she was perpetuating. I think it's a telling little anecdote; marriage-status discrimination is somewhat invisible. Debates about racial issues, foreign policy, or a hot subject like the environment, are prominent in the public domain. But marital-status discrimination goes largely unchecked. It's not on most people's radar screens. So those of us who have thought the issues through need to keep them alive: in print, in conversation. This doesn't make us gurus or role models of any sort - just people with a strong historical and ethical consciousness.

Source URL: http://www.psychologytoday.com/node/4031

Links:
[1] http://www.amazon.com/Here-Comes-Bride-Weddings-Marriage/dp/1568581939/ref=sr_1_1?ie=UTF8&s=books&qid=1232529547&sr=1-1 [2] http://blogs.psychologytoday.com/blog/living-single/200903/meet-brilliant-fearless-and-funny-satirist-the-marriage-mystique [3] http://www.amazon.com/Educated-Romance-Achievement-College-Culture/dp/0226349446/ref=sr_1_1?ie=UTF8&s=books&qid=1238038809&sr=1-1 [4] http://www.unmarried.org/ [5] http://www.amazon.com/Singled-Out-Singles-Stereotyped-Stigmatized/dp/0312340826/ref=ed_oe_p/102-4637341-6604139 [6] http://www.amazon.com/Symposium-Penguin-Classics-Plato/dp/0140449272/ref=sr_1_2?ie=UTF8&s=books&qid=1238039000&sr=1-2 [7] http://www.amazon.com/Good-Life-Penguin-Classics/dp/0140442448/ref=sr_1_1?ie=UTF8&s=books&qid=1238039071&sr=1-1 [8] http://www.amazon.com/Satires-Horace/dp/1931337012/ref=sr_1_7?ie=UTF8&s=books&qid=1238039152&sr=1-7 [9] http://www.unmarried.org/newsletter-archives.html [10] http://www3.interscience.wiley.com/journal/118584107/abstract?CRETRY=1&SRETRY=0

68.

Here's What Happens When You Publish an Unconventional Book about Single Life

Mar 30 2009

Conversations with Jaclyn Geller: PART 3 (of 3)

There is an episode of Sex and the City that readers of Singled Out love to tell me about. I've never seen it, but maybe it will sound familiar to you. Carrie goes to a baby shower, gift in hand, and complies with the house rules dictating that she take off her pricey Manolos before entering. The shoes get stolen, the hostess refuses to pay for them, and the cumulative inequities of all of the registry gifts that Carrie has given to this woman (with none in return) start to rankle. So Carrie registers for one thing - her pair of shoes - and sends the woman an invitation to her wedding to herself.

This is a long way of saying that considering how often that episode has been mentioned to me, I guess I should have anticipated the response my last post received. That was Part 2 of my interview with Jaclyn Geller, in which I asked her if newlyweds should get all the loot. Right away, there were hundreds of page views and a lively discussion in the Comments section is continuing still. Now on to the last and final part of our conversation.

Bella: One thing I did in preparing the questions I wanted to ask you during this interview was to look at the reader reviews of your book that were posted on Amazon.com. Some offered high praise, of course. The ones that I found more interesting were the negative ones. (Perverse of me, I know.) The offended reviewers seemed to dredge up every negative stereotype of unmarried women, describing you as bitter, angry, and all the rest. I think that means that your arguments were hitting a nerve. You don't stay in your place. You don't write in a reticent, deferential way, and you don't make conventional arguments. That, I suspect, drives some people over the edge, in a way that perhaps says more about them and our society than it does about you. As you look back at what was said about Here Comes the Bride over the years (not just the amazon.com reviews), what's your take on how other people reacted to your work?

Jaclyn: Bella, I tend to avoid reviews and summaries and responses posted anonymously on the Internet. That's where you find the extremes, both negative and positive. And it's such totally uncontrolled, inaccurate information that there's really no point in looking at it.

Samuel Johnson said that, in conversation with "the wits," he never felt he had hit his mark unless it rebounded back on him, and I guess that's true to some extent. The book did hit a nerve. There have been subsequent monographs that take on marriage; they haven't elicited the same hostility. I think mine may have cleared a bit of a path for other authors on this topic, and I'm grateful to have had the opportunity to do that. People who argue for change are often caricatured as being bitter and/or personally disturbed. We take the right of women to vote for granted, but early in the century suffragists were mocked and pathologized. They were derided as "mannish" and unhappy and abnormal. So I think it just comes with the territory. At the end of the day, lack of popularity is a small price to pay for having made even the smallest difference.

When the book was first published I did a lot of interviews and I had a lot of "off the record" conversations. I was sometimes surprised at the anger that greeted my suggestion that anyone who marries at least reads a history of the institution before signing those papers. That did not seem like a controversial suggestion; after all, as Santayana said, he who forgets the past is doomed to repeat it. If you want to marry, do so, but at least proceed in an informed manner. And why not take some time to learn about the legalities of matrimony in your state? But these were unpopular ideas. I guess the nature of a mystique is that it's supposed to remain unexamined --- shrouded in a romantic haze.

In retrospect, I also think that some of the more rational criticisms are accurate. The book has its problems. It's a first effort, after all, and some parts are rough, under-theorized. I want the next one to be more refined!

But the single biggest surprise about my book's reception was that people read it at all. I wrote it as a graduate student - at that time an unknown author. I published it with a distinguished small press that had a limited marketing department. It's an extended essay -- a piece of fairly dense prose. It expresses an unpopular point of view. But people read it. And they wrote to me: some were angry, some were grateful, some were ambivalent. But the letters and emails kept coming. They still do. Barnes and Noble even listed it as a selected nonfiction title, apparently, because an unmarried buyer really liked the chapter on wedding registries, in which I describe visiting the registry at Bloomingdale's department store as a would-be bride.

The book also brought some remarkable individuals into my life: men and women with whom I have enjoyed deep, enlivening conversations, who have pushed me to think about the subject in new ways. Writing can be a solitary business; I like doing it with collaborators. Right now I'm working, with a teacher and friend, on a volume about eighteenth-century satire. It's for specialists in our field. But I'm also thinking about the next trade project. I have written short collaborative pieces that flesh out some of the subjects touched on in Here Comes the Bride, and I'm looking forward to future projects that blend others' points of view with my own. I think even minimally worthwhile prose generates good discussion, which generates even better prose.

As far as anonymous respondents go, the most gratifying letter from a reader came from a Mormon woman who had grown up in Utah in a town she characterized as a "marriage factory." She described how women turning 20 would buy themselves engagement rings and invent nonexistent fiancés because they were so ashamed to be seen publicly without the prospect of a husband. She told me that as a result of her own thinking, and her reading, which included Here Comes the Bride, she was not going to marry her boyfriend, despite the fact that she adored him. They would live together and forge their own definition of love. That kind of response makes up for all the mudslinging.

Bella: Thanks again for doing this Q & A. And thanks again for all your great work.

Jaclyn: It was my pleasure, Bella. And thank you for your work.

Source URL: http://www.psychologytoday.com/node/4086

Links:
[1] http://www.hbo.com/city/episode/season6/episode83.shtml [2] http://www.amazon.com/Singled-Out-Singles-Stereotyped-Stigmatized/dp/0312340826/ref=ed_oe_p/102-4637341-6604139 [3] http://blogs.psychologytoday.com/blog/living-single/200903/should-newlyweds-get-all-the-loot-and-other-impolite-considerations [4] http://blogs.psychologytoday.com/blog/living-single/200903/meet-brilliant-fearless-and-funny-satirist-the-marriage-mystique [5] http://www.amazon.com/Here-Comes-Bride-Weddings-Marriage/dp/1568581939/ref=sr_1_1?ie=UTF8&s=books&qid=1232529547&sr=1-

1 [6] http://www.samueljohnson.com/arroganc.html [7]
http://answers.google.com/answers/threadview?id=495329

69.

The New York Times
nytimes.com

June 18, 2004

Sex and the Single Voter

By BELLA M. DEPAULO

Want to attract single voters? Drop the underpants.

This should be my moment. I'm a single woman, and at last, the political world has discovered me. People in my demographic, it has been reported, stayed away from the 2000 presidential election in droves, and wow, could we have made a difference if we had shown up. The single women who did make it to the polls supported Al Gore overwhelmingly -- about two-thirds voted for him, while a little less than one-third voted for George W. Bush, according to surveys.

In contrast, married women split their votes about evenly for Mr. Bush and Mr. Gore. But pollsters indicate that 68 percent of them showed up to vote, compared to just 52 percent of the women who were divorced, widowed, or had always been single.

In theory, I like where this is going. I have strong opinions about human health and well-being and about the place of America in the world, and I'm ready to voice them.

To appeal to me, though, the Democratic Party is offering me underwear. The panties sport slogans like "Kiss Bush Goodbye." I can pick them up at nightclubs or PantyWare parties.

Not to be outdone, CNN did a cute segment on "lipstick liberals." A reporter took to the streets to try out her guess about why single women do not vote more often. "Is it scary to think about politics?" she asked a young, successful, single woman.

No, it wasn't.

A pollster, Kellyanne Conway, offered her own explanation: "Women who have what we call the four magic M's -- marriage, munchkins, mortgages and mutual

174

funds -- are much more likely to vote than their unmarried, non-stake-holding, non-ownership counterparts." Ms. Conway also had a tip for single women to help them get to the polls: "Pretend it's a hair appointment we would not miss."

I get the message. The political players are not out to engage me in a serious discussion of the issues. As a single woman, I'm too preoccupied with lipstick, hair and underwear. They need to find a way to get me to the polls only this one time. Then, by the next presidential election, perhaps I'll be married and have a mortgage.

I have a different view about 2000. I don't think singles were cowering in fear of politics, or too dazzled by the whirl of their social lives, to get to the polls. I think they were singled out of a system that ignored them. In one of the debates in the 2000 election, a woman from the audience tried to focus the candidates on her demographic. "How will your tax proposals affect me as a middle-class, 24-year-old single person with no dependents?" she asked. Neither candidate acknowledged that she was one of millions of single voters. Neither promised to fight for the votes of single people. Mr. Bush had the facts on his side; the questioner would keep more of her money under his plan rather than under Mr. Gore's. But Mr. Bush did not mention that. He did, though, describe the great prescription drug plan she would get under Medicare.

Singles are getting another message this year. No matter how many thousands of lives you may have saved with your lifelong, relentless advocacy for safer cars and workplaces, and purer food and water; no matter how doggedly you have pursued the causes of government and corporate accountability, and inspired countless others to do the same, you can still be dismissed as immature and irresponsible if you are not married.

Chris Matthews, host of the MSNBC program "Hardball," captured that sentiment when he said this to Ralph Nader about the current president: "He's raised two daughters; he's had a happy marriage. You've never been married. Isn't he more mature in his lifestyle than you are?" The unmarried Mr. Nader, Mr. Matthews said, lives "a life that's about as responsible as what's on the movies tonight."

So what's a candidate to do? Here are four suggestions.

1. Hit the books. Learn about the real place of singles in contemporary American society. Singles account for more than 40 percent of the electorate and work force. Households consisting of two parents and their children are slightly outnumbered by households comprised of a single person living alone. And most singles do not live alone. About nine million households are single-parent homes. Singles are also homeowners. Last year, they accounted for 46.7 percent of house sales. Singles are not predominantly youthful; only a third are aged 18 to 29. Singlehood is no longer a way station on the road to marriage. Women on average now spend more years of their adult lives single than married, and men are not far behind.

2. Learn the actual voting patterns. Despite the hype, it was not single women who had the lowest rate of voting in 2000, but single men. In their candidate preferences,

the men stood out in their support of Ralph Nader (7 percent, compared to 4 percent for single women, and 2 percent for married men and women).

3. Master the issues of concern to singles. You will find, for example, that singles would like to make a decent living, have affordable health care and enjoy retirement. Their values are not antifamily -- they are human values. The language of singles is the language of inclusiveness. Here is an example: "If you are willing to work hard and play by the rules, you are part of our family, and we're proud to be with you." It is from Bill Clinton's 1996 speech accepting the Democratic nomination for president.

4. Oh, and about those panties? Kiss them goodbye.

70.

Talk to me, I'm Single

October 27, 2006

Want to Win Elections? Talk to Me - I'm Single

I'm single. Always have been. I'm also an educated and informed participant in the political process. Even when all of the candidate choices are dismal, I still show up at the polls and cast my ballot for the least disappointing person. But millions of other single people do not seem to share my enthusiasm.

To many progressives, it is exasperating, frustrating, and bewildering that so many single people are with them on the issues but just don't vote. I think there are lots of reasons for this, and I've written about some of them during the 2004 campaign and in my new book, Singled Out: How Singles are Stereotyped, Stigmatized, and Ignored, and Still Live Happily Ever After. Here, I want to take you through a brief tour of some of this season's political outreach, narrated from the point of view of someone who is single. I hope you will start to see how even those candidates and groups whose positions I (mostly) favor and respect do not seem to have much respect or concern for me.

Here's what I hope is appealing about the suggestions I will make today: The interested candidates need to invest no extra time or money to implement them. All they need to do is rewrite their campaign materials so as to include all of their constituents, not just the married ones. (Oh, and when they claim to value human values and not just "family values," they should mean it.)

Exhibit #1. In a recent e-mail, Patty Wetterling let me know that Minnesota firefighters, police, and nurses stood at her side at the state Capitol. She promised to continue to "fight to keep children and families safe." Did she really mean to imply that she was concerned with the safety of all of her constituents, as long as they were not single people without children? Why not pledge to work for the safety of every single person in her district? (Double meaning intended.)

Exhibit #2 (a collection that just keeps growing). Earlier in the year, Bob Menendez posted a blog on Give 'Em Hell Harry in which he proclaimed that he was "Standing Up for Working Families." At the website of the Democratic Party, I learn that the "Bush Economy Fails Working Families." Over at the home page of the Massachusetts AFL-CIO, I find the "2006 Fight for Working Families Headquarters." Why don't we all declare our support for workers instead of "working families"? The trite byte isn't even sensible; employers don't hire working families, they hire workers.

Exhibit #3. Consider, too, the deeply shameful television ad designed to smear Harold Ford. Watching the scantily clad white woman wiggle and wink as she asked the black candidate to come hither was excruciating. But something else alienated me, too - the implication elsewhere in the ad that the only candidates worth supporting are those who are devoted to the elimination of the so-called "marriage penalty." The mantra-like pledges to relieve married people of their burdens, without any comparable concern for single people, would be off-putting even if the "penalty" really did fall disproportionately on married people. It doesn't.

Exhibit #4. Here's another e-mail I got. It seems to be from the Phil Angelides campaign, but the sender is not Phil but Julie. It begins, "Dear Bella, I have been married to Phil Angelides for 24 years." So the message seems to be, "Vote for Phil Angelides; his wife thinks he's great." Or maybe it is even simpler: "Vote for Phil Angelides; he's married."

I understand the temptation to reach for the images of the sturdy "working families" or the warm and fuzzy loving wives. Married people are the low-hanging fruit. They vote more often, and that tastes good now. But is this a wise long-term plan for a party that wants to sustain itself for decades to come?

Maybe candidates and parties figure that since most people eventually do marry, their appeals to marriage and traditional family will reach single people once they have become unsingle. Or maybe they believe that most single people want nothing more than to be married, and so singles will identify with the matrimaniacal messages on the basis of their longing.

Wrong.

The Pew Internet & American Life Project surveyed thousands of American adults late last year (2005). They found that the biggest group of single people, 55 percent, said that they were not in a committed relationship and that they were not looking for a partner. And while it is true that most Americans do try marriage at some point in their lives, there is another statistic that I find even more compelling. On the average, Americans now spend more of their adult years unmarried than married. It is now marriage that is the transitional stage - connecting one singlehood to the next - and it is transitional only for those people who do marry.

177

The rising tide of single people has been building for decades, and it has not yet crested. The current mid-term campaign will be over in days, but the importance of people who are single to politics and to our nation will long endure.

Source URL: http://www.huffingtonpost.com/bella-depaulo/talk-to-me-im-single_b_32663.html

---

71.

Which Religions Are Welcoming to Singles? Part I: Introduction

January 18, 2009

I'm mad at religion. I don't mean that just personally, though that applies, too. I'm mad on behalf of the single people who e-mail me with their stories of feeling excluded or devalued in their places of worship.

Not everyone who writes to me about this expresses anger. Some simply ask how to find a church or other place of worship that is accepting of single people. Others wonder how singles are regarded in the teachings of different religions.

I don't know the answers, so a few months ago, I set out to find people from various religions who might be willing to address such questions for readers of this blog. That has been a challenge, as some of the people I've approached have declined or simply never responded.

Happily, though, I now have the first set of responses to my questions. They have been provided by Professor Vanessa Ochs, Associate Professor of Religious Studies at the University of Virginia. Her area of expertise is Judaism. Her discussion will be the topic of my next post.

For subsequent posts in this series on religion, I hope to find experts who are willing to address the issues singles have raised from the perspectives of other religions. (One more person has tentatively agreed, and I have e-mails out to several others. Feel free to send me your suggestions or post them in the Comments section.) In the meantime, you may want to look at Religion Link. There are some promising resources in the section, "As singles increase, ministries adapt and mature."

My Own Religious Backstory

I was raised Catholic in the tiny town of Dunmore, Pennsylvania (outside of Scranton), where there were basically three kinds of people - Italian, Irish, and

Polish - and all of them were Catholic. In my grade school classes of about 25 kids each, there was typically one boy who was Protestant, and we all felt sorry for him.

When I took my first college anthropology class, I was stunned to discover that the world was not overwhelmingly Catholic. (Seriously, I didn't know that.) I think one of the readings referred to Catholic mass as a "primitive ritual." That sure was news, too.

I was a committed Catholic in my childhood. Every May, I created my own <u>May Altar</u> in my bedroom, complete with flowers, candles and a statue of the Blessed Virgin Mary (affectionately called The BVM). I even persuaded an aunt I adored, a lapsed Catholic, to go back to Mass.

By around the time of junior high, I confided to a nun that I did not believe in God or Catholicism or any of the rest of it (I felt guilty about it at the time), and asked if she could recommend anything to read that might persuade me. She gave me a few things. I don't remember any of them, but none did the trick. The only Catholic reading I can recall from those youthful days was a pamphlet filled with questions and answers such as this one (paraphrased): *Question:* Why does God put hair on your most personal part? *Answer:* To protect it from even your own eyes.

The junior high version of my religious skepticism was based on a suspicion that most of the people attending St. Anthony's did not really believe any of it, either - they were just there to see friends and family and fellow parishioners, and to be seen. They were there to share stories over the spaghetti suppers in the church basement; for the cookies and coffee in the same church basement after midnight Mass on Christmas Eve; and for the grilled-on-the-spot sausage and pepper sandwiches, the "pasta e fagioli" (pasta with beans), and "pizza fritte" (fried dough) sold at the Church picnics that went on for days each summer.

I never did become religious again. For decades, I've been a true atheist. What's different now, though, is that I think I have a better understanding of what religion has to offer to those who do believe. I've seen the comfort it brings in the worst of times, and the structure and sense of meaning and of community that it can bring at almost any time. I think it was especially important to my grandparents and parents, first or second generation immigrants, who thought therapy was shameful. Their priests were their therapists.

I've reappraised some of my skepticism, too. Suppose some - or even many - of the Catholics of my childhood were there for the spaghetti suppers and the midnight Mass cookies or the church picnics or the camaraderie? Why not consider that a good thing?

The irony of the feelings of marginalization many singles experience in their places of worship is that, so far as I can tell, it doesn't have to be that way. When I think back to those church picnics, I'm struck by just how singles-friendly they really were. People were more likely to wander around in groups of friends than in pairs of romantic partners. Even married couples were not enmeshed; he might be grilling sausages at one booth, she serving up the pizza fritte at another.

But like I said, I'm mad at religion. The way religion has been used in politics to demean and divide people - well, I think that should be a sin. In places of worship, too many singles end up feeling shut out or put down. Is that inherent in the teachings of the religion, or is it possible, within at least some religious traditions, to be true to the theology and also welcoming to singles? Those are some of the kinds of questions that I hope will be answered in this series. Maybe I will even find someone to take on the question of the place in single people's lives of the kind of spirituality that is not defined by organized religion.

Source URL: http://www.psychologytoday.com/node/3029

Links:
[1] http://artsandsciences.virginia.edu/religiousstudies/people/vlo4n.html [2] http://www.religionlink.org [3] http://www.religionlink.org/tip_080114.php [4] http://www.city-data.com/city/Dunmore-Pennsylvania.html [5] http://campus.udayton.edu/mary/questions/yq2/yq369.html [6] http://www.huffingtonpost.com/bella-depaulo/im-a-values-voter-too_b_71685.html

72.

Which Religions Are Welcoming to Singles? Part II: Judaism

Jan 19 2009

Professor Vanessa Ochs on the Place of Singles in Judaism

"Traditional Judaism is not geared for the set of unattached adults we now call 'singles.' The ideal and only thinkable state for the traditional Jew is to be married, and not just for the sake of increasing and multiplying -- though that is considered a mitzvah, a sacred obligation that needs to be fulfilled. (Technically, it is incumbent only upon men--the assumption is that women want children so badly that they don't need to be commanded to have them). Marriage is considered desirable because it alleviates loneliness.

"So what if you are a 'single' and you attend synagogue--are you apt to feel comfortable? Yes and no: If you are new in town, and the community is small and cohesive enough to notice you, they may take you on as a 'project' and fix you up with eligible members of their community who are 'looking.' You might appreciate their matchmaking efforts or find them intrusive. If it's a larger community, chances are you will feel somewhat marginalized--synagogue life seems to privilege families. The exception to the rule would be big cities, such as NY, where particular synagogues (Bnai Jeshurun in NYC is one) are known to be especially welcoming to singles--if I recall, they have an early service for families on Sabbath eves, and a later one that gathers hundreds of folks, and many many singles.

"I should add that the modern Orthodox community finds itself in an interesting predicament, as far as singles are concerned. On one hand, they want their singles to feel welcome in the community. On the other hand, they don't want the singles to feel SO at home (say, by being regularly invited to meals with families, or by having tight networks of other religious single friends with whom to celebrate holy days) that they fail to feel the communal pressure to 'get going' and get married."

More About Vanessa Ochs
Vanessa Ochs is an anthropologist and the author of several books on Judaism. They include (among others) Inventing Jewish Ritual and Words on Fire: One Woman's Journey into the Sacred. I thank her for sharing her insights with the "Living Single" community.

Source URL: http://www.psychologytoday.com/node/3043

Links:
[1] http://www.psychologytoday.com/blog/living-single/200901/which-religions-are-welcoming-singles-part-i-introduction [2]
http://artsandsciences.virginia.edu/religiousstudies/people/vlo4n.html [3] http://www.bj.org/
[4] http://www.amazon.com/Inventing-Jewish-Ritual-American-Traditions/dp/0827608349/sr=1-2/qid=1168970721/ref=pd_bbs_sr_2/104-3455528-4391145?ie=UTF8&s=books [5] http://www.amazon.com/Words-Fire-Womans-Journey-Sacred/dp/0813367182/sr=1-1/qid=1163136698/ref=sr_1_1/103-6601117-4420602?ie=UTF8&s=books

---

73.

Which Religions Are Welcoming to Singles? Part III: Christian Ministries

Jan 30 2009

Monique Moultrie on the Place of Singles in Christian Ministries

"In the feminist tradition of naming one's social location, my answers arise from my personal wrestling with sexuality and my participation in the progressive Protestant church. From my queries on whether I could love sex and God to my doubts as to whether I could afford as a woman to live sexually free, sexuality and religion have always been intertwined for me.

"I research in the area of faith-based/Christian ministries that explore singles' sexuality. These ministries have turned into a multi-million dollar industry-with books, classes, Internet and gospel radio dating services, and conferences all designed to help singles, and especially women, come to terms with their sexuality and spiritual walk with God. In fact, I argue these ministries have begun to take the place of church discussions with singles. For example, it is common for singles ministries in some Protestant churches to serve only as a tool to provide "marriage matches" for church-goers rather than deal with the complexities of single Christian lives.

"This is perhaps the case because there is an emphasis on marriage in the Christian faith. The 'Adam and Eve' Genesis biblical narrative is widely viewed as a foreshadowing of contemporary marriage and sexual relations are usually deemed only acceptable in a marital bond. Despite all the religious rhetoric to the contrary, there are actually only a few accounts in the New Testament that actually discourage premarital sex. However, the prevalent consensus in many Christian churches is that marriage is the ultimate union of two individuals.

"Yet, in these encouragements to marry the lived realities of Christian believers are often forgotten. While the universal church claims to have no hierarchy, many of the structures of the church implicitly depend on couples. For example, church leaders are usually married as it is presumed that this prevents sexual misconduct (and for those who are biblical literalists it is also a requirement for leadership). Thus, singles, which make up a substantial population of churches, are often shamed and shunned out of the spotlight.

"Hence, the allure of singles ministries as a place where singles can be leaders, can be productive contributors to the church, and socialize with others. Many churches provide singles conferences, workshops, singles bible studies, worship services, retreats, etc. Not all are oriented towards pushing the members towards the altar. In fact, some emphasize working on oneself and getting more centered and more aligned with God before seeking a partner. Some of the better ministries will tackle head on the complexity of singles, allowing space to discuss sex when single or at least how to balance sexual desires when the church is encouraging marriage. The attention to singles does not have to be solely puritanical or conservative!

"For me, the major downfall of these ministries is that they promote heterosexual unions and naturally assume everyone is looking for an opposite sex partner to eventually marry. But if you are openly gay/lesbian in many Christian churches, I'm sure you've got other issues to deal with other than being single!

"The best way to find churches with ministries that fit one's needs is to attend their singles functions. I advocate 'church-hopping' or visiting congregations until you find a church that fits where you are in the world. If you are happy with the other resources in your congregation but want to feel more valued as a single, then speak up! Go the church leadership with the idea for a singles ministry. (My personal suggestion is a book group on Donna Marie Williams' Sensual Celibacy-it urges more than just celibacy!) If you're in an area with active church ministries, buddy up with other congregations doing the same. Attend singles conferences in your area. Most importantly, never settle for being a second-class citizen in the household of faith!"

More about Monique Moultrie:

Monique Moultrie is a Ph.D. candidate in the Graduate Department of Religion at Vanderbilt University. She is specializing in the field of ethics. Her doctoral research investigates black women's ethical responses to sexual messages provided in faith-based Christian movements. She received a Bachelor of Arts in Religion and Sociology from Duke University and a Master of Arts in Theological Studies from Harvard Divinity School, where her concentration was in the sexual ethics of Christianity and Islam.

Thank-you, Monique Moultrie, for sharing your experiences, knowledge, and wisdom with the "Living Single" readership.

Source URL: http://www.psychologytoday.com/node/3199

Links:
[1] http://www.psychologytoday.com/blog/living-single/200901/which-religions-are-welcoming-singles-part-i-introduction [2] http://www.psychologytoday.com/blog/living-single/200901/which-religions-are-welcoming-singles-part-ii-judaism [3] http://www.bartleby.com/108/01/ [4] http://www.amazon.com/Sensual-Celibacy-Abstinence-Discovering-Relationship/dp/0684833514/ref=sr_1_1?ie=UTF8&s=books&qid=1233294292&sr=1-1 [5] http://geneva.rutgers.edu/src/christianity/ [6] http://www.religionlink.org/tip_060807.php

74.

Which Religions Are Welcoming to Singles? Part IV: Catholicism

July 20, 2009

The person who generously shared his insights on Catholicism for this series is Jack Clark Robinson, who is a Roman Catholic priest and a Franciscan Friar at the historic Old Mission of Santa Barbara. He has worked with Native Americans and was also a pastor of a mostly Hispanic church in New Mexico. He also just finished his dissertation in the History department here at UC Santa Barbara. I've never met him, even though I'm a permanent visitor at the same university, but as these things go, once I announced my interest in starting this series, referrals led me to him. That's fortunate, as he has provided some very thoughtful answers, as you will see.

Jack Clark Robinson on the Place of Singles in Catholicism

Bella: Let's start with a distinction - if you think it is one worth making - between the formal teachings of a religion and the actual services offered at various places of worship. Starting with the formal teachings, can you tell us briefly about how single people are regarded in Catholicism.

Jack Clark Robinson: The formal teaching of the Roman Catholic Church with regard to human relationships begins with the dignity of each individual human being. In the Gospel according to Matthew (Matthew 22:19-23), Jesus was asked what is the greatest of the commandments. He replied by quoting two verses from the Jewish Scriptures. "You shall love the Lord your God with all your heart, with all your soul and with all your mind," came from Deuteronomy, and "You shall love your neighbor as yourself," came from Leviticus. Those two verses indicate three rules: 1) Love God; 2) Love your neighbor, and 3) Love yourself. The last one, "Love yourself," is best understood not as affirmation of egocentrism, but rather as an indication of the worth, value and dignity with which every human being has been endowed by their individual creation in the image and likeness of God. The essential value of human beings comes from the relationship of every human being to God, whether consciously acknowledged or not, rather than from human relationships. All properly ordered human relationships then begin with the spiritual equality and worth of every human being as an individual.

With that said, even though the formal Catholic teaching emphasizes the value of individuals, when it comes to practical application of resources, most parishes place far more emphasis on married folk and families than on singles. First, the three sacraments administered at parishes (baptism, confirmation and matrimony) either deal directly, as in matrimony, or indirectly, as in the baptism of infants or confirmation of teenagers, with couples. Second, historically, many parishes in the United States were heavily invested in elementary education leading them to work extensively with young families. So though the formal teaching of the Catholic Church does not allow for discrimination between young single people and young married couples, as a result of other factors, in most parishes, young singles receive scant attention in comparison to young married couples, especially those who have children.

Bella: Single people have sometimes shared with me their stories of feeling unappreciated in their places of worship. They tell me, for example, that their particular places of worship are so focused on married couples and families that they feel either devalued, or even sometimes completely excluded from various events. Do you have any suggestions for how single people can figure out whether a particular place of worship may be welcoming to them?

Jack Clark Robinson: Check the website. Most Catholic parishes in an urban setting which are going to be with it enough to be welcoming to single people will also be with it enough to say so on their web sites.

Beyond the obvious, that is activities targeted at singles, there are other opportunities for singles in parishes. Almost any activity from liturgical ministries to social service and social justice ministries in most parishes can often use any help that they can get and would welcome volunteers. It is a way to get connected with people who share similar interests, whether in making music or making a better world.

Bella: This is overly optimistic of me, but in case any priests may be reading this, do you have any suggestions for how they can create places of worship that are more welcoming to single people?

Jack Clark Robinson: I wish that I had a pocketful of good ideas, but in ten years of parish ministry, I was not overly successful in involving singles in parish activity. There are some activities, such as "Theology on Tap," which involves singles meeting on their own "turf," such as restaurants and bars, with religious professionals to talk about issues of interest. But I know of nothing which has been a great success in this area.

Bella: Do you have any advice as to how individual worshippers can approach their priests with suggestions for making their places of worship more inclusive and welcoming of people who are single?

Jack Clark Robinson: The number one rule in approaching a priest or any other professional staff member at a parish is to remember that these people do not need more work. The most effective way to approach a priest is to say, "Here is what I would like to do." If the priest is open, and some will be, though others will not be, then you are halfway to seeing your suggestion getting a try!

Bella: Many thanks, Jack Clark Robinson, for sharing your insights with Living Single readers.

Source URL: http://www.psychologytoday.com/node/31068

Links:
[1] http://www.psychologytoday.com/blog/living-single/200901/which-religions-are-welcoming-singles-part-i-introduction [2] http://www.psychologytoday.com/blog/living-single/200901/which-religions-are-welcoming-singles-part-ii-judaism [3] http://www.psychologytoday.com/blog/living-single/200901/which-religions-are-welcoming-singles-part-iii-christian-ministries [4] http://www.history.ucsb.edu/people/person.php?account_id=192 [5] http://santabarbaramission.org/

75.

USA Today's Big New Story on Marriage Peddles Same Old Fallacies

Feb 18 2009

USA Today is very excited about marriage. Splashed across the front page of the Health and Behavior section, set off by a colorful illustration, was this pom-pom raising headline: "Federally funded ad campaign holds up value of marriage."

You read that right - federal funds are being used in an ad campaign to promote marriage. The initiative was spearheaded by (surprise!) the Bush administration back in 2005. (The Obama team has not yet made a decision about continuing the funding for the ads.)

Never mind the appropriateness - fiscally or morally - of using federal funds to cheerlead for marriage. That's too easy. I care about the supposed scientific basis for the campaign.

Reporter Sharon Jayson, in one key sentence, perpetrates all the usual myths (and one truth) about the implications of getting married: "Research suggests a bevy of benefits for those who marry, including better health, greater wealth and more happiness for the couple, and improved well-being for children."

Actually, it doesn't, except for the wealth part. That claim is true. As I explained in Chapter 12 of *Singled Out*, there are 1,136 federal provisions that benefit and protect only those people who are officially married. So yes, getting married typically increases your take, since you get to tap into policies that financially favor married people at the expense of singles.

What are vastly overstated or just plain wrong are the claims that getting married makes you healthier and happier and rescues your children from doom. Here are just a few of the pervasive methods and mistakes that result in the perpetuation of the myths that getting married makes you healthier and happier and saves your kids from doom. (Many more are in *Singled Out*.)

• **The cheater method**. Claims that getting married makes people happier or healthier are sometimes based on comparisons between the currently married and the previously married - some of which favor the currently married. But the previously married people DID get married! Using the cheater method, you just pretend that people who are divorced or widowed never did get married.

• **The mistake an intro psych undergrad would not make**. Pretend that if married people look better than single people when they are measured at one point in time, that means that married people did better BECAUSE they got married.

• **The cheat-some-more method**. Include among the married people only those who have happy or healthy marriages; compare them to all single people (regardless of happiness or health).

• **The selective reporting method: Only mention those studies that support your favorite myths**. Have you heard about the studies showing: That single parents are friendlier to their children than married parents? That the children of single parents spend more time with extended family members than the children of married parents? That children of single and married parents in the U.S. do not differ in grades or in the quality of their relationships with siblings and friends? That in some countries, the children of single parents are better readers than the children of married parents? Probably not (unless you are a reader of this blog). That's because the scientific findings that run counter to the stigmatizing of singles and their children do not get much play in the popular press (or in the SmartMarriages e-mail blasts or in the National Healthy Marriage Resource Center).

Predictably, the SmartMarriages listserv was delighted by the *USA Today* story, and equally predictably, they puffed up their piece with under-informed and misinformed claims. Strong marriages, the group declares, help single people because "it takes a lot of strong, stable, healthy marriages to create and sustain a village." Actually, if you base your statements on science (and not pseudoscience or ideology), the opposite may be true. Often it takes single people to create a village - they are the ones doing more than their share of the work of maintaining family, community, and intergenerational ties. (That slippery sentence in the "Smart" Marriages e-mail about strong marriages helping single people was followed by a bit of underhanded bashing of the children of single parents. I've already debunked that.)

The *USA Today* story did not play entirely by the Marriage Mafia rules. Jayson included some voices of skeptics:

• Jeffrey Arnett, who provided a wonderful interview about emerging adulthood for Living Single readers, said that the adults he studies take their independent decisions very seriously. About the decision to marry, he adds: "I can't imagine they'd want the advice of a government agency."

• Nicky Grist, the very smart and savvy executive director of the *Alternatives to Marriage Project*, said that two questions were paramount: "Should government tell people when to get married? And should government and society privilege marriage over all other relationships? Our answer to both of those questions is no."

Let that be the last word.

Source URL: http://www.psychologytoday.com/node/3488

76.

USA Today **Reporter Responds to Living Single Blog Post**

Feb 24 2009

Last week, when *USA Today* ran a story titled, "Federally funded ad campaign holds up value of marriage," I immediately blogged about it here. The person who wrote that story, Sharon Jayson, called to talk to me yesterday about my post. So the first thing I want to say to Sharon Jayson and to *USA Today* is thank-you. I'm not trained in journalism but I have little doubt that responsiveness to criticism is a hallmark of high professional standards in that field.

I want to thank Jayson and *USA Today*, too, because blogs are still disputed territory in the media, so responding to a blog post is a way of taking this form of expression seriously.

Jayson and I discussed two issues: Was *USA Today* really coming down on the side of marriage or marriage-promotion? And, what does the science really say about the implications of getting married? I think that she was right about the first and I was right about the second.

Was *USA Today* really coming down on the side of marriage or marriage-promotion?

I said in my post that the headline, "Federally funded ad campaign holds up value of marriage," and the colorful graphic alongside it, was "pom-pom raising." I also noted that the SmartMarriages group took the *USA Today* story and ran with it as a celebration of their own marriage-promotion positions.

Jayson said that the headline was meant to convey the position of the federal ad campaign and not the position of *USA Today*. The illustration showed the statue of liberty holding a giant wedding cake in her hand, adorned with the typical bride-and-groom cake-topper. Jayson said that in the meeting that *USA Today* held to discuss the article and accompanying graphics, no one ever expressed a desire to promote marriage or marriage-promotion. (I still think the image is matrimaniacal, but I'll let it go.) Finally, she said that she has no control over what groups such as SmartMarriages do with her articles, and I surely agree with that.

What does the science really say about the implications of getting married?

My major objection to the *USA Today* story was Jayson's summary statement about the science of marriage: "Research suggests a bevy of benefits for those who marry, including better health, greater wealth and more happiness for the couple, and improved well-being for children."

About that statement, I said in my original post, "Actually, it doesn't, except for the wealth part. That claim is true.... What are vastly overstated or just plain wrong are the claims that getting married makes you healthier and happier and rescues your children from doom."

It has been one of the primary purposes of Singled Out and of this blog to show that many of the claims about getting married are exaggerations, misrepresentations, or flat-out falsehoods.

One of Jayson's responses to my claim was to acknowledge that there are studies here and there in which the currently married people do not look happier or healthier than the currently unmarried people. Basically, she was suggesting that any studies showing that marrying does *not* improve health or happiness are the exceptions.

I don't think those kinds of studies say ANYTHING about the implications of marrying. They can't, because they use a cheater methodology. They compare people who got married and stayed married to others, including those who got married and then got unmarried. They then say, "Look, people who are currently married are happier and healthier than other people, including people who got divorced. So hey, everyone, get married and stay that way!" As I've explained before (here and here), that would be like a drug company making claims about the effectiveness of its new drug, based on a study in which only those people who took the drug and liked it were included in the drug group!

I offered a challenge to Jayson, and now I will offer it to everyone else as well - all other reporters, scientists, marriage-promoters, marriage skeptics, and interested disinterested readers. Here it is: Find one study - just one - that shows, using a non-cheater methodology, that getting married results in greater health or happiness. I think that if you can find one or two (and I don't know that you can), they will be the exceptions.

Here's what such a study would need to look like. It would follow people over the course of their lives as they transitioned from being single to getting married. The group of people who got married would have to include all people who ever got married - not just the ones who got married and stayed married. Why? Because that's the claim that is being made. Look again at the quote from the USA Today article: "Research suggests a bevy of benefits **for those who marry**." The claim is that marrying makes you happier or healthier. Where's the evidence?

In Chapter 2 of Singled Out, I discussed in some detail, complete with graphs, the results of what is probably the largest and longest-lasting study of the happiness implications of getting married. The study has been going on for more than 20 years. The results showed that for those people who got married and stayed married, their happiness increased about a quarter of a point (on a 0 to 10 scale) around the year of the wedding. Within a few years, though, they went back to being about as happy as they were when they were single. So they got just a temporary blip in happiness, and that was only for those who got married and STAYED that way. Those who would eventually divorce did not experience the happiness honeymoon - on the average, they were already becoming less happy, not more so, as their wedding day approached. Their happiness continued to decline until the year before their divorce became official.

The authors did not report any analyses in which all of the people who ever got married were included (the proper test of the claim that if you get married, you get happy). Putting together the results of the people who stayed married and those who divorced, though, clearly does not add up to scientific evidence that getting married means getting happy. It may even suggest the reverse - we'd need to see the graph.

Conclusion
I'm not saying you shouldn't get married if that's what you want to do. I am saying, though - based on the scientific evidence, properly analyzed and interpreted - that you should not expect the act of marrying to transform you, magically, into a happier and healthier person. (And also, federal government, don't use my taxpayer money to try to persuade people to marry, based on bogus science. In fact, don't do it at all.)

About the claim that getting married makes you happier and healthier, I'm not just saying that there are exceptions here or there. I'm saying something much bolder: If there are any properly-conducted and analyzed studies showing that getting married makes you happier or healthier, THEY are the exceptions!

Finally, thanks again to Sharon Jayson and *USA Today* for following up on my critique of their story.

77.

Singles Are "Catching Up" in Health, But Who Is Really in the Lead?

Aug 15 2008

"Married adults report better health, but singles are catching up," proclaimed one of the many headlines touting the latest marital status study to make it into the media spotlight.

I'll give you my bottom line about this study first. Then I'll explain in greater detail.

BOTTOM LINE

Here's what the study really did show:

1. For people who had always been single, their health improved continuously from 1972 until the end of the study, 2003. This improvement was evident in all groups - men and women, Blacks and whites. (This was accurately reported.)

2. The other part of the headline, that married people are still the healthiest, was misleading in at least four ways:

A. The study does NOT show that differences between the currently-married and the always-single occurred BECAUSE the currently-married people got married. Instead, the data were analyzed in a way that gave the currently-married people an advantage it did not give the single people. (That is standard practice in cottage industry of marriage studies.)

B. Even allowing for the approach that makes marriage look better than it really is, the differences in health between the currently-married and the always-single are tiny. By the last year of the study (2003), the probability of reporting good health was about .928 for the currently married and about .926 for the always-single. If it is easier to think in terms of percentages, that means that about 92.8% of currently-married people said their health was good or excellent, compared to about 92.6% of always-single people. So the headlines saying that married people are still the healthiest are touting a difference of about two-tenths of one percent. And remember, that advantage did NOT come from getting married (as I explain below). Is that 0.2% what you imagined when you read headlines claiming that married people are the healthiest?

C. For the African-Americans, by 2003, there was no difference at all between the health of the currently-married and the always-single.

D. Women who had always been single were healthier than men who were currently married. In 2003, the likelihood that always-single women would report good or excellent health was about 92.8. For currently-married men, it was about 91.8. (This wasn't noted in any of the media reports I found.)

THE MORE DETAILED DISCUSSION

The authors crunched data collected over 32 years (from 1972 through 2003) from more than a million people, so this is a study worth taking seriously. Importantly, the same people were NOT followed that whole time. Each year, a different set of people participated. They described their overall perceptions of their own health, on a scale ranging from poor to excellent. Those reports were then linked to their marital status.

The key question was: How has the health of the different groups changed over the 32 years? So, for example, if you compared the health of the currently-married participants in 1972 to the health of the currently-married participants in 1973 and every other year up to the final one (2003), what would the change over time look like?

For the people who had always been single (or "never-married," as they are more often called), the answer was clear. Whether male or female, Black or white, their health steadily improved over time. The same could not be said for any of the other marital status groups (currently married, divorced, separated, or widowed).

191

Sounds good for singles, except when you keep in mind the headline. Sure, singles are doing better now than they were a few years ago, but they are still not as good as married people. The Washington Post headline was even more stark: "Married Folks Still the Healthiest." Singles did not even get the Most Improved Player Award in that story title.

The currently married people actually were the healthiest in most (though not all) of the analyses, so what's my problem? (You just know that I have one.) It is the implication that they are the healthiest because they got married (e.g., "marriage benefits health"). Again, sadly, the *Washington Post* was one of the worst offenders, recruiting an "expert" not involved in the study to comment, "This study provides confirmation that marriage does tend to make people healthier." Of course, it does nothing of the sort.

In the "Science and the Single Person" chapter of my book, Singled Out, I explained why studies like these do not and cannot demonstrate that getting married makes people healthier (or happier or anything else). I'll provide a quick recap here.

Here's the hypothetical example I like to use. Suppose a drug company did a study in which they let people decide for themselves whether to take the new drug (rather than randomly assigning them to a drug condition or a placebo condition). They also let people quit taking the drug whenever they wanted to. Some people started taking the drug and hated it, so they were removed from the Drug group and set aside into a different group (No Drug - intolerable). Others started taking the drug but eventually lost access to it (No Drug - withdrawn). The drug company removed them from the key Drug condition and set them aside, too.

So now the drug company takes the data from only those people who started on the drug and stayed on it. It compares how good those people felt to how good everyone else felt - the people who never did take the drug, those who hated it and stopped taking it, and those who were cut off from the drug. Their conclusion? Our drug works! Yeah!!! Everyone should take our drug and then they will feel so much better.

That's the logic of all of these studies of marital status that are not longitudinal (i.e., that do not follow the same people over a number of years as they get married, get unmarried, or stay single). You can claim that getting married is good for you, as long as you do not count the people who got married and found it not so good at all.

A previous study further illustrates how currently married people can end up with the best health scores even though getting married did NOT make them healthier. This is a study that was longitudinal: 10,000 people were followed for more than 4 years. They found that the married people who had more health problems early in the study were nearly twice as likely to divorce by the end of the study. See how this works? The married people who have health problems are more likely to get divorced. So now they are taken out of the married group and put into the unmarried group. The people who are left in the married group now have fewer health problems than the others. But that's not because they got married. Getting married did not cause them to get healthier. Getting unhealthy seemed to motivate some of the married people to get divorced.

I'm not saying that getting married never results in getting healthy. I am saying that there are lots of ways to account for results from the recent study and others like it. Typically, in our matrimaniacal culture, interpretations that make married people look better are favored over others, even when there is no good scientific reason to do so.

The marriage-centered point of view is evident not just in the framing of the results, but in the speculations that are offered to account for them. Let me illustrate with another finding. Over time, the health of people in the divorced, separated, and especially the widowed group got even worse. So, from 1972 to 2003, the health of people who had always been single looks better and better, while the health of the previously married looks worse. By the last year of the study (2003), the people who had always been single had a health advantage over the previously married that was greater than it had ever been before.

Why are the always-single people healthier than the previously-married? The authors offer one possible explanation that is called a "stress" or "crisis" or "loss" hypothesis: "the never-married are relatively immune to any apparent disadvantage associated with the stress of marital dissolution." Translation: People who have always been single have not dealt with a marital relationship that has ended in death or divorce, so of course they are better off.

Do you see any problem with that? Can you think of any other explanation for why the always-single might fare better than the previously-married? I think this issue is so important that I am going to highlight it in a future post. So for now, think about your answers, and I'll get back to you.

The question raised by the recent findings is not just why the always-single are healthier than the previously-married, but why the difference between them has grown larger between 1972 and 2003. Why would the dissolution of a marriage be harder on people in recent years than in decades past? The authors say more research is needed, and they are right. Here's one possible hypothesis: People who got married or unmarried in 1972 were not so caught up in the Soul Mate mentality that became so prevalent later. They did not expect their spouse to be their everything - to fulfill all of their wishes and hopes and dreams. They continued to value other important people, such as friends and relatives. People from more recent times who have bought into the myth of the Soul Mate and The One, and who expect the world of that one person, and who have relegated everyone else to the back burner, are going to be crushed when that one person is gone.

There are a few other points from the study that I'd like to clarify or underscore.

1. What is the magnitude of the difference between the currently-married and the always-single? If you can access the original article (unfortunately, it is behind a pay wall), look at the graphs on the bottom of p. 247. The BIGGEST difference was for men in 1972. For the always-single men, the likelihood that they would report good

or excellent health was about 89%. For the currently married men, it was about 91%. For the women, the difference was smaller than that (a few tenths of 1%) for all 32 years. (How can such a small difference be statistically meaningful? One reason is that there are more than a million people in the dataset.)

2. You may have read that "the gap between the married and the never-married is closing, especially for men." I want to clarify the "especially for men" part. Again, if you can, look at the graphs on the bottom of p. 247. The gap is closing more for men in part because it started out bigger. So in 1972, there is a bigger difference between the married men and the always-single men than there is in 2003. For women, there is a very small difference between the currently-married and the always-single at every point in time. Looking at the last year on the graphs (2003), the difference in health between the currently-married and the always-single appears to be about the same for the men as for the women.

3. Women who had always been single were healthier than men who had always been single for all 32 years. (Not a big difference.)

4. Women who had always been single were healthier than men who were currently-married; from the graphs, it appears that this was true for all 32 years as well. (Again, none of these differences are big.)

5. At the start of the study (in 1972), if you control for family income, all of the categories of unmarried people (always-single, divorced, separated, and widowed) were healthier than the currently-married. That suggests that if the currently-married people were healthier than the currently-unmarried people, it may have been because the married people had more money. If the unmarried had as much money as the married people did, they would probably have been healthier than the married people. (No, that wasn't reported anywhere either.)

The ways of presenting studies like this one are not unique to these authors. The kinds of explanations they entertain, such as the loss hypothesis, are the standard ones. The authors are, in fact, better than most. One of the points they were making in the article is that it is important to look separately at different categories of unmarried people, rather than glomming them all together. That's commendable.

The authors also end their paper in a way that is rare for scholars of marriage:

> "the self-rated health status of the never-married has improved for all race and gender groups examined, and it is more similar to the married for men now than ever before, which suggests that encouraging marriage in order to promote health may be misguided. In fact, getting married increases one's risk for eventual marital dissolution, and marital dissolution seems to be worse for self-rated health now than at any point in the past three decades."

Links:
[1] http://www.accessibility.com.au/news/married-adults-report-better-health-but-singles-are-catching-up [2]
http://www.ingentaconnect.com/content/asoca/jhsb/2008/00000049/00000003/art00001 [3]
http://www.washingtonpost.com/wp-dyn/content/article/2008/08/11/AR2008081100632_pf.html [4]
http://www.psychologytoday.com/blog/living-single/200808/cracking-the-code-how-think-critically-about-reports-the-alleged-superiori [5] http://www.amazon.com/Singled-Out-Singles-Stereotyped-Stigmatized/dp/0312340826/ref=ed_oe_p/102-4637341-6604139 [6]
http://www.ingentaconnect.com/content/els/02779536/1998/00000046/00000003/art00186

78.

Is MSNBC Really Recommending Marriage as a Treatment for Depression?

June 5, 2007

The headline on MSNBC was catchy: "New treatment for depression - marriage." It was also irresponsible.

I spent years checking out claims like this while working on my book, *Singled Out: How Singles Are Stereotyped, Stigmatized, and Ignored, and Still Live Happily Ever After*. At the urging of readers who had noticed this latest bit of matrimania, I checked out this pronouncement, too.

The MSNBC article was based on a study that will appear in the *Journal of Health and Social Behavior*. I asked one of the co-authors for an advanced copy. The authors described their work accurately and carefully. MSNBC reported it selectively.

First, here's what MSNBC got right. In the research, adults who started out single were interviewed in the first year of the study and then 5 years later. Both times, depression was measured on an 84-point scale. The people who were married by the time of the second interview scored about 3 points lower on the depression scale (out of the 84 points) than those who stayed single. That's an overall average. Breaking it down, the singles who started out depressed and then got married scored about 8 points lower in depression; those who started out happy scored about 2 points lower.

Now here are a few points from the original report that did not make it into the storyline whereby marriage is touted as a "new treatment for depression."

1. At the very longest, the people in this study were married for 5 years. This is important. Consider, for example, the results of a study in which people reported their happiness every year for 18 years (here and here). Those who got married and

stayed married enjoyed just a small increase in happiness (about a quarter of a point on an 11-point scale) around the year of the wedding. Then they went back to being as happy or as unhappy as they were when they were single.

2. MSNBC does not happen to mention that the people who married and then divorced within the 5-year period were excluded from the calculations. Do you think the people who got divorced were becoming less depressed as a result of marrying? Neither do I. The 18-year study of happiness reported some relevant data. On the average, the people who married and later divorced did not even get a small blip in happiness in their newlywed year. Instead, they were already becoming slightly less happy (rather than happier) as their wedding day drew nearer.

3. The people who were classified as depressed were about 20% of the people in the study. The other 80% were the ones who scored just 2 points lower on depression (out of 84) after they married. Here is a comment in the authors' own words: "Those with average levels of marital happiness who were not depressed prior to marrying do not experience significantly better psychological well-being than their continually never-married counterparts."

4. Here's something else from the authors: "In most cases, above-average marital happiness is necessary for conferring the psychological benefits of a transition into marriage." (So, getting married decreases depression as long as you end up in a marriage that is happier than most.)

5. Based on an interview with one of the authors, MSNBC suggests that marriage may provide "the companionship and emotional support needed to help alleviate depression." But if it is companionship and emotional support that is key, then wouldn't a close and caring friendship provide that?

So let's see. If you get married, you may end up less depressed if you start out among the 20% most depressed people to begin with, if you don't get divorced, if you end up in a marriage that is happier than most, and if no one asks how you feel after the first few years, and no one compares the marital relationship to any other relationship that offers companionship and emotional support.

On these grounds, you want to quit therapy, toss your meds, and just get married? I don't think so.

Exaggerated claims such as this MSNBC headline (that shot to the top of the most e-mailed stories) are obviously obnoxious to single people. But they are unfair to married people, too. Teeing up a fortune cookie expectation - Get Married, Be Happy - is setting readers up for disappointment and disillusionment. People have their reasons for marrying, but trying out a "new treatment for depression" is unlikely to be one of the sensible ones.

Source URL: http://www.huffingtonpost.com/bella-depaulo/is-msnbc-really-recommend_b_50703.html

79

If You Get Married, Will You Sleep Better?

Jun 13 2009

A new sleep study hit the press a few days ago, and my inbox is lighting up. Should I believe it, inquiring minds are asking. The study was presented at a SLEEP conference (SLEEP is what they call the Associated Professional Sleep Societies). Media reports flaunt headlines such as "Marriage linked with better sleep" and "Stable marriage is linked with better sleep in women."

Readers of this blog know how I feel about research studies - I want to read the published versions, not just abstracts, not just press releases, and surely not just what the media claims that the studies say. But this latest study has been a challenge. I can't find a published study corresponding to the press release. I can't find anything longer than an abstract. I emailed the author who is quoted in many of the stories, but she has not responded. My guess is that there is no published article. The results were presented at a conference, and maybe not even a conference paper (rather than just an abstract) is available. So I'll tell you what I think based on the information I can gather, but I still want to see a professional write-up.

Let me start with my hypothetical drug study example, because I think we are better at thinking intelligently, critically, and impartially about drugs than about marriage. A drug company - I'll call it Promarital - has come up with a new drug that is supposed to help you sleep better. I'll call the drug Sleeppiage. The Promarital drug company offered their Sleeppiage drug to 360 White, African-American, and Chinese women (average age of 51). The company measures the women's sleep when they first sign up for the study and again over the course of the next 6 to 8 years.

1. Some women **never do take Sleeppiage**. The Promarital company calls these women the **No Drug** group.

2. Some women **take Sleeppiage but hate it and refuse to continue taking it**. The company calls these women the **Losing the Drug** group. There are no published reports of the precise size of this group but from other research, we can estimate it as at least 43%.

3. Some women did not take the drug at first but did **start taking it later**. Promarital describes these women as "**Gaining the Drug**."

4. Finally, there is the drug company's favorite group. They took the drug from the start and stayed on it. Promarital calls it the **Sleeppiage** group, or just the **Drug** group.

Promarital reports, with great fanfare, that Sleeppiage works, because the women in the fourth group, the Drug group, sleep better than all the rest! The Drug group women sleep especially better than the women in the "Losing the Drug" group.

That's right, the Promarital drug company takes out of the Drug group all of the women who hated the drug - at least 43% of them! - and says about the remaining women, "Look at how well they are sleeping - Sleeppiage is just great!"

This, in its broadest strokes, is what the latest sleep study is saying. (I'll go into more detail below.) It is also an example of how decades of research on marital status has been used to suggest, falsely, that if only you get married, you will be happier, healthier, sleep better, live longer, and all the rest.

My Sleeppiage = Marriage equivalencies are probably obvious, but I'll spell them out just to be sure I'm clear:

1. The **No Drug** group corresponds to women who **stayed single** the whole time.

2. **Losing the Drug**: women who got married, then **divorced**.

3. **Gaining the Drug**: women who started out **single, then married**.

4. Drug, or **Sleeppiage** group: This is the **currently married** group, or everyone who is left of the people who got married, after setting aside all the people who got married, hated it, and got divorced.

Actually, it is even worse than I just suggested. That's because often, the people who marry, hate it and get divorced, are not just taken out of the marriage group and set aside. Instead, their distaste for the whole thing and their bad outcomes are used as evidence that marriage is good! Seriously. I'm not making this up. Every time you see someone argue (in the media or at professional meetings or in the journals) that divorced people do worse in some way (sleep or happiness or health or whatever) than people who are currently married, that's the case that is being made. It is the same as a drug company proclaiming that their new drug is great because people who take the drug and like it do better than people who take the drug, hate it, and therefore stop taking it.

Would you take a drug based on that evidence?

But can't you conclude that the moral is to get married and stay married? Well, that assumes that if all of those people who got married, hated it, and got divorced had just stayed married instead, they would now be sleeping just fine. Seems unlikely. The only definitive study cannot actually be done - you'd need to randomly assign people to stay married or get divorced and then assess sleep.

Another finding was that women who started out single and later got married and stayed married also slept almost as well as the women who were married the whole time. (Well, sort of. When they first married, their sleep was more restless.) Doesn't that indicate that if you get married, you will eventually sleep better? Again, not really. Because if you get married, you may or may not stay married. If you eventually divorce, you may not sleep any better than if you stayed single the whole time. (Unfortunately, not enough data were reported, so I can't find any precise numbers. In most studies of marital status - I reviewed them in Singled Out - people who were previously married do worse than people who have always been single.)

The Real Summary of the Results of the Sleep Study

From what I can tell from the paltry data that has been made available, here's what the sleep study really did show.

• If you get married, chances are pretty good (probably about 43%) that you will eventually divorce, and divorced people have some sleep problems.

• If you are among the remaining people who got married and did not divorce and did not become widowed over the course of the 8-year study, your sleep will be pretty good. (Again, we don't know how good - data are not reported.)

• If you start out single and then get married, you might eventually get divorced. See above. If you don't get divorced over the course of the study, your sleep will eventually improve, though at first you will sleep more restlessly.

• If you start out single and stay single, we don't know how your sleep will compare to all of the people who got married - that's not reported. Your sleep will not be as good as the people who are left in the married group once all the people who got married, hated it, and got divorced are taken out of that group. If the results of this study are like so many other marital status studies in the literature, then probably the always-single group will sleep better than the previously married group.

• Actually, there are some qualifications of these findings:

  • The study only reported on women.
  • The study included White, African-American, and Chinese women, but the results were mostly true only for the White participants.
  • Oh, and another thing - the currently married sleep better if they are also happily married. If they are having problems, forget about it. So the group that is already given an unfair advantage (because the people who didn't like marriage and got divorced are taken out of the group) still only looks good if you consider the happily married among them.

So start with women only. Set aside the African-Americans and the Chinese. Look at the people who got married. Not when they first got married, because their sleep is restless then. Not the people who got married and then divorced, because their sleep is not so good, either. Also, of the married group that is already rigged (because everyone who got married, hated it, and then got divorced have had their marriages statistically annulled - they are not included in the married group anymore), rig it

199

even more by underscoring just those who are happily married. There you go! That's the evidence that getting married makes you sleep better!

Let's all go out and buy Sleeppiage.

What Was GOOD about the Study

Actually, this study had one very important strength - it was longitudinal. The authors looked at the sleep patterns of the same people at the start of the study and again 6-8 years later. That way, we can see what happened to the same people as they went from being single to getting married, or being married to getting divorced, or any other pattern. That's the next best thing to the methodologically superior study that we cannot ethically do - randomly assign people to get married or stay single or get divorced or become widowed.

So the problem is not with the design of the study. It is with the misleading reports of the results and of the implications of those results.

What Was Good About the Reporting

Most reports that I found in the media used an important word: "linked." They said that marriage was linked with better sleep. That's good because it is not a word that implies causality. It is not the same as saying that getting married results in sleeping better. (My guess, though, is that many readers made that leap anyway. I'd love to see a study of how these headlines are interpreted.)

The best reporting, unsurprisingly, came from the website of the SLEEP group. They reported 3 sleep studies, with this headline: "It's Complicated: Sleep, Marriage, & Relationships."

I also got a kick out of something else I discovered while trying to figure out what the sleep study really did say: One of the best reports came from a website that describes itself as "Celebrity, Sex, Fashion for Women." That site is Jezebel. In the relevant post, all three studies are mentioned, including the one showing that people who earn a lot of money sleep a lot better than people who don't. Here's the closing line: "The study author recommends never going to bed mad, or, you know, just having huge amounts of money."

Once More, Because It Is So Important

If you hear someone say or imply, "get married because married people do better than divorced people," you are at risk for getting scammed. Divorced people DID get married. They didn't like it. They amount to about 43% of the people who got married. Imagine testing a new drug, or a new hypothesis, and letting yourself exclude from the key group the 43% of the people who hated the drug, or who behaved just the opposite to the way you predicted. Then imagine trying to publish that study, with the claim that it shows how great your drug or your hypothesis is!

Same for comparing the group that took the drug (minus the ones who hated it and stopped taking it) to those who never did take it, and saying that the drug wins. Or comparing your experimental group (minus the people in that group who behaved contrary to your hypothesis) to the people in the control group, and declaring your hypothesis has been supported. It wouldn't happen. Unless you were studying marital status.

Source URL: http://www.psychologytoday.com/node/29921

Links:
[1] http://www.eurekalert.org/pub_releases/2009-06/aaos-smi060309.php[2] http://firstpersonsingular.org/2009/06/10/why-im-not-getting-enough-sleep/ [3] http://well.blogs.nytimes.com/2009/06/10/marriage-linked-with-better-sleep [4] http://www.sciencedaily.com/releases/2009/06/090610091345.htm [5] http://www.aasmnet.org/Articles.aspx?id=891 [6] http://sleepmeeting.blogspot.com/2009/06/its-complicated-sleep-marriage.html [7] http://www3.interscience.wiley.com/journal/118586765/abstract?CRETRY=1&SRETRY=0 [8] http://www.amazon.com/Singled-Out-Singles-Stereotyped-Stigmatized/dp/0312340826/ref=ed_oe_p/102-4637341-6604139 [9] http://jezebel.com/ [10] http://jezebel.com/5285766/marriage-money-mean-better-sleep [11] http://www.eurekalert.org/pub_releases/2009-06/aaos-ssg060209.php

80.

Are Singles Doomed to High Blood Pressure? Only If They Read the Media Reports of the Latest Study

Mar 22 2008

Have you heard the one about marital status and blood pressure? The media has been abuzz about a study on that topic released a few days ago. The research has been featured on Good Morning America, CNN, MSNBC, in an Associated Press report, and many other places.

HERE ARE THE CLAIMS MADE IN THE MEDIA

I typed a few key words into Google to get a sense of the headlines. Here are a few:

1. "Happily married have lower blood pressure than singles."
2. "Marriage may lower blood pressure."
3. "Walk down the aisle for lower blood pressure, but be happy!"
4. "A happy marriage leads to low blood pressure."
5. "Happily marrieds have lower blood pressure than social singles."

Exhibit #6 comes from a pro-marriage listserv. The moderator introduced the study by noting, "This research is all the more reason to help couples learn how to get married..."

For years, I have been examining claims about the links between getting married and getting healthy. (See Chapter 2 of my book, <u>Singled Out</u>.) My approach is apparently different than that of many reporters: I actually go to the original journal article and read what the study really did show. Time and again, the results that make it into the media are a biased version of the actual results of the research, and in just about every instance, they are biased toward making married people look better and single people look worse.

I'll explain how that has happened with this particular study. Sometimes, though, you need look no further than the headline to realize that something is amiss. Take the very first headline, for example: "Happily married have lower blood pressure than singles." The claim is that if you compare only those married people who are happily married, to all singles (regardless of their happiness or anything else), the married people seem healthier.

HERE ARE THE ACTUAL RESULTS

Here's what I learned about the study from reading the <u>original journal article</u>:

Adults from the Provo, Utah community (mostly white) agreed to wear a blood pressure monitor for 24 hours. The married group was comprised of 204 heterosexuals. The 99 singles included 12 who were divorced and 1 who was widowed; the others had always been single.

From headlines such as "Marriage may lower blood pressure," you might guess that when blood pressure was averaged across the 24 hours of the study, the married people would have lower blood pressure than the singles. You would, however, be wrong. There were NO SIGNIFICANT DIFFERENCES in blood pressure between the married people and the single people.

Next, the authors looked at people's blood pressure only while they were awake. Maybe those waking hours, when married participants may have actually be interacting with their spouses, are the times when they look healthier than single people. Wrong again. There were NO SIGNIFICANT DIFFERENCES in blood pressure between the married people and the single people during waking hours.

What's left is blood pressure while sleeping. The authors looked at how much each person's blood pressure decreased while sleeping compared to when the person was awake. The married people had a greater reduction in blood pressure (not necessarily the same as a lower level of blood pressure), by about 3 points, than single people.

That is the key finding that you have been hearing all about: Married people look better than single people only if you compare reductions in blood pressure when the participants are unconscious.

I'm not saying that "nocturnal dips" are unimportant. But really, when you read those headlines, is that what you thought you were learning?

202

But suppose, hypothetically, that the results had been much stronger. Imagine that the married people had much lower blood pressure than the single people all day and all night. Would it then be okay to say that if you want to have lower blood pressure, you should get married?

Not on the basis of this study. Anyone who has taken a course in psychology or research methodology probably knows why. If married people differ from single people in blood pressure (or anything else), you cannot know, on the basis of this sort of study, whether they differ BECAUSE they are married. Maybe the people who got married already had lower blood pressure even before they married, and getting married made no difference.

Methodologically, there is a great way to figure out whether getting married helps your blood pressure. Unfortunately, it is unethical. You would have to assign people at random to get married or stay single.

The next best thing is to follow people over time. Richard Lucas and his colleagues have done this in a study of happiness that has been ongoing for at least 18 years. They found that people who got married and stayed married throughout the course of the study experienced a small increase in happiness around the time of the wedding. Then they went back to being as happy or as unhappy as they were when they were single. The people who married and eventually divorced did not even get the benefit of a honeymoon effect; they were already becoming less happy, not more so, as their wedding day approached.

There is no comparable study of changes in blood pressure as people transition from being single to being married (or from being married to being divorced or widowed).

WHAT'S WITH THE "HAPPILY MARRIED"?

I've already made fun of the headline claiming that happily married people have lower blood pressure than single people (whether happy or unhappy). The happy qualification covers another finding that some of the reports did mention: Unhappily married people had worse blood pressure readings across the 24-hrs than did the single people. They also had higher blood pressure during the day. Their "nocturnal dips" were not any different.

Hence, some main headings (e.g., "Good marriage equals good blood pressure") were qualified by a subheading: "Bad marriage worse than being single."

Fair is fair. The blood pressure of unhappy married people should be compared to the blood pressure of unhappy single people.

WHAT ABOUT THOSE "SOCIAL SINGLES"?

Headline #5, "Happily marrieds have lower blood pressure than social singles," introduces another factor - whether singles are "social" or not. The title of the published article poses the question, "Is there something unique about marriage?" The press release from Brigham Young University stated that "Having supportive friends did not translate into improved blood pressure for singles or unhappily marrieds." What that summary suggests is that even if you are single and you have supportive friends, you are still doomed to your non-dippy blood pressure.

Now once again, let me tell you what I read in the actual journal article. The measure of "supportive friends" was a 40-item scale. It consists of 10 items measuring your access to tangible, material help (sample item: "If for some reason I were put in jail, there is someone I could call to bail me out"); 10 items measuring whether you have people with whom you can discuss your problems (sample item: "There is really no one I can trust to give me good financial advice"); 10 items measuring whether you have people you can do things with (sample item: "Most people I know don't enjoy the same things I do"); and 10 items measuring your self-esteem (sample item: "I am able to do things as well as most other people").

Single people who had more access to support (as measured by this scale), compared to married people who had more access to support (again, as measured by this scale), had no better blood pressure readings than those who had less access to support. That's the basis for the conclusion that "there [is] something unique about marriage."

Here is the question that the study did NOT address: If you are single, and you have a close friend or a sibling or anyone else who is important to you (or if you have the number of close relationships and the degree of closeness that you desire), then how does your blood pressure compare to a married person's?

CONCLUSION

If you are single, I don't think you should decide to get married in order to lower your blood pressure. Just relax and get a good night's sleep.

Unfortunately, that probably won't work for me. I'm single, and media reports like these make my blood boil.

Source URL: http://www.psychologytoday.com/node/258

Links:
[1] http://www.newswise.com/articles/view/538727/?sc=dwhn [2] http://www.amazon.com/Singled-Out-Singles-Stereotyped-Stigmatized/dp/0312340826/ref=ed_oe_p/102-4637341-6604139 [3] http://www.springerlink.com/content/120893/?sortorder=asc&Online Date=In the last week [4] http://www.springerlink.com/content/v8j6w4q383356746/

81.

Single Men Have Good Hearts

Feb 22 2009

Have you heard the one about the wild and unhealthy single men and the better-behaved and healthy-living husbands? It is not a joke (though it should be) - it has been described as scientific fact. The book, *The Case for Marriage*, is full of misstatements and cheater methods that make married people look better than they really are and singles look worse. (These are described in detail in Singled Out.) But, sadly, *The Case* is often cited, so it is a good source of conventional (though dopey) wisdom about the implications of getting married.

The Conventional Wisdom about Getting Married and Getting Healthy

Here are a few choice quotes about single and married men from The Case:

• *"For men, a lot of the health advantages of marriage can be summed up in a single phrase: Fewer stupid bachelor tricks."*

• *"Wives not only discourage drinking, smoking, and speeding, but they cook low-fat or low-cholesterol meals, add more fruits and vegetables to the family diet, and encourage regular sleeping habits."*

• *"When men lose their wives, either to death or divorce, they once again resume their bachelor habits."*

Those poor single men. They must be keeling over from heart attacks and strokes, or waddling into old age with bloated bellies filled with a lifetime of beer and bratwurst. Since it's American Heart Month, I suppose we should pay attention.

Getting Married and Getting Heart Disease: A National Study

I like to fight singlism with science, so I was delighted to discover a report of an 8-year study of heart disease, based on a nationally representative sample of more than 9,000 people in late mid-life. When the study first started in 1992, the participants ranged in age from 51 to 60.

The participants were contacted five times from 1992 and 2000. Their marital status, cardiovascular health status, and health behaviors were assessed. Other information (for example, socioeconomic status) was also recorded.

There are five different marital statuses:
• Continuously married (i.e., first and only marriage)
• Remarried
• Widowed

• Divorced
• Always single

Let's look first at the prevalence of heart disease at the start of the study. (Heart disease = doctor diagnosis of heart attack, coronary heart disease, angina, congestive heart failure, or other heart problems, or stroke.) In the table below is the **percentage of people** (averaged across all ages) **who had heart disease at the start of the study**. Lower numbers indicate less prevalence of heart disease, so the group ranked #1 is the healthiest. The rank-ordering of heart disease for the 5 marital statuses was the same for the men as for the women. See if you can guess which marital status goes with each rank.

WOMEN MEN
1. 8.4   13.0
2. 8.7   13.5
3. 10.7   16.4
4. 10.8   16.5
5. 11.6   17.7

Okay, here are the answers:

1. Always single
2. Continuously married
3. Remarried
4. Widowed
5. Divorced

So there you have it. The lowest rate of heart disease is found among the women and men, ages 51-60, who had been single all their lives. The rates for the continuously married are higher, though not statistically so.

The study went on for years, and the authors calculated the probability of experiencing heart disease for each age, from 51 through 65. (See Table 5 in the article.) Of course, the probabilities increase with age for men and women of all marital statuses. Let's see where they end up at age 65. Here are the results for the **MEN**.

1. 29, always-single men
2. 33, widowed men
3. 42, remarried men
4. 46, continuously married men
5. 50, divorced men

Look at what has happened to the continuously married men. At 46%, the likelihood of having heart disease is greater for them than for any other group of men except the divorced. The always-single men are doing way better, at just 29%.

(For women at age 65, the probabilities were 32 for continuously married, 38 for always-single, 43 for widowed, 45 for remarried, and 47 for divorced. So even though men typically have higher rates of heart disease than women, the always-single men have the lowest rates of all 10 of the groups.)

The authors also looked at how the risk of heart disease changed for each successive year of marriage. Here, in their words, is what they found: "Each year in marriage increased rather than decreased the risk of cardiovascular disease by 2% for both men and women." The risk increased each year both in first marriages and in remarriages.

Because the authors collected data on health measures such as smoking and obesity, and on conditions described as morbid (really, that's the technical term), they could venture a data-based explanation as to why each year of marriage added to the risk of heart disease: "**Longer marriages were associated with less healthy behaviors and an accumulation of morbid conditions, such as hypertension, diabetes, and high cholesterol.**"

So much for *The Case for Marriage* with its wives preparing low-cholesterol meals for their husbands, with fresh fruit for dessert. (And yes, that book, published in the year 2000, envisions wives making all the meals for their husbands.) And about those "stupid bachelor tricks" - perhaps the authors would like to revisit that claim?

Where Were the Feature Stories about These Findings?

This national study of heart disease was published in a very reputable journal (*Journal of Marriage and Family*) in 2006. Do you remember seeing any headlines about it in the media? I don't either.

Can you imagine how many feature stories you would have seen if the results were reversed, and the continuously married men (rather than the always-single men) had lower rates of heart disease than all of the other men and even all of the other women?

Here's my guess about why the great results for single men did not get much attention: Matrimania sells, and the bashing of single men is in.

Here's another. If you look at the published summary (abstract) of the article, you will see that the results for the always-single men (or women) are not even mentioned. Instead, the focus is on the bad things that happen to your heart if you "lose" a marriage.

What about the Other Kind of Heart?

By medical measures, always-single men have good hearts. But what about the other sense of a "good heart," the meaning that is more about the kind of person you are than about the condition of your body parts?

I find this an especially interesting question in light of the recent books about single men that seem so demeaning (sometimes <u>unwittingly</u> so). In a conversation about one of those books (*Guyland*), Jeff Arnett told Living Single readers <u>what the research really does show about single men</u> during emerging adulthood:

> "What's really striking is how much less sexist, racist, and homophobic young guys are now than in the past. Most want an equal partner in a romantic and sexual relationship, not just someone who will serve them. Most have friends who are of different ethnic groups, and most have gay or lesbian friends and don't make a big deal out of it. What's more, rates of every type of 'guy problem' have declined sharply in the past 30 years among emerging adults--including alcohol use, crime, and unprotected sex. So the assertion that the typical young guy today is a drunken porno-mad potential rapist is nonsense. It's untrue and unfair."

Personally, since <u>Singled Out</u> was published, I've met many single men at my talks and book signings, and - minus the visuals - I've met many more in the e-mails I've received about issues of singlism and living single. I realize my experiences may be unrepresentative and my opinion may be biased, but I'll state it anyway. I believe that most single men have very good hearts.

Source URL: http://www.psychologytoday.com/node/3518

Links:
[1] http://www.amazon.com/Singled-Out-Singles-Stereotyped-Stigmatized/dp/0312340826/ref=ed_oe_p/102-4637341-6604139 [2] http://www.americanheart.org/presenter.jhtml?identifier=4441 [3] http://eric.ed.gov/ERICWebPortal/custom/portlets/recordDetails/detailmini.jsp?_nfpb=true&_&ERICExtSearch_SearchValue_0=EJ739619&ERICExtSearch_SearchType_0=no&accno=EJ739619 [4] http://www.psychologytoday.com/blog/living-single/200807/so-why-have-you-never-been-married-a-case-study-in-accidental-singlism [5] http://www.psychologytoday.com/blog/living-single/200812/those-pitied-mocked-envied-years-between-the-late-teens-and-late-twenties-

---

82.

Newsweek's Turn to Post Misleading Account of Latest Marriage Study

Jul 28 2009

A new day has dawned, and with it another study of marriage misrepresented in the media. As always, the inaccuracies are in one direction only - implying that getting married results in better outcomes than it actually does. I've been at this for a while, and I have yet to find a media report that misrepresents findings in a way that makes singles look better than they actually are. (I don't even want that - I want accuracy.)

Here are some of the headlines that WERE published, supposedly as descriptions of the latest study of marriage:

• "Getting married - and staying married - is good for your health" (from Health Behavior News Service)
• "Lasting marriage linked to better health" (from Reuters)
• "Divorce hurts health even after remarriage" (from MSNBC.com)
• "Another reason to stay married" (from Newsweek)

Here are some of the headlines you did NOT see, that actually would be accurate descriptions of the results of the study:

1. **People who have always been single are healthier than the previously married.** (The advantage held for all four measures of health: number of chronic conditions, number of mobility limitations, self-rated health, and depression. Significance tests were not reported.)

2. **People who have always been single have no more chronic health conditions than people who are currently married.** (This is especially noteworthy because this is not a comparison of all people who stayed single with all people who had ever gotten married. Instead, it just compares the ever-single to those who are currently married. Anyone who got married, hated it - maybe even suffered poor health during marriage - and got divorced and stayed that way - is taken out of the married group. Do you see how this makes marriage look better than it really is?)

3. **Women who have always been single report health that is just as good as women who got married and stayed married.** (This comparison uses a married group that is even more selective. Single women - all of them - are compared NOT to all currently married women - a group that would include those who were previously divorced or widowed and got remarried - but just to those who married and stayed married. In the study, the continuously married represent just about 57% of all those who ever did marry. Of course, there is no comparable selection of just a particular subgroup of singles. Yet, even by this rigged comparison, the always-single women [though not the men] do just fine.)

4. **Men who got married were LESS healthy the younger they married.** (This was true even for those who got married and stayed married. What's especially noteworthy about this is that the authors pursued this analysis in their attempt to show that marriage is so good for you, that the more years you spend married, the healthier you will be. Surprise! The opposite was true, even for the most select group of men who got married and stayed married. Among those who married and then got divorced or widowed, the results still were not as the authors expected. Those who got married at a later age - both men and women - reported better overall health and fewer chronic conditions and mobility limitations than those who married at a younger age.)

Now consider this quote, taken directly from the original report: "Those who have married once and remained married are consistently, strongly, and broadly advantaged." Considering results #2 and #3 above, this statement simply cannot be true.

I'm making two points. One, the media got this study wrong. Two, the authors were not entirely accurate either. They report one set of findings in the tables depicting their results, then say something else about those findings when they get to the end of the article and want to sum up their findings. Perhaps it is worth noting that one of the authors is Linda Waite, co-author of "The Case for Marriage," a book with one misleading and inaccurate statement about marriage after another - as I documented in detail in Chapter 2 of Singled Out.

The Basics of the Study

The authors analyzed interview data from a national sample of 8,809 Americans between the ages of 51 and 61. They were interested not just in the participants' current marital status, but their history of staying single or married, or transitioning in or out of marriage. These are all plusses - it is a big study, a representative study, and the authors are looking at the details of marital status history, not just big blobs of current marital-status categories. Moreover, their study included not just one but four measures of health. (The study was longitudinal, but the authors only look at one-point in time, with all the resulting interpretive ambiguities.)

In their sample, some stayed single the entire time (close to 4%). Of those who ever married, about 22% got widowed or divorced and did not remarry (they are the previously married); and about 20% got remarried after their previous marriage ended; the others stayed married.

The authors wanted to show that the previously married would have worse health than the currently married - and they did. They also thought that more marital disruptions would mean worse health, but they found little evidence for that. They also found that those who divorced and then remarried had worse health than those who stayed married, but better health than those who divorced and stayed that way. (What is also evident from Table 3 is that those who stayed single did just as well or better than the remarried with regard to chronic health conditions and mobility limitations, though not the other two measures.)

What the Media Reports Got Wrong

Sadly, *Newsweek*'s report of the study was the most egregious. Their headline was, "Another reason to stay married." Their tease was, "A new study shows that couples who split face health risks."

Reporters Barbara Kantrowitz and Pat Wingert use Governor Mark Sanford (he of Argentine soul-mate infamy) and Jon and Kate Gosselin as examples. The study, they claim, "suggests that the course the Sanfords are pursuing could ultimately work out better" because they are the ones who are trying to stay together.

ʼn the original study, those who got married and chose to stay that way had better ꞁth than those who got divorced. What the reporters seem to be implying is that if only all those people who divorced had just stayed married, their health would be better. But that study shows nothing of the sort. Nor does it in any way suggest that the Sanfords will have better health if they stay together and the Gosselins will end up decrepit, depressed, and diseased if they stay split. The only way we could know whether divorce results in worse health than staying married would be to randomly assign people to divorce or to stay married - which of course, we can't do. We can, though, be accurate and honest in reporting and extrapolating from the studies we do conduct.

Think about the people who get to the point of considering divorce. High-profile quips to the contrary, divorce isn't something most people do offhandedly because they can't be bothered to stay together. There might be relentless infidelity, constant arguing and conflict, emotional abuse, maybe even drug or alcohol abuse or violence. It is irresponsible to suggest that if only all the married people would just stay married, they'd be healthier.

Astonishingly, *Newsweek* will not even concede that much. After quoting Waite as saying that the currently widowed, divorced, and separated pretty consistently have worse health than the currently married, the reporters say this: "So does that mean that every troubled marriage should be saved? No one study could ever answer such a broad question." Many psychologists, they add (without naming any), would argue against continuing a marriage involving intense violence or untreated drug or alcohol addiction - that could "make it hard for a couple to repair a bad marriage." (Note the tentativeness. Apparently, it is an open question to the reporters as to whether a spouse who is being severely physically abused would have better health by staying in the marriage than by leaving it.)

The *Newsweek* reporters describe Waite's "Case for Marriage" book as influential (without noting any of the problems with it, as delineated here) and even invoke the debate over whether the government should fund marriage-promotion programs. They concede that such programs are controversial, but again, no one gets a say in this article except Linda Waite.

Let me clarify my position. I'm not arguing for divorce. I'm arguing for accuracy in reporting. I'm also cautioning against the needless stigmatizing of people who make difficult and painful choices, and against the piling up of bogus, stinky, pseudo-scientific arguments in supposed support of the gratuitous stigmatizing claims.

Lessons for Journalists and Cautionary Notes for Consumers of Media Reports About Marriage

Please, journalists, don't just read or reprint the press release. Go to the original report in the scientific journal. Once there, don't just look at the abstract or the discussion section, where the authors put their gloss on what they have found. LOOK AT THE NUMBERS. Think about the arguments the authors are trying to make, and whether the design of the study could ever have produced definitive results relevant to those arguments. When you do your interviews, don't talk only to the study authors. Talk to someone who may have a different point of view, AND who has read the original journal article. Readers, be wary of any media report that does not seem to have met these standards.

Quick Recap of Marriage and Health

Let's see if I can briefly summarize the results of this recent study.

• If you get married and then divorce, you will have worse health than if you never got married in the first place, or if you get married and stayed married.

• If you get married and you are miserable and you don't get divorced - well, we don't know from this study what will happen to your health. That's not tested.

• If you are a woman and you get married and stay married throughout the course of the study, you won't have any better health than if you stayed single. (You will if you're a man.)

• Beyond the study's end: When the interviews were conducted, participants were, at most, 62 years old. Even those who had married just once and stayed that way won't be married forever. Death happens. If it is your spouse who dies, then you will have worse health than the people who are still married. But if it is you who dies first, well - then you're dead!

Source URL: http://www.psychologytoday.com/node/31448

Links:
[1] http://www.newswise.com/articles/view/553874/?sc=mwtn [2] http://uk.reuters.com/article/idUKTRE56Q4OI20090727 [3] http://www.msnbc.msn.com/id/32174614/ns/health-more_health_news/ [4] http://www.newsweek.com/id/208544/ [5] http://www.amazon.com/Singled-Out-Singles-Stereotyped-Stigmatized/dp/0312340826/ref=ed_oe_p/102-4637341-6604139 [6] http://www.psychologytoday.com/blog/living-single/200808/cracking-the-code-how-think-critically-about-reports-the-alleged-superiori [7] http://www.psychologytoday.com/blog/living-single/200907/time-s-misleading-cover-story-marriage

---

83.

Marriage and Health: Eh Tu, *New York Times*?

Aug 4 2009

The *New York Times* has just published a piece on that same marriage and health study that Newsweek discussed so misleadingly. Sadly, this piece isn't what it should be either. I am especially disappointed with this one because I've read some of the reporter's previous work and liked it. But if she had read my post on this study (including the terrific comments that were posted by readers) - or Chapter 2 of Singled Out - I think she would have written a better piece. In fact, from the comments that Living Single readers posted to my take-down of the *Newsweek* story (and their other comments as well) I think many readers could critique this *New York Times* story without any help from me.

Nonetheless, here goes.

The first sentence of the story is, "Married people tend to be healthier than single people." I'll get to that in a moment.

A few paragraphs later, the reporter takes up the question that Living Single readers raised in their comments to my post about the study: If this is so, why does it happen? Here's the reporter's answer:

> "The health benefits of marriage, documented by a wealth of research, appear to stem from several factors. Married people tend to be better off financially and can share in a spouse's employer health benefits. And wives, in particular, act as gatekeepers for a husband's health, scheduling appointments and noticing changes that may signal a health problem. Spouses can offer logistical support, like taking care of children while a partner exercises or shuttling a partner to and from the doctor's office."

So what's the most important reason why married people tend to look healthier than unmarried people (**if** they do)? The study in question, like most others on the topic, looks at people of different marital statuses at one point in time. In one category are the people who are currently married, and in the others are the divorced, widowed, and always-single, and various permutations. The currently married people look healthier largely because all those people (probably at least 43%) who got married, hated it, and got divorced are taken out of the marriage group. In my favorite analogy, it is like a drug company claiming that taking their drug Shamster makes people healthier as long as you take out of the Shamster group all of the people who took it, hated it, and stopped taking it.

A few more points.

• If marriage is so good for health because wives nag their husbands to stay healthy, then why are married people fatter than everyone else?

• It is true that the currently married are better off financially than the currently unmarried and that they can get access to health care benefits by way of their spouse's plan at work. (The financial advantage is itself important - marital status discrimination is built right into our laws and policies.) The story focuses on the divorced and widowed, but those who have always been single are also disadvantaged with regard to money and access to health benefits. So isn't it interesting (as I pointed out in my last post) that in the very study that the reporter is describing, **people who have always been single have no more chronic health conditions than people who are currently married, and women who have always been single report heath that is just as good as women who got married**

and stayed married. People who have always been single have had a lifetime of economic disadvantages, and a lifetime of lesser access to health benefits, and a lifetime of figuring out for themselves how to stay healthy (no spousal nagging included), and yet they do just as well on some measures as people who are currently married. And remember, they are doing just as well according to the cheater-method that already gives a huge advantage to people who got married (by taking out of the group the big chunk of people who got married, hated it, and got divorced).

• There's also this result, not reported by the *Times*, from the same study: **People who have always been single are healthier than the previously married**. (The advantage held for all four measures of health: number of chronic conditions, number of mobility limitations, self-rated health, and depression. Significance tests were not reported.) [UPDATE: The *Times* did mention this result for one of the 4 measures, chronic conditions.] Some of the previously married had access to their spouse's health plan from work while they were married. So why are the always-single people, who never had any such access, healthier than the previously married are?

About that "Wealth of Research"

I think there is an important reason why so many reporters fall so readily for the "get married, get healthy" myth. The Marriage Mafia (including many scholars who have staked their careers on claims about the supposed benefits of marriage) insists that there are scads of studies showing that it is good to get married. There are libraries full of studies in which health (or happiness or sex or just about anything else you can think of) was measured at one point in time, and the currently married were compared to the currently unmarried. Many of those do show an advantage of the currently married. But the currently married are NOT healthier BECAUSE they got married. You'd need to look at longitudinal studies (studies of the same people over time) to get a good sense of that. When you do, the results are not exactly what the Marriage Mafia would like to claim. Again, one of the main reasons the currently married look better is because of those who got married, more than 40% couldn't stand their marriages and got divorced. When you remove more than 40% of the got-married group and count only those who are left, it is remarkable that their advantage is sometimes slender or nonexistent.

Again with the drug study analogy: Suppose the drug companies did not just one Shamster study but hundreds or even thousands. In each study, they remove from the Drug condition anyone who took Shamster, hated it, and stopped taking it. They want to claim that since the people currently taking Shamster are doing better than those not taking it, everyone should take Shamster. Yeah! Shamster is great!

It is obvious what a crock this is. It would not increase your faith in Shamster one bit to learn that there were thousands of studies just like this flawed one showing the "benefits" of taking Shamster. Now imagine that there were such a collection of studies of a Shamster drug, and a *New York Times* story opened with the sentence, "People taking Shamster tend to be healthier than people not taking Shamster." It wouldn't happen. (For one thing, Shamster would not be approved by the FDA based

214

on studies such as the one-point-in-time studies of the mythical benefits of marriage.)

What the *New York Times* Got Right

Fortunately, the *Times* reporter did not make all of the same mistakes that *Newsweek* did. Towards the end of her story, she includes this important qualifier:

> "None of this suggests that spouses should stay in a bad marriage for the sake of health. Marital troubles can lead to physical ones, too."

The reporter also talks to someone who may not be so matrimaniacal, and even gives her the last word:

> "I would argue that if you can't fix a marriage you're better off out of it," said Janice Kiecolt-Glaser, an Ohio State scientist who is an author of much of the research. "With a divorce you're disrupting your life, but a long-term acrimonious marriage also is very bad."

[To those interested in divorce rates and how they are calculated, here's a useful reference: Schoen, R., & Canudas-Romo, V. (2006). Timing effects on divorce: 20th century experience in the United States. Journal of Marriage and Family, 68, 749-758.]

Source URL: http://www.psychologytoday.com/node/31663

Links:
[1] http://www.nytimes.com/2009/08/04/health/04well.html?_r=1 [2] http://www.psychologytoday.com/blog/living-single/200907/newsweek-s-turn-post-misleading-account-latest-marriage-study [3] http://www.amazon.com/Singled-Out-Singles-Stereotyped-Stigmatized/dp/0312340826/ref=ed_oe_p/102-4637341-6604139 [4] http://www.psychologytoday.com/blog/living-single/200808/cracking-the-code-how-think-critically-about-reports-the-alleged-superiori [5] http://www.psychologytoday.com/blog/living-single/200804/the-marriage-promotion-claim-is-right-all-the-wrong-reasons [6] http://www.psychologytoday.com/blog/living-single/200810/the-economy-single-persons-vulnerability-is-real

84.

No, You Won't Live Longer If You Get Married

Feb 10 2009

Here's another myth about getting married that just won't die (pun intended). Yesterday, the *Washington Post* teased its Valentine's Day story with this online headline: "Want to live longer? Try marriage."

215

The money quote came from a research brief from RAND: "Numerous studies covering 140 years have shown that married persons tend to live longer than their unmarried counterparts."

As readers of this Living Single blog know, I don't take any quotes at face value. I read the RAND brief and found that it was based on one study of men-only published in 1996. I read that study, too. (The reference to 140 years was alluding to other studies on the topic, including some I'll describe below.)

A book often cited by the Marriage Mafia (Waite and Gallagher's "The Case for Marriage") claims that getting married "can literally save your life." In Chapter 2 of Singled Out, I scrutinized each of the studies cited in supposed support of that claim. Here I'll just briefly review some of the tricks the authors used to make the results of getting married look better than they really were.

The most popular cheater method is to pretend that people who are divorced or widowed never did get married. (It is the same method used most often to make the bogus claim that getting married makes you happier or healthier.) Practitioners of this bit of artifice are trying to make an argument that goes something like this: "Divorced people don't live as long as married people, so that shows that getting married expands your life span." But divorced and widowed people DID get married!

Neither the 1996 study based only on men, nor any of the studies cited in The Case for Marriage, compared all of the people who ever got married to the people who stayed single.

So when the authors of The Case claimed that getting married saved men's lives, they did so by acting as if the men who got divorced or widowed did not actually get married. I call that a statistical annulment.

Here's something else interesting from that book. Even after using the cheater method, the authors ended up admitting that getting married did not matter much to women's longevity. Even the women who got married and stayed married did not seem to live longer than the other women.

Now let me tell you the results of what is probably the longest-running study of longevity ever conducted. It is the Terman Life-Cycle Study, started in 1921. The 1,528 men and women, who were 11-years old when the study started, have been followed for as long as they lived. Two groups of people lived the longest: those who got married and stayed married, and those who stayed single. People who divorced, or who divorced and remarried, had shorter lives. What mattered was consistency, not marriage. The results were the same for the men and the women.

Does that mean that once married, you should stay that way in order to live longer? To answer that definitively, we'd have to do a study that could never be done: Randomly assign married people to stay married or get divorced. Maybe those who stayed married would live longer. Or maybe those who wanted to divorce, but were

216

assigned to stay married, would have lives that were even shorter (and more miserable) than those who did divorce. We just don't know.

Source URL: http://www.psychologytoday.com/node/3337

Links:
[1] http://www.washingtonpost.com/wp-dyn/content/graphic/2009/02/09/GR2009020901260.html?hpid=sec-health [2] http://www.rand.org/pubs/research_briefs/RB5018/index1.html [3] http://www.ncbi.nlm.nih.gov/pubmed/8875065 [4] http://www.amazon.com/Singled-Out-Singles-Stereotyped-Stigmatized/dp/0312340826/ref=ed_oe_p/102-4637341-6604139 [5] http://journals.indexcopernicus.com/abstracted.php?icid=587103

85.

"I Didn't Work This Hard Just to Get Married"

Jun 9 2009

There are so many groups of singles I'd love to hear from - singles who may have their own special take on single life, but (so far) have rarely make it into the book world. As I have often mentioned (as have others who post comments to this Living Single blog), I pine for more voices of single men. Plus, it would be wonderful to hear more from GLBT singles; amidst all the matrimania and same-sex marriage wars, the lives of uncoupled gay men and lesbians are too often invisible.

But my post today is not a complaint but a celebration. One of the groups of singles under-represented in anthologies and other nonfiction works now has its say. In I Didn't Work This Hard Just to Get Married (is that a great title or what?), we hear from successful single black women, thanks to author Nika Beamon who interviewed them and told their stories. Nika, who is herself an award-winning journalist and producer, talked to an interior designer, a movie producer, an author, an actress, a business owner, a publisher, and many more, and also told her own story along the way.

The people in this book are targets of a triple whammy of prejudices and stereotyping - they are black (so they get hit with racism), they are women (so, sexism), and they are single (hence, singlism). Yet, there is not one whiner in the collection. Oh, sure, they have experienced all these isms and sometimes they say so, but what is impressive is what they do about it.

Here's my favorite example. Author Deborah Gregory told Nika about this experience from her childhood: "When I went to bookstores, the characters in the books were so white. It was very hurtful." If you have ever heard of the Cheetah Girls, then you already know how Deborah Gregory dealt with the pain of exclusion.

She wrote the immensely popular books for preteens about a diverse group of girls who were gutsy, smart, and brave, and who cared about their friends. Eventually, the girls made it into a Disney Channel movie. Deborah Gregory gave herself the storybook characters she never had as a child, and shared them with the world.

There's something else I love about the Cheetah Girls. As Gregory puts it, not one of them has "this Cinderella thing." They don't fantasize about getting rescued by some prince. Neither does Gregory.

Here are a few more of my favorite things from Nika Beamon's book:

• One of my favorite quips is from actress and comedienne Kim Coles who said, "I don't have any regrets about being single. You know when I have regrets? When I need someone to climb up on a ladder and do something for me. But you know what I do? I call the handyman."

• My "best sense of balance" award goes to business owner Camille Young, who said, "I don't feel this [being single] is a trait to hold on to, to emulate or to honor, nor is it something to hide, regret, or be ashamed of."

• My favorite theme running through the book: These single women are not alone. They have friends and family who are important to them, and they are quick to say so.

• My favorite "I can relate" quote comes from Sheila Bridges, interior designer for celebrities such as Sean Combs, Tom Clancy, and her Harlem neighbor, Bill Clinton: "I've had so many friends over the years that had a vision of walking down the aisle in the white gown - what the dress would look like, sketching it out - but I never had that."

• My favorite statistic: "more than half of the fifty thousand kids placed in permanent homes in the United States were adopted by African American women without a spouse."

• My favorite insight: Divorce can be more difficult economically for black women than for white women because black women are more likely to be working long hours already and earning incomes similar to their husbands.

• My favorite quirky perspective is from movie producer Effie Brown (*Real Women Have Curves*) who said that if she ever gets married, she wouldn't mind having separate bedrooms. She would appreciate space of her own as well as shared space.

Finally, a true confession: I wrote the Foreword for the book. But I'm not profiting financially from sales so this post is not an ad. I have never even met author Nika Beamon. She just e-mailed me out of the blue, telling me her vision for this book, and I signed on immediately. My profits are emotional. This book represents more consciousness-raising about singles, and what could be better than that.

86.

But What About Single Men?

Jun 25 2008

When I was preparing to write Singled Out, I wanted to study the stacks of scientific studies based on thousands of people who filled out questionnaires. I did, but then I wanted more. I wanted to read rich and textured accounts based on in-depth interviews of single people who talked for hours about their lives, sometimes over the course of many years. Books like that about single women are not hard to find, and they have been around for decades.

Trying to find similar intensive studies of the lives of single men, though, was a whole different story. There just wasn't much out there.

The same thing happened when I tried to find scholarly writings about single people. Single women are of interest to academics, but as for single men - not so much.

Just say the word "single" and your listeners will probably make a quick mental leap to "single women." When my agent was shopping my proposal for *Singled Out* to publishers - a proposal that described myths specifically about single men - one editor said that I was trying "to write a book that will appeal to a market of singles who are a diverse population of women." Another said that his imprint had already published two books about single women and he was not interested in another.

Before I started doing systematic research of my own, I liked to ask people who they thought had it harder when it came to living single in a society so preoccupied with couples. I don't think anyone ever said it was men. Their reasoning made a lot of sense. The "extra" man, they would say, was always welcome at social events, whereas the "extra" woman was seen as a nuisance. The women I asked would point to all the wedding fantasies peddled to them from their babyhoods (filled with stories about princesses) to their adulthoods (dotted with sparkly bridal magazines and syrupy "reality" TV shows such as The Bachelor).

So when Wendy Morris and I designed our studies of the stereotyping of single people, we thought the single women would be singled out for special disparagement. They were disparaged all right, but so were the single men - and usually to about the same degree. There were a few qualified differences here or there, but not the big blatant divergences we expected.

I now think that there are differences in the particular ways that single men and single women are derogated, but the different myths translate into roughly equal doses of condescension and dismissiveness. Here's how I summarized the myths about single women and single men in two of the chapter titles of *Singled Out*.

Myths about single women:
"Your work won't love you back and your eggs will dry up. Also, you don't get any and you're promiscuous."

Myths about single men:
"You are horny, slovenly, and irresponsible, and you are the scary criminals. Or, you are sexy, fastidious, frivolous, and gay."

Pundits strut their singlism unselfconsciously. Consider, for example, a recent discussion on the TV show <u>Hardball</u> of one of the hottest political topics - who will snag the Vice-Presidential slots on the 2008 tickets? The guests were asked to consider the possibility that McCain would choose Florida Governor Charlie Crist, a single man. Roger Simon of *Politico* said of Crist: "He'll probably get engaged soon," then added that the engagement "will probably help put him on the ticket."

I'm on the listserv of a group called <u>Smart Marriages</u>; it's self-described goal is "strengthening marriages and families through marriage education." On their website, they tout much of the research that I debunk in *Singled Out*. Under their list of quotes, they include this one from Franz Kafka. I noticed it because it was also included in a recent mailing to the listserv.

> Bachelor's Ill Luck
> "It seems so dreadful to stay a bachelor, to become an old man struggling to keep one's dignity while begging for an invitation whenever one wants to spend an evening in company, to lie ill gazing for weeks into an empty room from the corner where one's bed is, always having to say good night at the front door, never to run up a stairway beside one's wife, to have only side doors in one's room leading into other people's living rooms, having to carry one's supper home in one's hand, having to admire other people's children and not even being allowed to go on saying: "I have none myself," modeling oneself in appearance and behavior on one or two bachelors remembered from one's youth.
>
> That's how it will be, except that in reality, both today and later, one will stand there with a palpable body and a real head, a real forehead, that is, for smiting on with one's hand."

So this, in the year 2008, is what passes under the banner of "strengthening marriages and families through marriage education."

Perceptions of single people (the stereotypes) aren't everything. What about evidence of discrimination? There's plenty of that, too (though singlism is less vicious than other isms such as racism or heterosexism). In one important domain, there are clear indications of greater discrimination against single men than single women: Single men are paid less than married men, even when their accomplishments are the same. The patterns for women are less consistent. (References are in Singled Out.)

Now here's what's truly remarkable: Despite all the stereotyping and discrimination, most single men (and single women) are doing just fine. Take happiness, for example. In every study I've read, the average happiness level of single men (and single women) is solidly on the happy end of the scale. And no, they would not become even happier, in any lasting way, if only they married.

Of course, I'm not saying that every last single person is happy. There are more than 42 million single men and more than 49 million single women, so some of them are going to be unhappy. But a study that has been ongoing for 20 years suggests that, on the average, they would not become any happier if they did marry (except perhaps for a brief honeymoon effect).

So here's the puzzle: Why is there such a disconnect between the negative perceptions of single men and the actual life experiences of those men?

Source URL: http://www.psychologytoday.com/node/1119

Links:
[1] http://www.amazon.com/Singled-Out-Singles-Stereotyped-Stigmatized/dp/0312340826/ref=ed_oe_p/102-4637341-6604139 [2] http://www.belladepaulo.com/otherdepaulo.htm#scholar [3] http://www.msnbc.msn.com/id/3036697/ [4] http://www.smartmarriages.com/marriage.quotes.html [5] http://www.ingentaconnect.com/content/klu/johs/2006/00000007/00000004/00009001

87.

Latest Study: Single People Do NOT Have More Attachment Problems (Part I)

Jan 5 2009

There's breaking news, and this time it is good: Single people don't have "issues" with attachment. In a study published in the latest issue of the journal Personal Relationships (described below), there were three attachment criteria, and single people did just as well as coupled people on all three.

• First, single people were no more likely than coupled people to feel anxious about rejection or abandonment.

• Second, they were no more likely than coupled people to try to avoid intimacy or interdependence.

• Attachment figures are people we like to be near in times of need, and who provide comfort and support in times of stress. That leads to the third criterion, the number of such people: Single people had about the same number of attachment figures as coupled people did.

The findings underscore what I have been trying to convey in <u>Singled Out</u> and here in this blog. Single people are not alone. Even when they live alone, they are not emotionally isolated. They have people in their lives who are important to them - people they like to be with, people who are there for them when they most need someone.

Single people, rather than having romantic partners as attachment figures, may instead develop secure attachments to friends, siblings, other relatives, or other categories of people. We should, once and for all, stop describing single people as "unattached."

Apparently, another study has reported similar findings, though I can't read it in my usual careful way (or at all, for that matter) because it is in Hebrew. In her thesis, Sharon Eisinger found no differences in the attachment styles of single and married people (all of whom were over the age of 30). She also found that singles were no more likely than married people to have maladaptive schemas.

This is important. If there is a Holy Grail in relationship research, or in developmental psychology, it may well be attachment. Initially, the main topic of attachment research was the child's attachment to her or his mother. The study of adult attachments came later, and (surprise!) at first focused primarily on attachments to romantic partners.

All across the lifespan, the nature of your attachments - whether they are secure attachments or insecure ones (anxious or avoidant) - is believed to be vitally important. In fact, there are probably thousands of published studies of attachment, most attesting to the importance to all of us of having a person (or persons) who is a safe haven in times of trouble. So if we can truly take attachment issues off the table as something to pin on single people as some sort of tragic flaw, then that's something we all should know.

That's the good news.

About the Study

Participants were 69 single and 73 coupled people, ages 25-55. The singles were recruited using ads placed in newspapers in Sacramento, CA. "Single" was defined as "not in a committed relationship for the past three or more years and not likely to become committed in the near future." The single participants were asked to nominate coupled people who might participate.

All of the measurements were taken at one point in time; it was not a longitudinal study. Participants completed a series of questionnaires, then they participated in a face-to-face interview. During the interview, they discussed topics such as their childhood relationships with their parents, their ideas about why they are single (or partnered), and how they handle stress.

The title of the article is "Attachment style and long-term singlehood." It appeared in the December 2008 issue of Personal Relationships, Vol. 15, pp. 479-491.

Preview of the Next Post: How the Authors Resisted Their Own Singles-Friendly Findings

What I'm going to do in my next post is to look at the subtext of the article (the one in English). I'll show how the authors seemed almost disappointed to have found that singles were not attachment-deficient, and how they presented their findings in ways that, to me, were not entirely even-handed.

In my opinion, many relationship researchers have invested all of their intellectual and emotional stock in romantic relationships, and they are resistant to the conclusion that plenty of single people may be doing just fine.

As part of the next post, I will look closely at a particular excerpt from the article. Here it is, if you want to start anticipating my points:

> "Future studies should more directly examine the determinants of long-term singlehood because adult attachment measures did not indicate that a particular form of insecurity is largely responsible (although this may be due to the reluctance of extremely avoidant people to get involved in our study, which required self-selection rather than random sampling among all adults). The hints in the data that single people experienced more troubled childhood relationships with parents compared to coupled people suggest that some aspect of relationships with parents might be partially responsible for long-term singlehood in later life." They then go on to add that insights from future research "should prove useful for clinical work with single adults and for those adults' own self-understanding."

Source URL: http://www.psychologytoday.com/node/2872

Links:
[1]
http://www3.interscience.wiley.com/journal/118506454/home?CRETRY=1&SRETRY=0
[2] http://www.amazon.com/Singled-Out-Singles-Stereotyped-Stigmatized/dp/0312340826/ref=ed_oe_p/102-4637341-6604139

88.

No Special Attachment Issues Among Single People (Part II): How to Make Even Good Findings Sound Bad

Jan 9 2009

Or, how to make lemons out of lemonade.

In my last post, I described the results of a recently published study showing that long-term single people are not any more likely than coupled people to have issues with attachment. They are not more anxious about rejection or more avoidant of intimacy, and they have no fewer people in their lives who serve as safe havens and sources of support in times of duress.

I also said that the authors seemed to be resisting their own singles-friendly findings throughout their article, and promised to say more about that in this post.

I'm using my analysis of this particular article as an example of a bigger point about what is still happening in academic psychology, and of course, well beyond the gates of academe. Even among very smart and accomplished people (and one of the authors of the article is a leading researcher and theorist in the study of adult attachment), unwitting singlism runs rampant. We as a society simply have little practice thinking about single people as anything but flawed. I don't think that these researchers (or the many others who talk about singles in similar ways) mean to exclude positive perspectives on singles - my guess is that those ways of thinking just don't occur to them.

Think about the examples in this post as practice in decoding the puzzles of singlism. I hope that what you will get out of reading it is not just the aha! experience of seeing a solution but also a broadened way of thinking that carries over to new examples you notice in your own lives.

I'm offering my debunking of this article as an emotional and intellectual inoculation. Maybe the next time you are faced with singlism, you can recognize it for what it is - not a true statement of what's "wrong" with you as a single person, but a reflection of what the practitioners of singlism have not yet figured out.

How the Authors Fought Their Own Findings, as Rendered in a Series of Tongue-in-Cheek Paraphrases

My Playful Paraphrase #1.
Let's Start by Stipulating That Single People Can't Possibly Do Better Than Coupled People

When, in the beginning of their article, the authors spell out their expectations for how their results might turn out, they come up with three possible hypotheses: (1) single people are more avoidant in their attachment styles than coupled people are; (2) single people are more anxious in their attachments than coupled people are, maybe because "they have been rejected by relationship partners who would not accept their anxiety, clinginess, and intrusiveness;" and (3) single and coupled people are similar in their attachment experiences.

Recognize that it is a step forward for the authors to concede that maybe the singles will not look worse than the coupled people. But also notice what is missing. There is no acknowledgment whatsoever that single people could have more secure attachment styles than coupled people.

The results showed that attachment was the same for the singles and the couples; I'm not arguing with that. But when scientists generate hypotheses, they should be open to many possibilities. Maybe, for instance, singles would be more secure because they don't place all of their relationship eggs into the one soul-mate basket. Maybe their attachments are to friends, and there are fewer anxiety-creating jealousies in friendships. I'm not saying that's so - I'm saying that scientists are supposed to have open minds and at least consider the possibilities.

Also notice the implication that only single people, and not anyone currently coupled, could have had the experience of having been "rejected by relationship partners who would not accept their anxiety, clinginess, and intrusiveness." Because, you know, only single people are ever clingy.

My Playful Paraphrase #2.
Let's Treat Singlehood as a Disease

The authors' main question was whether single and coupled people differed in their attachment styles. But that was just part of their framework. They had a whole childhood-to-singlehood model worked out. First, they thought the single people would describe more screwed-up childhood relationships with their parents. Single people's messed-up childhoods would then result in insecure attachments (or maybe no adult attachment figures at all). Those insecure or missing attachments would then result in a life of long-term singlehood.

This strikes me as a disease model of singlehood. The authors are trying to explain singlehood in terms of what got screwed up in single people's lives. Of course, that falls apart when the key link just isn't there - singles do not have attachment issues.

My Playful Paraphrase #3.
Here Are Some Other Things Wrong with Single People. Let's Take Them Seriously Even Though They Do Not Explain What They Were Supposed to - and, Oh, Let's Ignore Other Studies with Different Findings

Because the authors expected single people to have screwed-up childhoods, they asked their participants about their childhoods. They also looked at other bad things that might be ascribed to single people, such as loneliness, depression, general anxiety (different from attachment anxiety), and sexual dissatisfaction. In the abstract (summary) of their article, they claim to have found that, sure enough, all of these things are more of a problem for single people than for coupled people.

I have two responses to this. (A) Really? Are you sure about that? And (B), Okay, so suppose you are right that singles are screwed up in all these ways. Then how come they are just fine when it comes to attachment?

(A) All those bad things about single people: Are they really true?

Let's start with the "troubled childhood" hypothesis. The authors included 9 measures of the participants' retrospective reports of their relationships with their mothers and fathers. (Actually, there were 11, but they only report the results of 9 of them.) On 7 of the 9 measures, the single and coupled participants score about the same. On the other two, the single people report more negative experiences.

I could say about this finding - as well as the main finding of no differences between singles and couples in attachment issues - that the sample was unrepresentative (the singles were recruited by newspaper ads and the couples were recommended by the singles) and so we need to be cautious. That's true, and maybe future studies will show that singles have less troubled childhoods than coupled people do (or even more troubled ones) or that singles really do have attachment issues.

I'm giving the authors a pass on that problem because (so far as I know) this is the first study of childhood experiences of single and coupled people, so even a flawed study adds something important to our knowledge base. Plus, it is quite a challenge to try to get a large representative sample of single and coupled people, or to study people over time as they become coupled. (The report of another study showing no differences in attachment between single and married people, mentioned in my previous post, adds a bit more credence to the attachment results of this study, but we still need to learn more.)

With regard to loneliness or depression or sexual satisfaction, though, the state of the literature is entirely different. For example, the authors noted that the singles in their convenience sample reported greater depression than the coupled people, but they do not mention these results from a longitudinal study out of Stanford: "<u>Depression during adolescence was found to predict higher rates of marriage among younger women and subsequent marital dissatisfaction.</u>"

The authors reported that the singles in their convenience sample reporter less sexual satisfaction than the coupled people. But they did not mention the results of a nationally representative sample, in which the findings were not at all as straightforward as "married = sexually satisfied; single = sexually dissatisfied." (See Chapter 2 of <u>Singled Out</u> for an account of what the findings really did show.)

After reading in the abstract that the singles were lonelier than the coupled people, I was surprised to find in the results section that on the standardized measure of loneliness, the UCLA Loneliness Scale, there was actually no significant difference between the singles and the couples. What's that about? In the face-to-face interviews, single people said the word "lonely" more often than coupled people did. I think that's why the authors declared them lonelier, even though the standardized instrument demurred.

I wonder whether the authors are familiar with studies showing extraordinarily low levels of loneliness among lifelong single women, at a time when they are expected to be most lonely - in later life (also described in Singled Out). They don't mention those studies.

(B) Suppose singles really are screwed up in all those ways. Then why are they doing just fine when it comes to attachment?

The main point of the study was to examine differences in attachment between single and coupled people. There were none. The other variables were supposed to help explain the process.

The authors did find, for example, that people who were more depressed (whether single or coupled) were more anxious about attachments. They also found that in their convenience sample, the singles were more depressed than the coupled people. So doesn't that raise another question: So why didn't the single people have more attachment issues than the coupled people?

Here's one possibility: Maybe in their quest to document a sequence of sad and bad life experiences resulting in a long-term single status, the authors neglected to consider or measure what might be good and meaningful and rewarding in the lives of people who are single. What are their passions? What do they care about? If you only look for bad things, that's all you are going to find.

Here's another possibility: The authors seemed to assume that the couples would do better on attachment because they were coupled and the singles were not. But maybe this "sugar and spice and everything nice" view of couples and their attachment styles was overly optimistic. Why not hypothesize that some coupled people cling to their partners because they are insecure, and that some single people are secure enough not to cave to the pressure to couple when they are perfectly happy with their single lives? I'm just asking.

I need to add a clarification here. I'm not saying that there are no single people who had screwed up childhoods and who therefore became insecure about attachments and therefore stayed single. There are about 93 million single people in the United States alone. Whatever your stereotypes about single people, there are going to be some out of the 93 million who fit them. What I am saying is that just because you know a screwed up single person, or just because you are a scholar who can come up with a reason to predict that singles might be screwed up, does not mean that, as a general rule, single people really are screwed up.

My Playful Paraphrase #4.
Sure, Our Study Says Nothing about Causality, But That's Just an Aside

When studies show that currently married people are less lonely or depressed or happier than currently single people, readers and journalists (and sometimes the researchers themselves) sometimes jump to the conclusion that the married people look better because they are married, and that if the single people would marry, then they would live happily ever after, too. As I've explained in previous posts (and in Chapter 2 of Singled Out), that's totally bogus. People who got married, hated it, and then divorced, are not included in the currently married group. You can't say that getting married makes people less lonely or depressed (or anything else) if you don't count all the people who got married and did not get any less lonely or depressed. That's just cheating.

The attachment hypothesis in the study I've been describing is different. There, attachment (and childhood experiences) are used to explain how people end up single. The ideal study, methodologically, is one that cannot be conducted: Randomly assign newborns to good or bad childhood experiences, then see if that predicts who ends up single or coupled. Short of that, longitudinal research (following lives over time) is the next best thing.

The authors acknowledge the causality issue in the last point of the last section of their paper, almost as an aside. But it is not an aside. It is critical. (I would say this even if all of the results had favored the single people; science first.)

My Playful Paraphrase #5.
How's This Suggestion for Future Research: Find Something Bad about Single People

Journal articles in psychology almost always include suggestions for further research. Think about this paragraph from the authors:

> "Future studies should more directly examine the determinants of long-term singlehood because adult attachment measures did not indicate that a particular form of insecurity is largely responsible (although this may be due to the reluctance of extremely avoidant people to get involved in our study, which required self-selection rather than random sampling among all adults). The hints in the data that single people experienced more troubled childhood relationships with parents compared to coupled people suggest that some aspect of relationships with parents might be partially responsible for long-term singlehood in later life." They then go on to add that insights from future research "should prove useful for clinical work with single adults and for those adults' own self-understanding."

The authors wanted to know what was responsible for long-term singlehood. They guessed it was insecurity. It wasn't.

Now what? Now they try to salvage their insecurity hypothesis by suggesting that maybe the really screwed up single people did not sign up for their study. If they had, then single people would in fact have had insecure attachments, just like they expected.

It is fine for the authors to offer such a speculation, except for one thing: They do not apply the same standards to the coupled people. Apparently, it never occurred to them that maybe the really screwed up coupled people did not sign up for their study. This is not an even-handed inquiry. It is a "let's see if we can find something wrong with single people" study. (And still, singles' attachment looks just fine.)

Next, the authors move on to the "troubled childhood" hypothesis. See the previous sections for my comments on that.

My Playful Paraphrase #6.
Note to Single People - Get Help!

About those insights needed for "clinical work with single adults": I don't think anyone should be reluctant to get into therapy. Still, in a study in which single and coupled people were statistically indistinguishable in their attachments, why are the authors talking only about help for single people and not couples?

My Playful Paraphrase #7.
Bella's Book on Singles is Just a Bunch of Smiley-Faced Opinions

I admit my bias about this point. (I couldn't hide it if I wanted to.) I don't like the way the authors refer to my book, <u>Singled Out</u>. When they find something supposedly negative about single people, they say that their finding is "contrary to the tone" of my book. They refer to my "suggestions," but nowhere do they indicate that my book is based on data. I realize that many of the readers of this "Living Single" blog have read *Singled Out*, so you know what I'm saying. For others: Especially in chapter 2 (but also elsewhere), I describe studies of the implications of marital status, and explain in some detail what can and cannot be concluded from them. (The authors also belittle the importance of the prejudice and discrimination faced by single people - a topic I've addressed in <u>other posts here</u>.)

My Playful Paraphrase #8.
We Found that Singles Have Attachments; Now Let's Pretend They Don't

Here are two sentences from the article. See if you can pick out the one word that suggests that the authors are fighting their own findings. (This may be too easy for "Living Single" readers but none of the authors or reviewers caught it.)

> "as people pass through adolescence and enter early adulthood, many transfer their primary sense of attachment from parents to romantic or marital partners. But not everyone does this (and many who do later find themselves alone after a romantic relationship breakup, a divorce, or the loss of a partner to death)."

The word, of course, is "alone." The authors have shown in their very own study that single people are not alone. They are securely attached to friends, siblings, and others. But in the matrimaniacal world of contemporary relationship research, anyone who does not have a romantic partner is, by definition, alone.

Final Word

The authors expected to find something damning about long-term single people - that they have issues with attachment. Instead, they found no differences at all between the attachment styles of single and coupled people. Still, they never seriously entertained the possibility that their original model was wrong, and that perhaps for many people, living single is a meaningful, productive, healthy experience, filled with secure attachments to the important people in their lives.

It is not just the three authors of the article in question who seemed smitten by singlism and matrimania. Papers in peer-reviewed journals undergo rigorous assessment, typically by the journal editor and two or more additional scholars. The disease model of singlehood made it through all of those layers of scrutiny.

Source URL: http://www.psychologytoday.com/node/2925

Links:
[1] http://www.psychologytoday.com/blog/living-single/200901/latest-study-single-people-do-not-have-attachment-problems-part-i [2] http://www3.interscience.wiley.com/journal/118506454/home?CRETRY=1&SRETRY=0 [3] http://www.psychologytoday.com/blog/a-family-affair/200901/attachment-security-born-or-made [4] http://cat.inist.fr/?aModele=afficheN&cpsidt=1591381 [5] http://www.amazon.com/Singled-Out-Singles-Stereotyped-Stigmatized/dp/0312340826/ref=ed_oe_p/102-4637341-6604139 [6] http://www.psychologytoday.com/blog/living-single/200808/cracking-the-code-how-think-critically-about-reports-the-alleged-superiori [7] http://www.psychologytoday.com/blog/living-single/200805/is-it-bad-notice-discrimination

89.

The Chronicle of Higher Education
September 28, 2007

Make Room for Singles in Teaching and Research

By BELLA DEPAULO, RACHEL F. MORAN, and E. KAY TRIMBERGER

Over the past few decades, the demographics of the United States have changed markedly. In 1970, 28 percent of Americans over 17 were single — divorced, widowed, or never married. More than twice as many households consisted of mom, dad, and the kids than of single adults living on their own. In 2005 more than 40 percent of adults were single, and more households contained just one person than married couples with children. In another striking departure from the past, Americans now spend more years of their adult lives unmarried than married.

It is not just the proportions of married and single people that are changing; so too are the nature and functions of marriage and the family. The nuclear family — which united marriage, economic viability, bearing and rearing children, love, sex, and intimacy — is splitting apart. In July 2007, the Pew Research Center reported that "just 41 percent of Americans now say that children are 'very important' to a successful marriage." And marriage is no longer the gateway to adulthood and having a family. The same Pew report noted, "In the United States today, marriage exerts less influence over how adults organize their lives and how children are born and raised than at any time in the nation's history."

Ways of thinking about single and married people have not kept up with those rapid social changes. Like other groups considered to be outside the mainstream of American society, single people are often the targets of stereotyping and discrimination. As one of us has shown — in **Singled Out: How Singles Are Stereotyped, Stigmatized, and Ignored, and Still Live Happily Ever After** (St. Martin's Press, 2006), by Bella DePaulo — single men are often paid less than married men, even when their accomplishments are comparable; single people are often charged more than married people for health and automobile insurance; renters prefer married couples to single people as tenants; and so forth.

In the academy, much research and teaching is based on the outdated assumption that marriage and the nuclear family dominate adult life. As a result, people who are single, and perspectives not based on conventional marriage, are greatly underrepresented or misrepresented in scholarship and public policy.

Since 1970 significant additions to the curriculum — such as women's studies, ethnic studies, and environmental studies — have revealed missing perspectives and challenged distorted ones on important subjects. Those transformations were driven by social movements. Other curricular innovations, like the addition of a global perspective to many disciplines, emerged from a recognition that our students would be living and working in a changing world. Now we need to change the curriculum to reflect the demographic changes in marriage, singlehood, and family size and composition.

Because marriage is so deeply ensconced in our politics, laws, religion, and customs, fully integrating singles into our research and teaching would require a major transformation. It is not enough merely to append a section on the new group to existing courses. That has been noted by scholars such as Peggy McIntosh, in an in-fluential 1983 working paper from the Wellesley College Center for Research on Women, "Interactive Phases of Curriculum Re-Vision: A Feminist Perspective," and Elizabeth Kamarck Minnich, in Transforming Knowledge (2nd edition, Temple University Press, 2005). Instead, we need to change our thinking. The rewards would include fresh perspectives not just on the single life, but also on marriage and the family.

Our own disciplines, and others with which we are familiar, demonstrate how singles should be brought into scholarship and teaching. Marriage and family studies, for example, is a burgeoning, multidisciplinary field that has recently expanded to incorporate the study of nontraditional families. But single people are still likely to appear in its research and courses only if they have an important life experience in common with adults in nuclear families — for example, if they had been married, have children, or are cohabiting.

Scholars in psychology, sociology, and many other disciplines have contributed to the growing field of relationship science — which, in theory, is about all relationships and hence broader than the study of marriage and family. In practice, however, research in that field focuses on romantic and marital attachments, using "relationship" as a shorthand for conjugal ties.

The marriage-centered view of singles assumes that they are alone, and that the growth of one-person households means the nation is at risk of a national epidemic of loneliness. Research from a singles perspective by one of us — **The New Single Woman** (Beacon Press, 2005), by E. Kay Trimberger — and other scholars challenges such assumptions. It shows that singles have strong ties to their extended families, are adept at forming networks of friends, and are more involved in their communities than married people are.

The relationships that are important to single people, like close friendships and ties to members of the extended family, are invisible to or devalued by scholars who consider marriage the norm. Some of them might argue that singles have close friendships because they are compensating for not having a spouse. A singles perspective would generate other hypotheses — for example, that many single people prefer to maintain a diversified relationship portfolio, rather than investing most of their emotional capital in just one person.

That perspective would look at the entirety of adult life, rather than focusing on the years a person might have spent married. Consider, for instance, the many studies on how multiple roles (such as worker, housekeeper, caregiver) relate to the well-being of wives and husbands. A singles perspective would explore how the division of labor within a marriage shapes a spouse's life after separation, divorce, or widowhood. It would look at the implications of multiple roles and skills for all people — not just married ones — throughout their lives.

Even some of the most enduring topics in the social sciences are likely to be refreshed by a singles perspective. For example, research on stereotyping and discrimination has looked at different racial, ethnic, and religious groups, as well at people of different ages and physical conditions or characteristics. But until very recently, it was rare to study singles as a stigmatized group.

The fields of women's studies and ethnic studies pioneered ways to add new subject matter and viewpoints to established disciplines, and since the late 1970s have incorporated the perspectives of race, class, and sexuality. But neither women's studies nor gender studies has adequately investigated the social stigma against singles, especially single women. Only in the past decade or so have a few faculty members in those and related disciplines begun to confront bias against singles. It is important to teach students that the cultural imperatives to find a "soul mate" (ideas transmitted not only by the mass media, but by students' families and friends) represent just one viewpoint. Students also need to examine their negative stereotypes about older single women, childless single women, and single mothers, and reconsider the values of autonomy and solitude.

In the legal curriculum, courses as diverse as torts, property, evidence, estates and trusts, health-care law, insurance law, family law, and income taxation reflect the law's favoring of married couples over single people. As increasing numbers of Americans become or remain single, laws and policies — and the study of them — need to reflect that social change.

The debate over same-sex marriage has underscored the ways in which the law discriminates against same-sex couples. Husbands and wives have the legal right to share property, to make decisions about each other's medical care, and so forth. Gay couples not permitted to marry do not share those rights. And, as one of us has noted — in Rachel F. Moran's "**How Second-Wave Feminism Forgot the Single Woman**," in the 2004 Hofstra Law Review — single people are also unable to give such rights to friends, siblings, or others. A singles perspective would ask why adults need to be part of a couple in order to be afforded legal protections.

The changing demographics make rethinking of laws, policies, and scholarship an urgent matter. The shrinking size of the nuclear family means that adults have fewer siblings to turn to for help, and parents as they age cannot rely as heavily on their children. Government aid will become increasingly important, and it will need to be directed to individuals and the personal networks that support them, as well as to families or couples.

Because a singles perspective has been largely absent from the higher-education curriculum, universities have not led the way in analyzing policy and suggesting reform. Incorporating a singles perspective into many fields, including those we have mentioned, would broaden and deepen scholarship while enriching the intellectual life of the classroom.

About the Author

Bella DePaulo (Ph.D., Harvard, 1979) is a social psychologist and the author of *Singled Out: How Singles are Stereotyped, Stigmatized, and Ignored, and Still Live Happily Ever After* (St. Martin's Press). In *Singled Out*, and in her other work on people who are single, DePaulo has drawn from social science data to challenge the stereotypes of people who are single. DePaulo has also offered seminars and workshops on the science of singlehood. She is the recipient of a number of honors and awards, such as the James McKeen Cattell Award and the Research Scientist Development Award, and has served in various leadership positions in professional organizations. DePaulo has published more than 100 papers in professional journals and has written op-ed essays for publications such as the *New York Times*, the *Chronicle of Higher Education*, *Newsday*, *Forbes*.com, and the *San Francisco Chronicle*. She writes the "Living Single" blog for *Psychology Today*, and is also a contributor to the Huffington Post. Bella DePaulo has discussed the place of singles in society on radio and television, including NPR and CNN, and her work has been described in newspapers (such as the *New York Times* and the *Washington Post*) and magazines (such as *Time*, *Business Week*, and *Psychology Today*). Dr. DePaulo has also written extensively about the psychology of lying. She has been a Visiting Professor of Psychology at the University of California, Santa Barbara since the summer of 2000. Visit her website at www.BellaDePaulo.com.

Made in the USA
Lexington, KY
30 November 2009